A **NAOMI SCHNEIDER** BOOK

Highlighting the lives and experiences of marginalized communities, the select titles of this imprint draw from sociology, anthropology, law, and history, as well as from the traditions of journalism and advocacy, to reassess mainstream history and promote unconventional thinking about contemporary social and political issues. Their authors share the passion, commitment, and creativity of Executive Editor Naomi Schneider.

*The publisher gratefully acknowledges the
generous support of the following:*

*The General Endowment Fund of the University
of California Press Foundation*

*The Director's Circle of the University of California
Press Foundation, whose members are:*

Tom Benet
Nancy & Roger Boas
Earl & June Cheit
Carol & John Field
Michelle Lee Flores
Harriett & Richard Gold
Gary & Cary Hart
Betty Hine and Holly Suich
Carole & Ted Krumland
Marilyn Lee & Harvey Schneider
Judith & Kim Maxwell
Thomas & Barbara Metcalf
Alejandro Portes
Lucinda Reinold
Tommi & Roger Robinson
Meryl & Robert Selig
John & Priscilla Walton

My Name Is Jody Williams

CALIFORNIA SERIES
IN PUBLIC ANTHROPOLOGY

The California Series in Public Anthropology
emphasizes the anthropologist's role as an
engaged intellectual. It continues anthropology's
commitment to being an ethnographic witness, to
describing, in human terms, how life is lived beyond
the borders of many readers' experiences. But it
also adds a commitment, through ethnography, to
reframing the terms of public debate—transforming
received, accepted understandings of social issues
with new insights, new framings.

Series Editor: Robert Borofsky
(Hawaii Pacific University)

Contributing Editors:
Philippe Bourgois (University of Pennsylvania),
Paul Farmer (Partners in Health),
Alex Hinton (Rutgers University),
Carolyn Nordstrom (University of Notre Dame), and
Nancy Scheper-Hughes (UC Berkeley)

University of California Press Editor:
Naomi Schneider

My Name Is Jody Williams

*A Vermont Girl's Winding Path
to the Nobel Peace Prize*

Jody Williams

Foreword by Eve Ensler

UNIVERSITY OF CALIFORNIA PRESS

Berkeley   Los Angeles   London

University of California Press, one of the most distin-
guished university presses in the United States, enriches
lives around the world by advancing scholarship in the
humanities, social sciences, and natural sciences. Its
activities are supported by the UC Press Foundation and
by philanthropic contributions from individuals and institutions. For more information, visit www.ucpress.edu.

University of California Press
Berkeley and Los Angeles, California

University of California Press, Ltd.
London, England

Library of Congress Cataloging-in-Publication Data
Williams, Jody, 1950–
    My name is Jody Williams : a Vermont girl's winding
path to the Nobel Peace Prize / Jody Williams. — 1st
Edition.
        pages   cm. — (California series in public anthro-
pology ; 25)
    ISBN 978-0-520-27025-1 (alk. paper)
    1. Williams, Jody, 1950–   2. Pacifists—United States—
Biography.   3. Women Nobel Prize winners—United
States—Biography.   4. Nobel Prize winners—United
States—Biography.   I. Title.
    JZ5540.2.W56   2013
    327.1'743—dc23
    [B]   2012031155

Manufactured in the United States of America

22   21   20   19   18   17   16   15   14   13
10   9   8   7   6   5   4   3   2   1

In keeping with a commitment to support environmen-
tally responsible and sustainable printing practices, UC
Press has printed this book on Natures Natural, a fiber
that contains 30% post-consumer waste and meets the
minimum requirements of ANSI/NISO Z39.48–1992 (R 1997)
(*Permanence of Paper*).

For my family.

To activists everywhere who work for a world of sustainable peace, equality, and justice for us all.

And to those who want to contribute to change but aren't sure what they do will matter. Every action we take for the benefit of others matters deeply. Find your passion and work on it, even a couple of hours a month. It will change your world in ways you can't possibly imagine.

CONTENTS

Foreword by Eve Ensler ix

Prologue: October 10, 1997 xiii

PART I.
IF YOU COULD BE ANYONE

1. What Do You Mean I Can't Be the Pope?

3

2. A Special Place in Hell

15

3. Claude, Casey, and the Corvair Convertible

36

4. V-I-E-T-N-A-M, Marriage, and Mexico

55

PART II.
THE MAKING OF A GRASSROOTS ACTIVIST

5. The Pamphlet

79

6. Boots on the Ground: Sandinista Interlude

101

7. Dinner with the Death Squad

124

8. I Thought I Wanted a Straight Job—
Instead I Got Landmines

143

9. Landmines and Love

171

10. The Ottawa Process and the 1997 Landmine Ban
World Tour

200

11. Whirlwind: October 10 to December 10, 1997

227

Epilogue

246

Acknowledgments 259

Illustrations follow page 76

FOREWORD

Eve Ensler

Jody Williams is many things—a simple girl from Vermont, a sister of a disabled brother, a loving wife, an intense character full of fury and mischief, a great strategist, an excellent organizer, a brave and relentless advocate, and a Nobel Peace Prize winner. But to me Jody Williams is, first and foremost, an activist.

What is an activist? The dictionary says, "an especially active, vigorous advocate of a cause, especially a political cause." My sense—and I think it is most clear in this stirring memoir—is that an activist is someone who cannot help but fight for something. That person is not usually motivated by a need for power or money or fame, but in fact is driven slightly mad by some injustice, some cruelty, some unfairness, so much so that he or she is compelled by some internal moral engine to act to make it better.

I have often wondered at what moment one becomes an activist. Are we born with the activist gene, and then some event or incident catalyzes it into being? Is it a deaf brother, abused and cruelly treated? Is it witnessing unkindness to those we love or being raped or beaten and undone ourselves and surviving through the love of others and then feeling compelled to give back the same?

Many of us are accidental activists. We didn't necessarily or consciously choose to devote our lives to ending war or violence against women or racism or poverty or sexual oppression, or to fighting for the environment, but our survival became so clearly wrapped in the struggle, we had no choice.

The big question, of course, is why do some shut down and move away in the face of power and oppression and others move into action? I think if we could resolve this riddle, we would unlock millions of sleeping activists who could possibly help save this world and transform suffering. Some of the secrets are found in this book.

What is most compelling about Jody's writing about her remarkable life and deeds is how unremarkable she makes it sound. It is simple, straightforward, unembellished. It all seems logical, one thing growing out of another. There were landmines destroying the lives of thousands of people worldwide. There was a goal to ban them. There was the insane belief that this was possible. (By the way, I think another characteristic of activists is this dogged faith that change is possible even in the face of what on the surface seems like an utter impossibility.)

Jody had a goal she wanted to accomplish—banning land-mines—and she employed her powers, her smarts, her wisdom and engaged all those around her to bring about that end. I think one of the wonderful things about her winning the Nobel Peace Prize is that it honored all the activists in her project who made it happen, and for that matter, it honored activism everywhere.

I have pretty much lost faith in governments or world leaders or patriarchal institutions to reverse the sad and terrifying trajectory of human beings. My hope, my life, lies with activists. I think of the Occupy Wall Street movement, environmental activists in the rain forests, domestic workers' unions, Pussy Riot, LBGT workers, V-Day activists, antiviolence and antiwar activists, antiracist, fair trade, hunger, animal rights activists. The list is fortunately endless, and these activists are born every minute and are rising everywhere to reenvision and give birth to the new world. They are obsessed, unstoppable, passionate, creative in finding ways over and around obstacles. They are community builders, often humorous, sometimes and necessarily belligerent, insomniacs, usually dancers, celebrators of life.

This book charts Jody's activist journey with a whole lot of other amazing people to successfully ban landmines. It will inspire you to believe that what you do matters a lot and to follow your path and trust your outrage and sorrow. If we are to find a way out of the current madness, it will take a whole lot more of us filled with the spirit, mischief, fury, and determination of Jody Williams.

PROLOGUE

October 10, 1997

The phone did not ring at 3 A.M. on Friday, October 10, 1997. It didn't ring at 3:15. It didn't ring at 3:30 either. If we didn't *expect* it to ring, we certainly *hoped* it would. But it didn't. Deflated, at least Goose and I could finally let it go and go to sleep. Since we'd finished cleaning the kitchen around midnight, we'd been tossing and turning in bed for hours.

We dozed off only to be woken up by the harsh ringing of the phone. I looked at the clock. It was 4 A.M. My heart was pounding. It was a combination of adrenaline from being startled awake and weird expectation. I picked up the phone to hear the singsong accent of a man who said he was calling from a Norwegian TV station.

He asked if I was me. When I said I was, he asked where I'd be in another forty minutes. As if I'd be leaping out of bed now and driving around the country roads of Putney, Vermont? I bit back any number of smart-ass retorts and simply said, "Here." The phone went dead in my ear.

Goose and I looked at each other, wide-eyed and unsettled.

Why had a call come at 4 A.M.? And why was it from Norwegian television and not the Nobel Committee?

Just a few weeks before, we'd spent a month in Oslo during the successful negotiations of the treaty banning antipersonnel landmines. Some of our Norwegian friends had told us then that the International Campaign to Ban Landmines, which I'd coordinated since getting it off the ground in 1992, was a front-runner for the 1997 Nobel Peace Prize. Media had buzzed about it the entire time we were there, even though we'd deflected their questions.

The last night in Oslo, we'd been out celebrating the success of the treaty negotiations. One of the Norwegian diplomats had whispered to us that if we were awarded the Peace Prize, we'd get a call from the Nobel Committee around 3 A.M. our time. They tried to give recipients time to prepare themselves before the chair of the committee made the announcement at a press conference a couple of hours later in Oslo.

But no call had come at 3 A.M. And when the phone rang an hour later, it was a cryptic exchange with someone from Norwegian television, *not* the Nobel Committee. Goose and I started speculating, and the only thing that seemed reasonable to us was that the media wanted to know where we were so they could get the ICBL's reaction to *not* receiving the Nobel Peace Prize after so much hype and expectation. Now we had about forty minutes to try not to fret.

The phone rang again promptly at 4:40 A.M. It was the same guy, who again identified himself as being with a Norwegian TV station. There was no dramatic pause, he quickly went on to say that he'd been "authorized" to inform me that the "International Campaign to Ban Landmines and its coordinator Jody Williams" were the recipients of the 1997 Nobel Peace Prize.

I repeated the words so Goose would know what was going on, then asked the guy who had authorized him to say that. He only repeated that he'd been authorized to let me know. He told me to turn on my television in about twenty minutes to hear the announcement live on CNN. I told him we didn't have a TV. "Well," he said, "turn on the radio."

When I told him there was no radio either, he laughed and said he'd keep me on the line so I could hear it directly from Norway. Stunned, I wouldn't be able to believe it until I heard the Nobel Committee say it out loud. I asked for about ten minutes to call my family. He said he'd call back then.

Mom screamed, "Hoo-hoo and yippeee!" It was obvious she'd not slept any better than Goose and I that night. My father could sleep through almost anything. I asked Mom to call my sisters, Mary Beth and Janet, and my brother Mark to tell them to turn on their televisions and watch the announcement live. Then Goose and I waited until the phone rang again. We sat in bed with the receiver between our ears and listened as the press conference began. Francis Sejersted, then chair of the Nobel Committee, read the announcement, which captures the essence of our work in the Landmine Campaign:

> The Norwegian Nobel Committee has decided to award the Nobel Peace Prize for 1997, in two equal parts, to the International Campaign to Ban Landmines (ICBL) and to the campaign's coordinator Jody Williams for their work for the banning and clearing of antipersonnel mines.
>
> There are at present probably over one hundred million antipersonnel mines scattered over large areas on several continents. Such mines maim and kill indiscriminately and are a major threat to the civilian populations and to the social and economic development of the many countries affected.

The ICBL and Jody Williams started a process which in the space of a few years changed a ban on antipersonnel mines from a vision to a feasible reality. The Convention which will be signed in Ottawa in December this year is to a considerable extent a result of their important work.

There are already over 1,000 organizations, large and small, affiliated to the ICBL, making up a network through which it has been possible to express and mediate a broad wave of popular commitment in an unprecedented way. With the governments of several small and medium-sized countries taking the issue up and taking steps to deal with it, this work has grown into a convincing example of an effective policy for peace.

The Norwegian Nobel Committee wishes to express the hope that the Ottawa process will win even wider support. As a model for similar processes in the future, it could prove of decisive importance to the international effort for disarmament and peace.

I can't remember our immediate reaction when I hung up the phone, because we heard people outside. I crept to the window to see several cars parked in the driveway. Panicky, we threw on the clothes we'd taken off only a few hours earlier and went out to see who they were.

Journalists? The house sat at the end of a mile-long unmarked dirt road in the-middle-of-nowhere-Putney. We weren't prepared for them, and even less so for the onslaught that would follow. By 5:15 I was serving coffee to them in my kitchen. They were the first and last journalists we let in the house that day.

I was so thankful it turned out to be a glorious eighty-degree Indian summer day in Vermont. I kept wondering what we would have done with all the people if it had been raining.

By midmorning, the field in front of the house overlooking the beaver pond was studded with satellite feed trucks. Eight or nine of them. There were TV cameras dotting the field. On the deck. At my front steps. The day didn't stop, except for one ten-minute break, until the last TV truck rolled out at 8 P.M.

The interviews flowed from one to the next almost seamlessly. Journalists arrived from all of the morning TV news shows in the United States. From several in Norway, Canada, Sweden, and other places I can't begin to remember. There were some from several different shows on the BBC. We had local media. National media. International media.

All of them wanted to know how we'd use the Nobel Prize to pressure the Clinton administration especially, and other holdout states, to get on board. For the whole day we had media attention resulting from the Nobel announcement to further the message of the ICBL: Come to Ottawa. Sign the treaty. Ratify it as soon as possible. Join the tide of history.

I had no time that day to think about the course of my life and how I'd come to be surrounded by journalists, talking about antipersonnel landmines and the Nobel Peace Prize. No one would ever have predicted it. That a quiet kid from Vermont had become a hardheaded, straight-talking woman who'd helped change our world. But I did, and this is my story.

PART I

If You Could Be Anyone

CHAPTER ONE

What Do You Mean
I Can't Be the Pope?

At some point in grade school, I finally realized I didn't have a snowball's chance in hell of becoming the first woman pope. Then again, I'd also been slow in noticing I couldn't even be an altar boy. Perhaps that turned out to be not such a bad thing, but at the time it felt unfair. Why boys only? What was so special about them?

I so wanted to be clothed in magnificent vestments one day, head bowed to receive the Papal Crown. And of course, I'd be fluent in Latin. At church on Sundays, I'd imagine myself gloriously robed, standing at the altar, cloaked in incense. The tiniest whiff of its burning fragrance still summons vestiges of my religious upbringing.

Even after my papal dreams were shattered, I remained mystified by the pageantry, the drama, and the majesty of the Holy Roman Catholic Church. Simply saying those four words made me feel transported. I was enthralled by the stories of the lives of our brave and tragic saints and martyrs. I, too, wanted to be resolute and heroic and leave a big mark on the world. No one would ever have guessed that one day I would manage something of a lasting mark, but it most definitely wasn't in the category of saint or martyr.

As a young child I'd breathlessly awaited my chance to begin attending catechism, where I'd learn about sin and how to avoid it. The Ten Commandments, the categories of sins and their implications, and Church rules would be taught to us to help guide us in life. Then, in my little white dress and veil, I'd march down the center aisle in church and receive my First Communion. I would be absolved of my sins, Catholic ground zero. It came fast. We received First Communion around the age of seven, at which point we were supposedly able to reason clearly and therefore reliably exercise our free will to avoid sin.

My younger sister, Mary Beth, who is now the nurse in the family, insists that studies demonstrate today's youth aren't fully capable of understanding the consequences of their actions, religious or otherwise, until their early twenties. Ages ago, we were expected to get on with it at seven. Now they can't manage until they reach drinking age? Would that mean they shouldn't have their First Communion until reaching twenty-one?

In any case, and unfortunately for my seven-year-old head, catechism had its downside. I was a quiet kid with a tendency to fear authority. It didn't come from my parents, Ruth and John. Disinclined to exact punishment, they were also very bad at "no." But once I'd begun catechism, life smacked of "no." Almost everything in my world seemed to be a sin or to threaten one. Sometimes the simple act of living felt like running temptation's gauntlet, as if hydra-headed demons of evil were waiting at every turn, trying to lead me sinfully astray.

If Mom corrected me for some minor wrongdoing, like trying to beat up my younger siblings, I worried I was earning a one-way ticket to hell. With catechism's emphasis on sin rather than the compassion and forgiveness of Jesus, avoiding the inferno sometimes felt impossibly beyond my reach. Fear trumped reason, and I lived with it for years.

I prayed every night before bed. There was the standard "Now I lay me down to sleep . . ." and then you could mention your specific issues to God. I always prayed hard for a miracle so my older brother, Steve, would become able to hear. I added my own little pleas to the multitudinous ones of my parents, who'd been praying for the same thing almost from the day of his birth. My dad stopped by church every day for solitude and consolation. Although at some point Mom gave up praying for the Steve miracle—her knees raw from novenas on his behalf—Saint Jude, the patron saint of lost causes, remains her primary saint.

At some point in the lives of all five of her offspring, each of us either became or threatened to become the particular lost cause Mom prayed to save. While no patron of her saints, these days I am convinced my mother has powerful energy that she prays into her universe. When I need a little extra protection or strength, I get Mom on the phone and ask for her prayers to Saint Jude. It makes both of us feel better. Also, from time to time—and even though we've had amusing debates about religion—I fire off an email to Archbishop Desmond Tutu and ask for his prayerful support, too. So far he hasn't turned me down.

Perhaps surprisingly, these days I find satisfaction in contemplating Ganesh, the elephant-headed Hindu god. He is revered as a remover of obstacles, an attribute that seems to parallel Jude's intervention on behalf of lost causes. Ganesh makes me smile, in contrast to my unhappy recollections of sin and Catholic hellfire. But when I was a kid, even the dashing of my papal hopes didn't alter the fact that being Catholic was a central element of my life. I came by it naturally.

My grandmother, Marianna Bertolino, whose name was ultimately shortened to Anna or Ann after she came to America, was born in Italy. At the beginning of the 1900s, when she was about a year old, her parents left that seat of the Church's power for the tiny village of Poultney, Vermont. It didn't matter that years later my grandmother married my grandfather, Ralph Colvin, a self-proclaimed heathen. To get her hand, Ralph had to solemnly agree that any offspring would be raised Catholic. The same promise was required of any of the other heathens who wanted to marry my grandmother's seven sisters: it was the Catholic way or no way.

Therefore, my mother, Ruth, and her younger brother, Chuck, were raised in the Church. As was I and my two brothers and two sisters. It didn't matter that my father's side of the family, who we almost never saw in any case, was Scottish-Welsh Presbyterian. Despite the small percentage of our blood that is Italian, we kids all cleaved to that heritage and its religion. Ralph and Anna B. Colvin were my "real" grandparents. Dad's parents didn't figure hardly at all in our family equation. He didn't particularly like them himself.

· · ·

My father, John Clarence Williams, was drop-dead gorgeous. I have a picture of him at around age eighteen, and to my eyes he's virtually smoldering from beneath its sepia tint. To me he smacks of James Dean. When fifteen-year-old Ruth Colvin first saw him, her heart did a triple somersault, and it never stopped. She's related the story a million jillion times, but it always feels fresh in her telling.

"Jody," she says, seeing her past through luminous eyes. "When I first saw John, he was just home from World War II, walking downtown in his navy whites. He was so handsome I ran myself ragged trying to 'casually' appear in his line of sight no matter where he was." She bounces around the living room in imitation of her teenage self trying to nonchalantly chase down my father. Throughout their fifty-eight years together, anytime Mom saw my father unexpectedly, she got butterflies in her stomach. "Just like the very first time I saw him," she says.

Two months after they met, Dad asked my grandfather for permission to give Mom an engagement ring for her sixteenth birthday. Uninspired at the thought, and predictably, Ralph said flat-out no. He wasn't mean about it, but he said there'd be plenty of time for that once his daughter finished college. And, he pointed out, she wasn't even out of high school yet.

No fool, my father knew if Ruth went to college unattached, it would spell their end. Not long after my grandfather quashed the engagement hopes, my parents went to New York—easy because you can spit into New York State from Poultney—lied about my mom's age, and got themselves married by a justice of the peace. Later that evening, after the stark little ceremony, Dad dropped Mom off at her house and went back to his own place.

They supposedly envisioned carrying on as before and keeping their marriage a secret indefinitely. Ridiculous. In any case, some months later, Mom noticed that her period was late. She tried jumping rope, hard, to make it start. It didn't, and soon the impending need to tell her parents that she might be pregnant ended that delusion. Stephen John Williams wasn't part of any official strategy of outing the secret marriage, at least not that I know of. But some years ago I began to wonder if the thought hadn't been playing around somewhere in my dad's subconscious.

Despite the shock, there were no recriminations in the Colvin household—you stand with family. And much like I do, my grandfather tended to make more noise at life's more inconsequential irritants. With things that really mattered, he was straight, calm, and solid. After the requisite Catholic marriage ceremony to sanctify the union, Dad moved into my grandparents' home, carrying all his belongings in one brown paper bag. My grandparents and Mom's younger brother, Chuck, fully embraced my dad, and they became the loving family he'd always dreamed about.

. . .

Steve came howling into the world about six months later. Mom's undetected German measles during her pregnancy had left my brother stone deaf. His vocal cords worked, but Steve would never accurately pronounce words he couldn't hear. His ability to scream was unmatched, however. Four decades after his birth, sometimes it didn't feel all that different, although that was for very different reasons. And still it took more years before proper medication was prescribed that finally began to help him.

Even if my parents had known Mom had measles and considered the possible impact on a fetus, the course of their history wouldn't have changed. Their fate had been sealed from the moment Ruth Colvin first set eyes on John Williams in downtown Poultney in 1946. Notwithstanding their difficult first child.

Steve was the kind of night crier who makes all young parents want to scream themselves. He rarely granted a night of uninterrupted sleep. In those days, my father was earning twenty dollars a week shoveling coal. He left home early in the morning and came back late at night covered in coal dust. Mom says my six-foot-tall father's weight dropped to 137 pounds in those days. He looked like a scarecrow dusted in black, a far cry from the dashing navy man she'd drooled over.

Always exhausted, my father could fall asleep instantly. But even Dad couldn't sleep through Steve's screaming, and he'd take his turn walking his son around the dark bedroom trying to lull him to sleep. What my grandparents and Chuck did to block it all out, I do not know.

After about a year and a half of interminable crying, Steve began to calm down. Life was finally finding balance when Mom began her campaign for another baby. It seems insane. All I can imagine is that the screaming had something in common with giving birth—it was like the horrible pain that mothers soon forget or they'd never want another child. Apparently, once Steve was sleeping consistently, Mom forgot the tension and distress of eighteen months spent with a shrieking baby.

My dad didn't share the enthusiasm. After growing up extremely poor with seven siblings during the Great Depression, he was frightened and oppressed by the thought of a large family. He worried constantly about how he'd ever be able to give his family all the things he'd never had as a child. My parents and Steve were still living with my grandparents. But Mom was relentless in pursuit of her objective. I was born two months after Steve turned three.

By then they'd managed to move to a second-floor apartment in a house directly across the narrow street from my grandparents. When hugely pregnant with me, Mom gained fifty pounds, and she'd sit in the window of the apartment weeping as she stared longingly at her home. No one knew it then, but all that crying presaged worse things to come with another move. Mom wept not only for the loss of her life as it had been but also for how it might have been, despite her passionate love for my father and her continuing desire for more kids.

By the time she was twenty-three, my mother had four children. Mark was the youngest of them; then Mary Beth, who is eighteen months older than him; then me, twenty months older than Mary Beth; and Steve, three years older than I am. The youngest in our family is Janet, who wasn't born until after the trauma of our move to Brattleboro, a town two hours from Poultney. She's almost nine years younger than I am.

In my mother's place, with all those kids, I'd have gone stark raving mad. Her nervous breakdown would have looked mild by comparison. By the time I was thirteen, I knew I wasn't cut out for parenting. I'd felt it almost from the first time I performed the adolescent-girl job of babysitting, for the princessly sum of fifty cents an hour.

As soon as the door would close behind the happy parents going out for the evening, I'd feel trapped and desperate. It was as if all the air had been sucked out of me. A couple of hours later, at the sound of the parents' key in the door, I would feel an almost palpable sense of liberation. And I would be close to euphoric when I could leave. I knew then, on the cusp of abandoning my short-lived babysitting career, that motherhood and I would never ever be a good fit. It was demonstrated again when I was an adult.

When I was in my early forties, I made a gift of myself to my sister Janet and her husband, Dan, and also to Mary Beth and her husband, Paul. I offered each couple a week of free babysitting so they could go off on adult vacations. I stayed with Janet's kids first. Riley was a baby and his sister, Devan, was just walking. The next week, it was Emma, also a baby, and her sister, Libby, who was about four.

Even though they are my nieces and nephew and I love them like crazy, they drove me crazy. I felt exactly the way I had when babysitting in my youth. It may be hard for most people to understand, but two weeks with kids almost did me in. Creating the landmine campaign was less fraught with stress than trying to be a stand-in parent. Mom had to come and spell me from time to time over those two weeks, and she laughed at me every time she did. When the last day of my ordeal finally arrived, as Mary Beth and Paul pulled into their driveway, I was already standing in the door, bottle of champagne in my hand (for myself, to celebrate my liberation) and ready to flee. They, too, laughed at me.

Occasionally, and despite that experience, Mom still tries to tell me how different it would have been if I'd had my own. She'll always believe that if I'd had kids, I would have "loved it." "Just look at how you are with your animals," she insists. "Imagine if they were your children." The fact is, I've never understood why she'd had four of us almost in a row when she was still practically a kid herself, or why she'd still wanted more.

My father never tried to sell me on having children. He loved all of us every bit as much as my mom did; but given his experiences as a child, he empathized with my desire not to have kids.

· · ·

My father's mother, Jean Buchanan, was an immigrant like my Italian great-grandparents. She'd arrived in America from Scotland at the age of seventeen, quite a looker and with some money in her purse. My dad said both details were true. I never saw any photographic evidence of the former; the woman I knew was hard, cold, and bitter. Any traces of beauty were long gone, if they'd ever been there in the first place.

Perpetually squinting through a haze of cigarette smoke, Jean uttered harsh commentary in a harsh brogue. She was always complaining about her lot in life or one or another of her eight children. I never met Dad's father. He lived with his second wife only a few miles away in another village, but he never cared enough to meet us.

By the time Jean married Roy Williams, she had blown through whatever money she'd brought to America. I remain ignorant of how they met and why they married. When I think of Jean, in particular, and Roy, from how my parents described him, I can easily imagine them as unsympathetic and broken characters from the *Grapes of Wrath*.

Roy and Jean scraped by while Roy managed a run-down farm in the town of Hampton, New York, which is across the bridge from Poultney. While our village had a population of twelve hundred people, the only thing that marked Hampton was a grocery store by the side of the road that ran north through the state to the Canadian border. Hampton was a town that wasn't. My father was born in an old bed in the sad old rented farmhouse in a town that existed only as lines on a map.

My mother says that Jean was a sharp and unloving mother. The words "I love you" did not pass her lips, and she never held or hugged her kids. When my father reached ninth grade, Jean made him quit school and go to work to help support his seven younger siblings. She required that of all her children, each in turn. Before the others were old enough to help, my dad was the one who had to collect water from the farm's well every day for the family's needs.

My father didn't live in a place with electricity, indoor plumbing, or bathrooms until he was seventeen years old, which was when he joined the navy, with his mother's permission. Until then, he'd always used an outhouse. I didn't know this until after he died in 2004, because he had been too ashamed to talk about it. It wasn't until then that his weird jokes about chamber pots, which he referred to as "piss pots," made any sense to me at all.

When they first got married, Dad told my mom that he would never, ever go camping. Not that I can imagine for a second my mother ever wanting to either. It isn't her style. He said that he'd camped out the first seventeen years of his life and he'd never do it again.

My father was a kid when he developed his deep-in-the-gut hatred of inequality. In part it manifested itself through his profound dislike of the Republican Party, a dislike born in the grocery store in Hampton. He had the humiliating chore of going there to pick up the Depression-era support checks that helped the family survive.

The store's owner and his sons happened to be Republicans; they also happened to be men who abused the system and took a cut of families' support checks for "administering" the relief money. Those who dared to complain found even less money in their hands the next time. If they complained too much, there might be no money at all. And not only were those desperate families stolen from, they were treated like dirt in the process.

For my dad, these men epitomized greed, corruption, and—maybe the worst thing in his estimation—a complete lack of regard for the common man. Or as he put it, the "little guy." For his entire life, that family rode the waves of my father's psyche like wraiths. Whenever any of us accomplished something grand, something unexpected, he'd wish he could transport himself back in time and stride into their long-closed store, puff out his chest, and brag like mad. He'd show them. How could he possibly be trash if his family could do such great things? Imagine when I received the Nobel Peace Prize.

A few years after Mom and Dad were married, they managed to buy a grocery store in Poultney from one of Mom's Italian aunts and her husband, who'd taught Dad to be a butcher in the store. As soon as it was his, my father defiantly hung Democratic Party posters in its two big windows, which faced directly onto Main Street. When Roy saw the posters, he rushed into the store and tried to take them down, fearful that people would no longer shop there. All those in Poultney who mattered, and most of those who didn't, were Republican in those days.

Dad turned on his father. He didn't give a *damn* if no one shopped there. He was a Democrat, and he wasn't going to hide his beliefs from anyone. He didn't care what anyone thought. The signs stayed put. And no one stopped buying their food at my father's grocery store.

I inherited that attitude from my father and from my grandfather Ralph. When I was younger I didn't realize, or couldn't acknowledge, that it had come from both of them. As I grew up, I increasingly identified with my Grampa Ralph. He was strong, confident, and didn't suffer fools lightly. He laughed as easily and quickly as he angered. Once the anger passed, also quickly, he didn't think about it again.

I have Ralph's jaw and my dad's blue eyes. I didn't understand how much I identify with my father's lifelong concern for the everyman. Part of that is what helped shape me into the grassroots activist that I am today. That, and trying to protect my brother.

CHAPTER TWO

A Special Place in Hell

When they took increasing pleasure in harassing Steve, I became certain Billy and Bobby, the boys who lived next door, merited a special place in hell. Certainly their souls must be dark if they could act like that toward my handicapped brother. He hadn't chosen to be deaf. He couldn't help it if he couldn't talk. The brothers morphed from simply irritating next door neighbors into nasty nemeses we'd escape only with our move away from Poultney.

Billy and Bobby etched themselves into my memory on a day that started out innocuously enough when Steve and I set out for a bike ride. We pedaled away from our house on Norton Avenue toward the hill at the end of the street, which seemed immense at the time. There, we turned left at the corner where our cousins lived and continued around the block and back to the front of the house. One spin around that small block was never enough, but we weren't allowed to venture farther into the wild reaches of Poultney; my mom could conjure up too many potentially dangerous scenarios. So we often went round and round the block until we got dizzy.

That afternoon, as we rounded the corner for the third or fourth time and rode along the side of the hill, Billy and Bobby came charging at us from behind thick bushes. Running along the hillside above us, they rained down stones and empty tin cans on us. We were either too shocked or too stupid to swerve out of their range before a can caught Steve in the head, cutting a long gash in his scalp. Yelping as blood poured down his face, he managed a shaky U-turn and pedaled home as fast as he could, certain I was right behind him.

If he'd looked back, he'd have seen my bike in the middle of the street, its front wheel spinning madly. Instead of my mousy self standing mutely by, shaking in my sneakers while they picked on my brother, righteous indignation overpowered my fear and I went after them, screaming like a banshee. I wanted to catch them and beat the crap out of them and make them pay for hurting Steve.

It didn't occur to me at the moment I'd be the one who'd likely get the beating, but that was irrelevant anyway. Before I even reached the ambush site, they were crowing at me from the top of the hill. Panting, bathed in tears of frustrated impotence, I watched them disappear. As their voices faded away, I picked up my bike and, exhausted and deflated, pushed it home.

Mom was standing in the front yard hugging Steve tight, pressing a towel to his head. She was looking at me as if some other kid had taken over my body. When I was young I never raised my voice. Mom swears that when I was a baby, I almost never cried. I was such a good girl growing up that I drove rebellious Mary Beth mad. She saw me as the boring, brownnosing, goody-two-shoes of the family. But I remember myself that day as a girl transformed.

Once we'd left Poultney, the bullies next door became just a very unpleasant memory, less and less important with time and distance. Maybe my feeble attempt to defend my brother had been a once-only, out-of-body sort of episode, and now that he was safe and secure I'd never have to worry about coming out of my quiet shell again.

$$\bullet \qquad \bullet \qquad \bullet$$

I'd just begun second grade when our Poultney bubble burst. Dad sold the grocery store and our house, and right before my seventh birthday, we'd be moving to Brattleboro, Vermont. By Poultney standards, Brattleboro, ten times its size with a population of about twelve thousand, was a megalopolis. At least my mother viewed it that way. She also acted like we were moving to the ends of the earth rather than ninety miles southeast of Poultney.

None of us wanted to move, but Steve needed to go to school, and the Austine School for the Deaf, in Brattleboro, was the only one my parents could find where he could be a day student. Most schools for the deaf at the time required students to live at the school. My family had already suffered through one such fiasco with Steve, and Mom and Dad weren't about to make him or any of us relive the experience.

Just before Steve turned six, they'd started looking for schools for him. They'd decided against the Austine School at the time. Back then, it consisted of one ancient building that looked like something out of Dickens, and its headmaster, nearly as old, didn't exude any apparent love for his calling. With few options, my parents finally settled on a boarding school in Connecticut.

The first time they dropped him off at that school, Steve broke loose from the people holding his hands and tried to claw his way over its eight-foot-high chain-link fence. That unsuccessful attempt to get back to my parents as they slowly drove away marked the beginning of the complete disaster that the boarding school experience was, not only for my brother but also for the rest of us.

As Mom's endless novenas to Saint Jude made their way toward the heavens, Steve showed no signs of settling in. In their equivalent of a Hail Mary pass, my parents decided that every Friday they'd drive the pre-interstate, two-lane roads to Connecticut to see him. Sometimes they'd stay there, and other times they'd bring him home for the weekend. Either way, I felt unsettled by the constant comings and goings of my always-tense parents. It's probably then that Mary Beth started sucking the middle fingers of her left hand while pulling out her already sparse hair with the right. Even with the end of those torturous trips, she didn't spare her hair.

Steve was wasting away. At school he'd barely eat, and everyone was concerned about his deteriorating health. Already a slight kid, he began to look ever more waiflike. He became extremely pale and totally passive. My brother no longer had the energy or spirit to fight, a result of the medications he'd been prescribed to calm him enough to adjust to the school.

Mom's novenas continued wafting upward, but apparently no one heard them. The intolerable situation came to an end when everyone agreed it was in Steve's best interests that he return home. He'd not even made it to Christmas vacation. Boarding school was not his solution.

Once he knew he was home to stay and the meds washed out of his system, my brother was a boy transformed. I have a black-and-white studio photograph of him, Mary Beth, and me taken not long after the Connecticut misadventure. My sister looks under two, I'd have been three, and Steve six; it must have proved too much of an effort to try to include infant Mark in the shot. Actually we have no pictures of Mark until the requisite grade-school photographs.

Wearing a white shirt with a bow tie, Steve shines handsomely in the picture, and his huge smile reveals no vestiges of the Connecticut nightmare. Mary Beth looks out, pathetically appealing with her slightly crossed eye and ragged hair. She was born anxious, and her anxiety had only been exacerbated with the dramas of Steve's time away at school. As a kid she was string-bean skinny. I, on the other hand, was born round and topped with a bald pumpkin head like Charlie Brown's. I also had an eye that moved about on its own terms. I sucked my thumb until I was nine, but kept my hands out of my hair. This was a good thing, because I've never had much.

By the time this photo of the three of us was taken, Mom either hadn't discovered home permanents or had decided I wasn't old enough to have one yet, because my white-blond hair is in a little flip. She'd already started attacking my bangs, however. In that picture I have raggedy bangs chopped so short that they almost didn't exist. But at least to my own eyes, the bangs and my new horn-rimmed glasses in no way diminish my round cuteness.

With Steve's return home and familial harmony restored for the time being, my parents found a tutor for him who used mail-order guides to teach the deaf at home. By the end of three years, she'd reached the limits of what she could teach him. Mom and Dad had to renew the search for a school for the deaf that would accept him as a day student. And that was how we ended up moving to Brattleboro.

The choices were still discouragingly few, but my parents had heard positive things about changes at the school they'd first visited in Brattleboro before the doomed Connecticut decision. New classrooms and a gymnasium had been built at the Austine School, and they'd also hired a dynamic, innovative headmaster. After long discussions with him and much deliberation at home, my parents agreed that Austine was the place for Steve and we'd be moving to Brattleboro.

·   ·   ·

We couldn't manage to leave Poultney without drama. Since we were moving right before my birthday, Mom planned my party early so my friends and cousins could help me celebrate. It was a grand birthday and good-bye party all rolled into one. Everyone was caught up in high-energy, sugar-fueled excitement.

As I was blowing out the candles on the cake, five-year-old Mary Beth jumped out of her chair and began teasing Mark, who was a few months shy of four. He had a sourball in his mouth, and my sister was dangling the bag of hard, round candies over his head, just out of his reach. As he looked up and stretched to grab the bag, he inhaled the sourball.

Clutching at his throat, Mark immediately began coughing and choking, but gasping for breath only lodged the candy more firmly in his throat. The festive party atmosphere dissolved instantly. Mom started slapping his back to try to dislodge the candy. It didn't work. She flipped him upside down and shook him by the heels. That didn't work either. Turning him right side up again, she slapped his back another time. No luck, and Mark was turning a distinct shade of blue.

Desperate, my mother stuck her finger as far down his throat as humanly possible and managed to get the edge of her long, beautiful, red fingernail under the candy and flip it free. By that time, Mark's eyes had rolled back in his head and he wasn't quite conscious, but at least he started breathing again.

Through it all Mom wept in fear, but she never stopped trying to get that damn candy out of her son's throat. The rest of us were her hysterical chorus. When the town's doctor arrived, Mark was lying on the sofa, still dazed. By then his normal color had been restored, and he was declared sound. Not long ago Mary Beth told me that once Mark had started choking, she'd fled and taken refuge under our bed, trying not to cry out loud. Long after the event, she continued to feel upset and guilty because she'd "almost killed her brother." None of us had ever noticed her part in the drama.

Mark's near-death experience frayed whatever resolve Mom might have had to try to make our move to Brattleboro as smooth as possible. Instead, it was sheer hell. My mother was immediately and totally miserable, and *every single weekend without fail* we'd pile into the family's blue-and-white Ford and drive home to Poultney to stay with my grandparents. In between those trips, Dad would continue his search for a job.

The two-hour ride was mostly a nightmare. My stressed out parents took turns hollering at the four of us in the back seat to "behave" or "be quiet" or, in desperation, "shut up or we'll stop this car and spank you." The threats were idle, but sometimes Mom would completely lose patience and make weak efforts to slap at us over her shoulder while Dad focused ever more intently on driving.

Much of our misbehavior in the car, if that's what it was, was a battle for space. Sometimes one of us would lie down in the rear window, above the back seat. Another would get on the floor and try to find comfort stretching out over the hump in the middle. That left the two others vying for the back seat itself. And somebody was always carsick. The worst case was when Mary Beth lurched forward to be sick on the floor, only to throw up on sleeping Mark's face. His mouth happened to be open at the time.

Just as it seemed like the road trips from hell were never going to end, they did. Unfortunately, it wasn't because the family had happily adjusted to Brattleboro. We no longer went to Poultney, because my mother couldn't. She couldn't get out of bed. In the terminology of the time, Mom had a complete nervous breakdown.

·   ·   ·

After half a year without work, my father had finally found a job as a salesman for General Electric and would cover a three-state area. This meant he'd be traveling all week, leaving the house early Monday mornings and not getting back home again until late Friday evenings. While it was a huge economic relief that Dad finally had a job, my mother felt completely abandoned while trying to cope with four kids in an alien town, with no friends or support network. My father had to take their only car, which left her feeling further trapped. Mom was angry at my father and envious at the same time. He'd get to hop in the car and drive off for five days of peace and quiet while she struggled to manage everything alone.

If I'd been in my father's position, I'd have been thrilled to drive away from that distressed, chaotic house. If I'd been in my mother's shoes, I would have been a raging maniac. Mom didn't have the energy to rage. Instead she descended into a profound clinical depression, where she lingered for about a year. It was a no-win situation.

Dad couldn't stop working, so he hired a woman to stay with us while he was gone. Mrs. Day must have been competent enough and not unpleasant, because I have no bad memories of her. I think of her in shades of gray. The rest of life around that time is sepia colored. If my mother emerged from her bedroom at all, I don't remember it. The only clear memory I have of her from that year is watching her sleep when Dad would let me tip-toe into the room to look at her and make sure she was still there.

I don't know how my mother pulled herself back from her abyss. She had no antidepressants, and they couldn't afford counseling. Even if they could have, at that point in my parent's lives, help of that kind, outside the family, would have been out of the question. Probably her acute depression just ran its course as most do, helped along by the fact that, for my mother's sanity and the sake of the family, my father stopped working for General Electric.

Dad found a job in town with a local vending company that provided food machines for factories in town and at some of the ski lodges around Mount Snow. They also had jukeboxes and pinball games. A few years later, my father bought the business, which he owned for the next three decades.

As far as I could see, he wasn't around all that much more than when he'd been a traveling salesman. Along with his full-time work with Brattleboro Vending Corporation, Dad held a variety of part-time jobs on the side. He sold used cars; and he sold mobile homes, which we were never supposed to call trailers but did anyway. Just to poke fun, which he didn't find funny at all.

My father was an insurance investigator once and, later, a

bartender. At one point he owned his own bar, until my mother told him it was the bar or her. There were too many late nights there, after he'd worked all day, and too many women interested in hanging around the handsome bartender.

Dad's long workdays weren't only a result of our puritanical New England work ethic; he cobbled jobs together to make ends meet. He was gone by the time we got up for school, and he often worked late into the night. But he was always home for the family dinner at 5:30 every night.

Only recently has my mother finally recognized that what she lived through was acute clinical depression. Curiously, despite the move to Brattleboro and its terrible impact on my mom, I've always considered her to be the rock of stability in the family. I was never one of the kids who hid things from her. To the contrary, there were many times throughout my life she wished I *wouldn't* share my adventures with her. Sometimes when I'd start to tell her something she didn't want to hear, she'd stick her fingers in her ears and start humming. I'd just wait her out. I always wanted her to know the entire me, not just the good parts.

Mom was always deeply embarrassed about her nervous breakdown, even though no one seemed to resent her for it, covertly or openly. It wasn't until we were young adults that we could try joking with her about it. Sometimes she could laugh, but usually she'd end up describing all of the factors that had contributed to the breakdown—as if we hadn't lived them ourselves.

And even though having four young kids was part of what had crushed her ability to cope, it was just on the other side of her depression that she became pregnant with Janet, who was born about six months before I turned nine. We all think getting pregnant again helped bring her back. She was totally excited. We moved to a bigger and nicer apartment just up the street, where there'd be more room for the baby. And when Janet arrived, we were all overjoyed. A new sister. Mom was happy again, finally. Dad smiled because Mom was smiling. We didn't know it was a brief interlude, and that not too long after Janet was born, Steve would begin his long descent into insanity.

. . .

When we moved to Brattleboro, I started going to Green Street School. It was just down the hill from the rented apartment where we lived. Despite my being a good student, school was sometimes an anxiety-provoking proposition. Like so many kids, I never felt I was smart enough, and I worried about it all the time. I fretted about the possibility of bad grades, but more than that I worried about looking stupid. Fourth grade arithmetic with Miss Larkin (although my friend Judy insists it was Miss Lawrence *not* Miss Larkin) was especially torturous. When it came to memorizing the multiplication tables, I was bound in knots of misery. We'd work on them in class, study them at home, and work on them more in class.

Miss Larkin's favored technique was to randomly call on students to stand up and recite whichever table she dictated: "Wally, recite the 7s table for us." Or "Joyce, the 9s table." The lucky ones got the 2s or 3s. She'd stand at the front of the class, stout and gray-haired, peering at her victims through steel-rimmed eyeglasses.

Most would try to avoid her eyes, hoping she'd call on someone else. Sooner or later Miss Larkin would get to everyone, and you'd be the one standing up—a deer in the headlights of her piercing eyes. How I hated that part of class with its potential for public humiliation. Not surprisingly at all, I hate math. However, I do remember my times tables.

Miss Larkin made a lasting mark on me and looms large in my psyche. To this day there are times when I'm asked a direct question and I go into deer-in-the-headlights mode and blank out. Most recently, this happened when I was part of a small editing team working on an annual landmine report with my husband, Steve Goose, who created the report and, for its first six years, served as its editor in chief.

Once I'd finish editing a chapter, he'd go over it, peppering me with questions: "How do you know this is correct?" "What's the source of this fact?" "This paragraph actually makes sense to you as it's written? You left it like this?"

At first frustrated and then angry as the questions kept coming, I could sometimes answer them and sometimes not. After all, I wasn't the researcher; I was just helping edit. But Goose's machinelike dissection of the issues and command of the information produced an endless barrage that would send me over the edge. My face would flush and I'd start to sweat.

Suddenly, in the midst of one such editorial inquisition, a vision of Miss Larkin popped into my head. And I started to laugh. Goose wasn't particularly amused when I first explained the comparison. Now when I feel like I'm being harangued with questions on any topic, I give him my fish-eye look of disdain and call him "Miss Larkin." He doesn't miss the point.

·   ·   ·

During the year of Miss Larkin, a new kid moved to town. Michael was an especially pathetic specimen of gawky grade-school youth. His ears stuck straight out from his head like those of Dumbo the flying elephant, or like Mary Beth's when she was young. The poor kid was also so pale he was nearly translucent, was incredibly skinny, and had no redeeming athletic abilities whatsoever. No one ever wanted to get stuck on a team with Michael during recess. He was the kind of kid who always got picked last.

David, on the other hand, was the blond, blue-eyed stud of Green Street School. He was the biggest, most athletic, smartest boy there. It's likely that every girl in grade school had a crush on him, and maybe even I did too, but that's not why I remember him.

He lorded it over everyone on the playground. Self-appointed king of recess, David was always team captain no matter what the game, and he chose the best players for his own team. He played to win. Not a gracious winner, he was likely an even worse loser. But who'd know? David never lost at anything.

One day, our class was making a large circle in order to play kick ball. As Michael shuffled his way into line, David, with a dash of machismo tinged with nasty, jumped in front of him. He chortled as his chest bump sent Michael out of the circle, arms swinging wildly as he tried to keep his balance. Michael's head was already hanging in shame, and he seemed to get even smaller as he backed farther away without a word.

I wasn't a friend of geeky Michael, but I couldn't stand to watch David humiliate him so brazenly. I wanted Michael to defend himself. He could talk! But he wouldn't. And why did we let David get away with it, sheep in the presence of the big guy's power, which we conceded to him by doing nothing?

That we all stood mute and watched his obnoxious behavior said as much about us as it did about him, and it made me sick. Suddenly I knew if I did nothing, I'd feel like less of a human being, even if I couldn't put it that way at the time. All those catechism lessons—do for others what you would want them to do for you—must have taken root.

Quivering with anger and fear, in unequal proportion, I stepped in front of David. Struggling to control my voice, I asked why he bullied people who couldn't stand up to him. I expected a barbed-tongue response, but David surprised us all when he backed down without protest. He opened up the circle and waved Michael back in.

My insides trembled for the rest of recess, but David seemed to take it in stride. He never harassed me for defending Michael, and he didn't treat him unfairly again. I began to wonder how many others could be helped as easily if people had the courage to stand up to their own fear and take action when they knew it was the right thing to do. It took a long, long time but eventually I recognized that each time I did it, it was easier the next time. (Just for the record, David peaked in grade school.)

.   .   .

Not long after I'd conquered my times tables, Steve started to complain about school. The other kids were mean, or they were stupid, or they pushed him during basketball—pretty much the normal complaints of many kids in school. But my brother began losing his unique sense of humor that had developed after the boarding school fiasco. As humor retreated, anger filled its space.

Much of his rising fury was focused on Mom. After all, he thought, it was clearly her fault that he was deaf. "Why me?" he'd sign while yelling at her. "Why can all the rest of your kids hear and talk and not me"? As his anger and complaints increased, he began trying to avoid school.

Steve would come into the kitchen as Mom was rushing to fix us breakfast and make sure we were ready for school. Knowing she was too busy to pay close attention, he'd start signing that he didn't feel well. She fell for it a few times before realizing it was his get-out-of-going-to-school strategy. When Mom began to ignore his complaints and make him go to school, he got more dramatic. He'd come into the kitchen, feign a swoon, and drop to the floor.

Mom would continue whatever she was doing, walking around him or stepping over him without acknowledging him on the floor. The first couple of times he did it, the rest of us thought it was funny and laughed at him. But when she continued to ignore him, he'd jump up and gesticulate furiously, using our family's homemade signing, "Didn't you see what just happened? Didn't you see me faint? Can't you see that I'm sick?" Then we'd sit at the table, trying to be invisible while eating breakfast and hoping his bomb wouldn't go off.

It sounds kind of amusing now, but then there was nothing funny about it. Each time Steve didn't get what he wanted, his outbursts became a little louder and more frightening. He'd get in Mom's face and scream. By the time we moved to our new house at 10 Chapin Street, he'd started threatening my mother physically. He was fifteen and crazy strong.

Nobody could understand why Steve turned from the relatively normal-seeming kid into the raging teenager he'd become. We believed he was an angry deaf kid who'd outgrow it sooner or later. But as time went on, his thwarted attempts to avoid school were not all that enraged him, and we could never be sure what would be the trigger.

Two topics—divorce and communism—could really set my brother off. He was a Catholic true believer, primarily because Catholicism taught him that the disabled would be whole in heaven and he was counting on it. Since Elizabeth Taylor was the divorce queen of the era, and divorce is a mortal sin, few things could throw him into a frenzy like fresh news of her love life. If it wasn't her, then some transgression by the godless Soviets or Cubans would make him fly into a rage.

"Why does he care what Elizabeth Taylor does?" I'd wonder aloud during his outbursts. Or: "Why does he care about the communists?" I started standing behind him and chanting provocative responses at him that he couldn't hear anyway. Perversely, it made me feel better.

Whether it was communism, Elizabeth Taylor, or high school, when Steve blew up, Mom was his target. At least once he tried to strangle her with the telephone cord. Another time, as she was trying to call my father for help, he ripped the telephone off the wall. The chain lock Dad put on their bedroom door didn't provide the refuge Mom sought. Steve simply kicked the door open.

With his new volatility, it was impossible to predict how quickly his rage would pass and he'd be the same old Steve, begging my mother's forgiveness for being a "bad boy." He'd mouth the words *bad boy* over and over as he gave the family sign for *bad,* which was a light slap at his rear end—sort of mimicking a parent spanking a misbehaving child. He was as bewildered by the mood swings as we were.

Steve and I began to have our own run-ins too. Once I reached high school, I started to challenge his outbursts. Making fun of him behind his back wasn't enough anymore. I was carrying around my own pent-up anger and frustration because no one "stood up to him." I was ready to try.

One time when I was around sixteen, we were both in the living room, and he was sitting where he always did, on an ottoman just inches from the TV screen. We never understood why he sat so close; maybe he was trying to lip-read. More likely it was because he knew it irritated everyone else when he sat in their line of sight like that. Often he'd also turn the sound off.

If he couldn't hear the TV, nobody was going to. No fan of the medium, I didn't care about the shows themselves. It was the principle.

That particular day I was ironing behind him. The ironing board didn't live in the TV room, but since Mom always ironed in front of the television, that was where I did it. It was Pavlovian. Every time I set the iron down on the ironing board, he could feel the vibration, and it was getting on his nerves. After a while, each time the iron hit the board, he'd holler and sign at me to stop ironing. Finally, I flipped him a furiously shaking bird and told him to buzz off because I was working and had to get it done.

Within seconds he was standing on the other side of the ironing board, bellowing at me, just inches from my face. I signed for him to back off and threatened to slap his face. Instead of moving away, he furiously egged me on: "Slap me, slap me, slap me." Suddenly, without thought, I surprised both of us and obliged him. Mom ran into the room just as he wound up and slapped me right back, hard, across the face. I did see stars as I staggered but managed not to fall, and Mom yanked on Steve's arm. The shock of it all snapped him back to normal, and again he was sorry. Bad, bad, bad.

.　　.　　.

My brother had the great misfortune of being born in 1947, when the guiding philosophy in teaching the deaf was to force them into the hearing world. Since they live in a hearing world, the theory went, they must learn how to operate in it. If allowed to live in an insular world of sign language, which so few people spoke, how could they ever function in the "real" world? That meant reading lips, learning how to talk.

Families of the deaf were discouraged from learning sign language, because that would only serve to isolate the deaf family member. We somehow managed with a rudimentary, homemade sign language and signing the alphabet. Mom was the best at it, and Mary Beth and I did okay. My father was always clueless about signing, and Mark and Steve couldn't really communicate with each other before they were adults. In the early years, Janet was so young and afraid that all she wanted to do was hide from Steve.

When I try to think about my brother's world of minimal communication with the most important people in his life, our family, my mind closes down. It loses the ability to tread that path. I can't handle imagining his existence and don't want to try to put myself there now. All that does is stir up memories I don't want to relive, since I can't change a thing.

One image that frequently forces itself into my mind, however, and which captures the isolation, is the family dinner, which we ate together every night until we all were grown and out of the house. We're seated around the table, talking on top of each other—the females of the family, that is—and then there's Steve sitting there, watching. He's unable to follow anything we're talking about and is involved only in the mechanics of passing food, eating. But until he changed, I believed he was really there, part of the family, just like the rest of us, except he couldn't hear.

A memory of his being forced to speak makes me quiver. Steve wasn't excused from confession. The deaf were given no special dispensation, although the routine was somewhat different for them since they couldn't whisper their sins through the screen in a darkened confessional. Before the regular confessions began, my brother (and any other deaf Catholic in town) would meet with the priest at the front of the church, in a small room off to the side. There he'd present his sins, which he literally checked off on the sin list. The priest would indicate what his penance would be and then motion for Steve to recite the Act of Contrition.

Maybe if you were familiar with the ritual, you could identify the prayer. If you stumbled into the church unknowing, you'd hear eerie sounds echoing through the house of the Lord. Since he'd never heard sound, Steve couldn't modulate the volume or tone of his voice. It wasn't that he was yelling, but somehow the combination of the peculiar pitch and tone resulted in his prayer reverberating off the walls of the church.

Perhaps my brother felt nothing but joy at being freed of his sins, because he certainly had no idea about the sound. Sitting in the back of the church, however, waiting for his torturous prayer to end, I'd be in agony. How much was for him and how much was about my own embarrassment, I honestly don't know.

But so much for the philosophy of forcing the deaf into the "real" world of the hearing. The first time I saw *Children of a Lesser God,* a movie about an angry young deaf woman fighting for the right to express herself as a deaf woman, not as a hearing woman might, I sobbed through much of the film.

Once, some years later, I cried throughout most of a weekend after watching it. Twice. Guilt induced masochism? Unfortunately, the book I was reading at the time, about the life experiences of children born completely deaf, didn't provide escape and instead underscored the depth of the sadness I was feeling.

.   .   .

One thing Steve and I had in common as kids was that we both were terrified of the Soviet Union and the nuclear threat. I first learned about nuclear bombs at Green Street School. We were part of what is now known as the "duck and cover" generation.

During emergency tests, we'd have to get under our desks and curl into a near-fetal position. Our legs had to be tucked into our chests, our arms wrapped tightly around our legs, and our heads on our knees, to be ready in case the bomb ever fell. Sometimes we'd file into the gym and line up against the walls in the same curled-up position. Because the gym didn't have any windows, the idea was that it would be harder for the bomb blast to reach us. Right. Have you ever been to Hiroshima?

I don't know who developed these fabulous exercises in "nuclear safety," but we felt anything but safe. The possibility of nuclear war felt like much more than just an unpleasant thing to worry about. Fear seeped deep into the marrow of my bones.

At that time in my very young life, if I wished that my family had tons of money, it wasn't so that I could have lots of beautiful clothes that matched, and toys, and a fabulous house with a built-in swimming pool. What I wanted was our own bomb shelter in the backyard so we might really be safe. I tried hard to focus on the fantasy of the security a bomb shelter offered, and not on what the world would be like once we dared emerge from it. I especially wished we had one when Russia tried to put nukes in Cuba.

The image of President Kennedy on the television screen during the Cuban Missile Crisis is seared into my brain. Young and handsome, yet presidential and somber, he spoke to the nation about the possibility of war because the Soviet Union was threatening our hemisphere with nuclear weapons in Cuba. America was demanding their immediate removal. Each day of the crisis was more tense than the last, until finally we were told the Soviet Union had backed down. The world had edged away from the nuclear abyss.

Though I had just turned twelve at the time, I was furious at Khrushchev and "the communists." I had visions of storming into the United Nations and addressing the General Assembly, where I'd get Khrushchev to "admit" that he was indeed a communist. Somehow, through the force of my eloquence, and before the world, I'd convert him into a freedom-loving democrat who would then return to the Soviet Union and liberate all its citizens.

I should be embarrassed at the memory. My only defense is that I was young and obviously had an unsophisticated understanding of the world. At least I knew about the United Nations, even if I did embrace the fantasy that it was a world body where people actually put aside national interests and worked together to resolve issues for the good of us all.

Once the crisis had passed and stability in the Cold-War world was restored, my U.N.-peacemaker fantasy passed as well. Little did I know how much the U.N. and weapons would feature in my adult world.

CHAPTER THREE

Claude, Casey,
and the Corvair Convertible

In the last days of summer in 1967, I fell in love with Claude. It was an August afternoon before the start of our senior year in high school when we first noticed each other. I was sixteen. Everybody was at the bowling alley. I hated bowling, but it was a place to hang out when the day wasn't nice enough to spend at the lake. So there I was at the Brattleboro Bowl with a bunch of girls, watching the boys watching us back.

Claude and I had seen each other in school over the years and never given each other a thought. That afternoon, seemingly out of nowhere, I became viscerally aware of him as he played pool. I knew he was feeling something, too, because, when I'd try to glance surreptitiously in his direction, he would be looking right back at me. The air felt charged.

The attraction I felt that day wasn't a figment of my hyper-stimulated imagination. Shortly after the bowling alley, we had our first date and then became inseparable—until the trauma of my going off to college a year later. Until then, it was Claude and me and his turquoise-and-white Thunderbird.

The car was an older model with fins sweeping up in back. Its interior was more beat-up than the exterior and had great tears in the upholstery that continuously spewed foam stuffing, which clung tenaciously to anything it touched. Janet, eight at the time, apparently was mortified by the car and its stuffing, and when she rode with us she tried to hide in the backseat so no one would see her. I never noticed. From my perspective the car was a blessing and a curse. Claude drove my siblings and me to and from school every day, but the Thunderbird was also a convenient place for the possibility of "sin" followed by shame and confession angst.

.   .   .

By the time Claude and I were kissing in the Thunderbird, I was visiting the confessional less and less frequently. At seventeen, I found that the underpinnings of my faith were collapsing after years of questioning.

One night a few years earlier, when I was thirteen and sleeping over at a friend's house, we were lying in sleeping bags on the attic floor. Through the windows, I could see stars spread across a broad expanse of the sky, layer after layer, from the brightest to mere pinpricks of light. I started trying to imagine the expanse of the universe. Struggling to grasp infinity and where it all came from made my brain feel like it was hyperventilating. The correct answer, of course, was God, who had created heaven and earth. But that night, for the first time, the rote answer didn't feel right.

Maybe the universe existed simply because it existed. Maybe God was the creation of humans and not the other way around. This wasn't original, breakthrough thinking, but that night it was for me, and it excited and scared me in equal measure. As those excommunication-worthy thoughts crystallized, I panicked. According to the faith, and as in many other religions, its adherents are the chosen ones. If you choose to deny the existence of God, you're damned to hell for all eternity.

Eternity and infinity were equally incomprehensible, but the hellfire that plagued my mind for years felt very real. Even though I thought a truly just God would prefer honesty to lies about believing, I balked. Thinking about burning in hell was just too frightening, and I beat a terrified retreat. But it was only a matter of time before questions resurfaced.

During the time I was with Claude, the priests who ran our church were of a particularly militant order. Forget about the compassion and mercy of the New Testament, they were stuck in the older books of the Bible. Keeping the flock in line was, for them, about fire and brimstone and fear.

The head priest, with his close-cropped white hair, square jaw, and rigid posture, could almost be taken for a marine. He must have prided himself on being a stalwart soldier of Christ. (Pride is one of the seven deadly sins . . .) I could envision him smiting idolaters for Yahweh. One thing young girls definitely didn't want to experience was time in his confessional. He simply hated women.

After a close encounter in the Thunderbird, I had to confess for the first time that I'd "let my boyfriend touch me." I'd had all my clothes on, so there wasn't much to be excited about, but that didn't count for anything. Unfortunately, the confessor that day was the marine-priest of God. The incident itself had been traumatizing. I felt dirty, guilty, and conflicted enough without that man telling me it was all my fault because women were temptresses who led men down the path of sin. Apparently in his book, men were completely defenseless before our charms.

I emerged from the confessional more livid than shamed. He couldn't know who did the tempting; he hadn't been there. And he was a priest and didn't know anything about male-female relationships anyway. I disliked him intensely, and his lack of compassion only made me feel more and more alienated from the Church. His colleague wasn't much better.

I was continuing to attend catechism, although I was increasingly at odds with the other parish priest, who taught the classes. We fought over sin and just about everything else. For example, I asked why, if the intention to sin was so important, taking birth control pills was a deadly sin, while the "natural method" was perfectly fine. In both cases the intention was to sin by avoiding pregnancy.

Because, I was told, with the natural method a couple could still receive God's gift of a child. But if God were omnipotent, I said, he wouldn't be hindered by a little pill if he were really intent on giving that gift. The flustered and angry priest was adamant: pill bad, natural good. I was equally adamant that it wasn't logical.

We also fought over the infallibility of the pope. How could a mere human be infallible? The priest assured us that the pope was infallible only in questions of the Church. But if popes were infallible, why did they change the laws of the Church seemingly willy-nilly? Priests could marry, for example, until the twelfth century, when a pope then declared they couldn't, and they still couldn't. But why could married Episcopal priests become Catholic priests and remain married? And suddenly, after 1966, eating meat on Friday was no longer a grave sin? What happened to all the poor fools who'd committed the sin before 1966?

My pope questions were the ones that exceeded the priest's tolerance, because he threatened that if I didn't accept the infallibility of the pope, I was "excommunicable." If that was the case, then excommunicated I was at seventeen years of age. I never went to catechism again or to Mass. I was liberated from confession and no longer worried about adding new sins to the sin list.

·   ·   ·

The Thunderbird might have been a hotbed of high school sin, but once I left for the University of Vermont, about three hours northwest of Brattleboro, it didn't manage to bring Claude to see me on the weekends. Back then there were strict and early curfews in the dorms, which were not coed. With no friends at the university, Claude had no free place to stay, and he couldn't afford a hotel room. That meant it fell to me to find ways to get home to see him as often as I could.

When my parents had driven our empty station wagon away from my dorm after helping me move in, I'd seen my world coming to an end. No family. No Claude. I was bereft. But moping around, homesick and weeping over my faraway boyfriend, helped me maintain my good-girl status through my first semester at college.

As I'd set out for my first day of classes in 1968, I'd thought myself a picture, albeit a sad and distracted one, primly attired in a blue-and-white checked A-line skirt with matching blue sweater. I can't say for sure what the classes were, but I have no trouble remembering the outfit. It seemed to define me as I began my college career.

I made my life at school as small as possible. I always went to class, then scurried back to my room to study. Signing in and out of my dorm as required and never missing curfew, I was a model of propriety. My desperate energy was always focused on those weekends when I could get home to my beloved. I was so distraught that I considered moving back there and going to a community college so I could be near him.

My parents weren't happy about it. They wanted me to have the education they never had and a broad and open future. But they never pushed back hard or tried to stop me from talking about how sad I was and how much I "hated" the University of Vermont. They tolerated my whining, hoping I'd get over it.

Because I was such a pitiful homesick and lovesick creature, I managed to wangle the family's "extra" car out of my parents. It was a blue Corvair convertible Dad had fallen in love with and picked up cheap during one of his stints as a part-time used car salesman. When he later got my mother a newer used car, he couldn't give up the Corvair.

Whenever I went to Brattleboro, there'd be a list of other townies needing a ride. It was a boon because they'd share the gas bill. One deep-winter weekend, the townie was Pat Casey. I had no idea then that one of the most important friendships of my life was being forged in the Corvair as we struggled our way back north through an unexpectedly intense snowstorm.

At one point in the ride, I found myself spinning in a 360-degree circle, twice, while avoiding the two cars I was passing at the time *and* the car coming at us from the other direction. Stunningly, not one car slid off the road and everyone continued driving as if nothing had happened. Casey and I shrieked, screamed, and laughed like maniacs through the entire episode. We recognized in each other a weird sense of humor and a predilection for risk taking. With that fear-inspired adrenaline rush, our bond was forged.

We hadn't been friends in high school, which we still joke about. Casey was part of the so-called wild crowd, even though she was *Irish Catholic*. Where were her guilt and shame? I'd never seen her at confession. By the time we were friends and I could jokingly ask her about it, it didn't really matter because we'd both left the church. In any case, her response was always punctuated with a funny little giggle, revealing the gap between her two front teeth. All our lives she's maintained that the gap is sexy, like Lauren Hutton's; I tell her she'd benefit from braces.

Casey was always more interested in extracurricular activities than schoolwork, until she found her passion in nursing school at UVM. In high school, she smoked, drank, and swore and sometimes even went parking with boys! She'd cut classes if she found them boring, or out of sheer bravado. In my little worldview, she seemed provocative and dangerous.

In high school, I didn't smoke, I didn't drink, I didn't swear, and most definitely, I did not cut classes. In fact I finished assignments almost as soon as they were given. I'd have English papers that weren't due for a month written within a few days so I wouldn't have to fret about them. Casey thought I was an uptight, somewhat snooty, boring asshole who worried too much about school and didn't care about having real fun. Neither of us had been particularly excited about being stuck with each other in a car for a long ride back to Burlington—even though she can and will talk to absolutely anyone.

But that ride changed everything. Under Casey's tutelage (at least that's what Mom wanted to believe at the time), I began to drink beer, the most readily available beverage at college. With the beer came twenty additional pounds that I had to struggle to get rid of. I began to pick up more "colorful" language; and by my junior year, *fuck* had become my favorite word. Think about its versatility. It can be a verb, adverb, noun, and adjective. I still love the word even though Mom has struggled to get me not to use it in public since the Nobel. She worries my language might tarnish my public image.

Casey and that Corvair sparked a sense of freedom that went beyond my initial joy at the thought of seeing Claude more easily. Perhaps the feeling also grew because other friends and I started talking about sororities. (Casey, of course, thought sororities completely lame and wouldn't give them a second of her time.) Maybe it was being invited to a frat party, and going. The boyfriend back home, now working for my father's vending company, seemed more and more mundane.

If Claude noticed any changes, he let them slide. He said nothing and I offered nothing. It would be the pattern of our communication during all our years together and not so together. The relationship dragged on painfully through the holidays before I escaped back to school for the second semester. I was a coward. Trips home became less frequent. I wanted the situation over with no pain involved. I wanted him to somehow intuit that we were broken up without my having to say a word. Couldn't he just kind of disappear?

Lacking the grace or guts to tell him in person, I got up the weak-kneed nerve to dump him over the phone. That way it would be easier to cut off the conversation if it got too difficult. Anyone who knows me now would swear I am lying through my teeth when I say that. No one believes that, when I was young, I'd do most anything to avoid confrontation. In those days, my escape techniques were fraught with hurt feelings, anger, and broken hearts.

Maybe we talked one more time by phone before school was out, but I didn't see Claude again until I was home for the summer. We dated some, and it went that way for the next couple of years. I'd give him little thought at school but go out with him when I was in Brattleboro. The fit was never the same as it had been during our first year of teenage love, but our story dragged on. And on.

· · ·

One night during the summer of 1969, Casey and I wandered downtown to a dance party outside the town's recreation center. We ran into Steve, one of Claude's best friends throughout high school. He wasn't the handsomest guy in high school, but he was one smooth talker and extremely well built. His nickname was Atty, after Charles Atlas, the best-known body builder of the time. It didn't take long for him to convince us to leave the dance and go have a couple of beers.

Atty drove us to the top of Memorial Park, the hill where I'd first learned to ski. We got out of the car and sat on the grass. After one beer, he pulled out a joint. I stiffened. I'd never smoked pot in my life and until then had never even been in its proximity. I almost believed a joint was the beginning of an inevitable path to heroin addiction. They both knew I didn't smoke, and I chattered worriedly about how it might make me feel. I had the sense to stop short of mentioning the road to heroin. They laughed and mocked me as they passed the joint.

The pot smelled sweet and inviting. I'm still drawn to the odor if not the substance itself; perhaps it reminds me of incense. While we sat around and talked, I didn't notice the smoke transforming them into raving lunatics. They only seemed to be laughing more. That didn't seem so bad, so I took a toke. Like every neophyte smoker you've ever seen, and to the amusement of Casey and Atty, I began hacking like my lungs were in danger of falling out. But they were willing teachers, and it didn't take long before I could successfully inhale, hold in the smoke, and not erupt.

Just as I was proclaiming that I didn't feel a thing, the night seemed richer and the air velvety. The stars shone more brightly and looked magical in the sky. Casey and Atty were simply hilarious, two of the funniest people I'd ever heard in my life. We were brilliant, fantastically attractive, and life was wonderful and full of adventure! Right then and there, Casey and I decided we absolutely *had* to go to the Newport Jazz Festival. We weren't into jazz, but in '69 the festival was going to be a fusion of jazz and rock, and the bands were ones we wanted to hear.

The plan was to borrow my dad's station wagon so we could sleep in the back. We'd take off early Friday and spend the long Fourth of July weekend there. When I talked to my dad about it, I made the festival sound as innocuous as possible, and it was easy to get the car. The truth of the matter is that my parents remained pathetic at saying no, my father in particular. In a typical parent-child scenario, he said yes if Mom agreed. Mom agreed because I told her Dad had already said yes. Mary Beth heard it all, and suddenly we were a trio. Casey, my sister, and I packed up the car and roared off to Newport.

It was one hell of a weekend. It wasn't the first concert I'd heard, but Newport was the first weekend-long music festival any of us had been to. Some of the jazz greats played, such as Miles Davis, but we were there for the rock and roll: Jethro Tull; Johnny Winter; Blood, Sweat and Tears; and Frank Zappa and the Mothers of Invention, capped off by Led Zeppelin. None of us can remember if we were still there for that closing act. In any case, the band that brought down my house was Sly and the Family Stone. They took us "high-igh-er. Baby, baby, baby light my fi-re. High-igh-igh-igh-higher!"

Maybe we slept in the back of the station wagon; Casey and Mary Beth insist we slept on the side of a hill. But sleeping didn't matter. It was the thousands of people, tens of thousands of people. It was the bands and the music. It was the dawning of the age of Aquarius! You didn't have to have pot, the air was pot. We left Newport committed to going to every music event we could possibly get to. For the rest of our lives. Watch out, Woodstock, here we come!

I have no idea what we looked like when we pulled into Brattleboro, but whatever it was did not impress my parents. No to our using the car. No to our commitment to music. And most definitely no to Woodstock. It proved to be one of the few times when my parents held firm to "no." We couldn't even make an attempt to sneak off in the Corvair, because somehow I'd managed to render it inoperable by the end of the school year. Something my father never let me forget.

But if my parents thought they would stave off my transformation to college hippie by making Woodstock off-limits, they were wrong. Eventually.

·   ·   ·

Although I'd started my college career while pining away for Claude and most of the family, Steve wasn't one I missed. He'd made it through high school at Austine but just barely. After that, he had only two different jobs, neither of which lasted for more than a couple of weeks.

First, he went to Poultney and stayed with my grandparents while Grampa tried to teach him to run the big presses at his printing business. The horrible noise they generated wouldn't bother Steve, but routine did. He couldn't or wouldn't focus, and he never made it to work on time or stayed there until the end of the workday. Quickly, he ended up back at home with my parents. He fared just as badly in the second job and has never worked since.

My brother's pleasures in life have been few. In addition to smoking cigarettes, he has watched endless hours of television, often way into the night, while eating nonstop. His rhythm was often out of synch with the family's, which in many ways was a blessing. He'd sleep all day and be up all night. He'd take the car and drive endlessly. My parents worried he'd get into a serious accident somewhere and it would take forever to find him. There were times we all hoped that, if he did crash, he'd never see it coming, that it would be blessedly painless and instantly fatal.

As Steve's physical violence toward Mom had accelerated, Dad began to say that if he ever knew he was terminally ill, he'd take Steve with him before he died so Mom wouldn't have to face him alone. I think my father believed he meant it. We all knew he'd never be able to do such a thing. And of course Mom already had to face Steve alone whenever my father was working. My brother's tirades grew, and the tense calm between them shrank.

Not long before I was to go back to UVM for my sophomore year, Steve completely lost control, with no perceptible provocation. Had he seen a picture of Castro somewhere? Had Elizabeth Taylor's lusty life set him off again? Maybe, maybe not.

Mom and I were in the kitchen with Steve, who was showing signs of going off, and as usual she was trying to calm him down. I, on the other hand, was fairly certain I knew all things in the world better than anyone else, and I had little tolerance for her feeble attempts at soothing him. I believed it was way past time to tell him to fuck off and to approach him head-on.

Steve was working himself into a lather, and he was in Mom's face. But this time he raised a hand toward her. I threw myself at him, not only to get him away from my mother, but also because I wanted to smash him one for myself. It became generalized chaos. Mom managed to break through to me, and we started backing away from the scuffle through the kitchen door into the dining room. Suddenly Steve grabbed a butcher knife and was coming our way.

We scrambled out the front door and locked ourselves in her car in the driveway. It was blisteringly hot, one of the few times in a Vermont summer back then when it got really hot. Mom and I sat sweating in the car, too scared to roll down the windows and get some air, even though he'd not followed us out.

Steve appeared in one of the dining room windows overlooking the driveway. He stood there flailing about with the knife and yelling, yelling, yelling. Then he turned the knife toward his chest, indicating he was going to kill himself. Mom might have been crying, but I lifted my arms to make sure he could see them and began to clap. I was egging him on, hoping he might actually do it and give us all some relief.

But we all knew he'd never kill himself. It was so much more satisfying to torture the entire family. Besides, suicide was a mortal sin, and he'd go straight to hell and never achieve his dream of being like everyone else. How come the world got Helen Keller and we got Stephen John Williams? It's a question that still crosses my mind.

A couple of days later, he went after Mom again. This time I wasn't home. She ran upstairs to her bedroom, closed the door, and locked it with the chain lock Dad had installed. As she was calling my father, Steve threw himself against the door and crashed through, splitting one of the door panels in the process and ripping the lock out of the wood. He looked ready to strangle her.

This time it was Mark who jumped in. Mark was a little over fifteen, still short and slight and no match for Steve. But the fact that his little brother was standing up to him stopped Steve that day.

Ten-year-old Janet was probably hiding behind the living room sofa or under her bed, and Mary Beth was out somewhere escaping the chaos. As much as possible during the summer, Mary Beth stayed with friends at the lake. Mom and I were usually in the house, making the potato and macaroni salads and the sandwiches to fill Dad's vending machines.

A few days later, Steve tried to strangle Mom in the kitchen with the telephone cord. Somehow we managed to call my father and the police. By the time the police arrived, followed by the county sheriff, my brother's fury had abated. He was shaken and full of agitated remorse. He was confused and couldn't understand why the police were there. When the sheriff put him in the car to take him to the county jail in Newfane, he was exhausted, deflated, and terrified. No one in the family was in a much better state, and it only got worse.

Mom and Dad went to see him in Newfane, where he cried and begged to come home, promising that he'd never be "bad" again. They returned from the jail without him and emotionally in shambles. Both of them cried for their son. They cried for their inability to make him happy. They cried for his inexplicable anger and for their self-perceived failings as parents. I cried for them, but I didn't cry for Steve. Not yet.

The court determined my brother to be a danger to himself and to others and incapable of making his own decisions. He was to be taken directly to Waterbury, the state mental institution, for observation and supposedly for help. Dad was made my adult brother's legal guardian by order of the court and remained so until he died at the beginning of 2004, when Mom took on the role.

My parents felt acute agony tinged with hope. Maybe, just maybe, someone at Waterbury would be able to figure out the root of Steve's anger. But Mom's novenas didn't work that time either.

Mom and Dad couldn't face seeing their son in Waterbury. I don't remember how I felt about that at the time. Although I wanted Steve to quietly disappear from the face of the earth without a trace, it was impossible to leave him alone and afraid. He'd been absolutely terrified just a few miles from Brattleboro at the county jail, and he knew Newfane. Nobody wanted to think about what he was going through at Waterbury, but it had to be much worse. So countless times over the year that he was there, I borrowed a friend's car and drove the twenty-one miles south to Waterbury to see my brother.

A few weeks after he'd been admitted, Steve was permitted to go out on the hospital grounds during the day. But the only thing my brother wanted after he got to Waterbury was to go home. The minute he was out the door, he walked straight over to the interstate, which you could see from the hospital, and hitchhiked back to Brattleboro.

When my startled and frightened mother saw him come in the front door, she immediately called Waterbury, only to find they hadn't noticed he'd left. This happened several more times until the powers that be, in their eternal enlightenment, decided to lock my brother up with the seriously insane. My first visit to him then mirrored scenes from Ken Kesey's *One Flew Over the Cuckoo's Nest.*

Big locked doors slid open to let me into a large open room. As they clicked shut behind me, I saw my brother on the other side of the room, just as he saw me. He watched me make my way to him. The room was peopled with ravaged examples of humanity, many of them shuffling about, in various states of disarray. Others slouched in chairs, open eyes fixed on nothing as they drooled through their day. I wondered what drugs they were given to keep them that way.

It was too agitating to look around and take everything in, so I tried to breathe deeply and move through it. I couldn't avoid seeing two men sitting on the floor, propped against the wall, vigorously handling their exposed genitals. They howled when they saw me, and Steve could see I was freaked out. He stepped between me and the men and told me not to worry, that he'd protect me. He flexed his muscles to show me he was man enough to take on all the crazies, as he put it. Maybe he could protect me if need be, but who in that hellhole was protecting him?

That day after I left Steve there, I did cry in horror and empathy and anger. This time my anger wasn't directed at my brother but at those who ran Waterbury. What exactly were they doing for him? There were no psychiatrists or social workers there who understood sign language. The administration didn't have the presence of mind or the interest or will to bring in sign interpreters so the "mental health care professionals" could, at a minimum, try to communicate with my brother. Steve was never diagnosed, nor was he given medication. He simply did his time and, one year later, was released. He returned to Brattleboro and resumed life with the family.

The mere passage of time had not magically cured him. His curse was not acute, like Mom's depression when we first moved to Brattleboro, nor was he simply an "angry deaf man." His condition was chronic. But what the hell was it, and how was he ever going to have a life? His rage had not dissipated, but it was held in check for some time by his terror at the thought of going back to Waterbury. That threat was the only real weapon my parents could wield to manage his violence.

•   •   •

My brother was released from Waterbury shortly before I got home for summer vacation. But I had a plan. I wasn't going to make sandwiches with Mom all summer for my father's vending machines. I got a job waitressing at Howard Johnson's. I'd spend less time near Steve, and maybe, since Claude and I wouldn't both be working for my father, I'd manage *not* to go out with him over the summer.

I was looking forward to renewed summer fun with Casey, but she had other plans. On the spur of the moment, she'd decided to stay in Burlington to work for the summer and had found someone to share an apartment with. I was stuck home with my parents. With Steve. Who was I going to mess around with; where was my escape?

It was a dismal prognosis. Nor did I excel at being a waitress—then or a decade later, when I got fired after two weeks of "wait training" at a new restaurant on Capitol Hill in Washington, D.C. Waiting on people is not my forte. Howard Johnson's was particularly uninspiring. One week, I managed to get a few days off, tacked onto a long weekend, and went to Burlington. I wanted to hang out with Casey and meet her roommate, Linda, at their apartment on Monroe Street in a less-than-great neighborhood (although, that didn't have much meaning in Burlington, Vermont, in 1970).

When Casey opened the door to their apartment, my view of the place was consumed by Linda, who was draped across an old sofa in the living room decorated with an Indian-print bedspread. She was wrapped in a sheet and engaged in intense conversation with a man, also wearing only a sheet, who was at least twenty-five years older than she was. His salt-and-pepper hair was wavy and full and he spoke with an indeterminate European accent. They were smoking Gauloises cigarettes and discussing poetry or philosophy or freedom or the lack of it. They could have been talking about waste management and it would have sounded heady to me.

Linda was the most exotic person I'd ever met. She was slim with huge breasts for her size and liquid brown eyes that filled her thin face. Her beautiful cheekbones were objects of envy, and her fine, wavy brown hair framed her face perfectly. And how did a girl from Burlington, Vermont, get to be so worldly?

I was taking all this in as Casey, who, thankfully, was fully dressed, broke into their conversation to introduce us. They were friendly enough but immediately returned to their conversation as Casey took me to her room and showed me the mattress on the floor where I'd be sleeping.

Those first few hours in Burlington, I felt awkward, drab, and pedestrian, like a kid in junior high school trying to fit in with adults. By the end of my stay, I felt more or less comfortable in a sheet myself. I'd also smoked my first cigarette, which made me so faint and ill I had to take to my mattress. (Fortunately, I never became a smoker.) Most important, I'd engaged in what I considered to be mind-broadening discussions with Casey and Linda and her European friend.

With each passing hour my dread at having to return home to my parents and Steve increased. The thought of waiting on people at Howard Johnson's and the seeming inevitability of dates with Claude bored and depressed me. And almost from the minute I'd gotten to Burlington, Casey had been badgering me to stay with her and Linda for the rest of the summer. The spare mattress in her room was mine if I wanted it.

For the rest of that summer and my last two years at the university, I lived off campus in apartments I rented with friends.

Monroe Street for those few weeks in the summer was fine, but when the three of us returned to school, it wasn't going to work. Fortunately I was able to move in with Judy Rand, another friend from home in need of a roommate. She had been one of Mary Beth's closest friends since fourth grade. It was Judy who taught my sister to smoke and swear—my mother's preferred take, again, on who'd done the teaching—so I knew her well.

Then, senior year, it was Casey, Judy, and me sharing an apartment just down the street from where Mary Beth lived with yet another friend of hers from home. She'd hated the first college she'd gone to and had dropped out after the first semester. After deciding that working for a living with just a high school diploma wouldn't do, she came to UVM to begin her nurse's training as I entered my last year there.

Fragments of memories from each of those apartments linger in my mind, but no place could ever compare with Monroe Street, where my transformation from button-down almost-sorority girl to genuine, barefoot, ripped-dungaree-wearing college hippie was seemingly completed.

CHAPTER FOUR

V-I-E-T-N-A-M, Marriage, and Mexico

The courses I cobbled together at school served mostly as a backdrop for events that would have lasting impact on my life. Increasingly I focused on the social turmoil in the country. And for me that was expressed by protests about the war in Vietnam. My college years weren't only a time of my metamorphosis from prim and proper freshman to college hippie. I also changed from a fairly uncritical product of our culture and history books to embryonic activist.

Vietnam became emblematic for a complex storm made up of the civil rights movement, feminism, and full-scale U.S. military intervention and the increasingly volatile reaction to it. Many of us experienced those years as a time apart, a time filled with expectations of great change. When the war ended, things didn't return to the status quo ante, but neither did the social upheaval usher in the transformation of America that so many in the streets hoped for.

When I'd left for school, I was living comfortably in the fog of our mythologized history. Within a couple years, I was a college hippie grappling with a shattered view of American benevolence in the world. How people come to grips with changing understandings of American myth and reality is in fact something I think about all the time. I understand the reluctance to confront all sides of a story. Particularly when it means tackling long-held and unchallenged beliefs without much experience to base one's questions on.

At first, I didn't understand that all countries create their own myths. Even in our personal histories we tend to emphasize the good, minimize or erase the bad, and reshape events for our own benefit. Nations do the same. Undying, epic stories about a country and what it stands for are part of what binds people together in a national identity. The stronger and better the stories, the more the people want to identify with them and defend them, even against evidence to the contrary.

More than once I've been amazed by how angry people can get when confronted with the darker side of their national history. I've listened as people take refuge in the belief that the parts of the stories they never heard before, or which were grossly underplayed in history books, are simply lies. Certainly parts of a country's patriotic stories are based on historical reality. But what happens when people begin to explore other aspects of that history? For me, the Vietnam War was a shock of epic proportions that helped shatter my unquestioned beliefs about America. The war brought to mind a teacher I'd been fortunate enough to have in high school. His name was Chip Porter.

It was his first year teaching. Mr. Porter was standing in for a social studies teacher on sabbatical, and he took us all by storm. He was young and hip, cool in his white, dashiki-type shirts. He was the only male teacher in high school who didn't wear a suit. Nor did he teach from notes he'd been using for years.

I wasn't sure what *social studies* meant. It was just one of the courses you took. I looked it up recently and found that the National Council for the Social Studies defines it this way: "The primary purpose of social studies is to help young people develop the ability to make informed and reasoned decisions for the public good as citizens of a culturally diverse, democratic society in an interdependent world." I doubt it was defined that way forty-five years ago. Interdependent? I don't think so; then the world was simply the communists and us.

However the subject matter was described, Chip Porter's teaching showed me that making "informed and reasoned decisions for the public good" often meant challenging conventional wisdom. Not necessarily accepting the official story. It meant not being afraid to ask questions even when the topic was one that others wanted to ignore.

Mr. Porter's class offered me the tools for critical thinking. I didn't exercise those skills consistently until some time later, but he helped me understand the fundamentals. I thought of him often as I became more involved in the unavoidable Vietnam debate at school and at home. The war was a subject my father and I roundly disagreed on. But neither of us could or would shut up about it.

Anytime I was home, Dad and I had raging arguments about the war at the dinner table. We made Mom completely nauseous. She pleaded with us not to discuss politics during dinner. We ignored her. Dad was pro-war, invoking his experience in "the Big One" and the domino theory of communism taking over the world. I argued that the war was wrong, the domino theory was bullshit, and that U.S. intervention in Vietnam couldn't and shouldn't be compared to World War II.

As the number of U.S. casualties grew, and we watched the

war on television and the protests spreading across the country, Dad began to soften. Revelations that the 1964 Gulf of Tonkin Incident, the pretext for President Lyndon Johnson's escalation of U.S. involvement in Vietnam, was largely fabricated shocked him. My father couldn't believe an American president would lie to the nation about war. What other lies were out there that we didn't know about?

As the war dragged on, what finally got to him was my brother Mark getting closer and closer to draft age. I regularly badgered my dad about how he'd feel sending his own son into that mess. Finally it penetrated his brain that this unpleasant scenario was entirely possible. Mark could be drafted and sent off to war in the hellhole that the United States had made of Vietnam.

That growing perception became tangible when Claude was called up. No one in my family wanted to believe it, but Dad especially was shaken. He strongly related to Claude's hard-scrabble family background and appreciated that he was a hard and diligent worker. My father couldn't believe that the kid who worked for him, my on-again off-again boyfriend, was going to have to go to Vietnam. If it could happen to Claude . . .

Dad's concern wasn't lessened much when Claude managed to escape the military. Once he knew his draft fate, Claude got as much medical documentation as he could describing a "weak back" from summer jobs in construction during high school. His supplemental plan, as advised by a draft counselor, was to have the words FUCK YOU boldly tattooed along the outside of his saluting hand. The contention was that no drill sergeant or military officer would want to have those words staring him in the face every time Claude saluted, and he'd be summarily rejected. I still wonder why it wasn't just as likely that they'd take him and then pound the crap out of him for the tattoo during boot camp and beyond.

We were never sure why but Claude was rejected during his induction physical and didn't have to do time in the military. What he did spend a lot of time on was trying to remove the tattoo with a pumice stone. After Claude's close call, my dad began to say that he'd take Mark to Canada himself before letting him go to Vietnam.

· · ·

Fiery debate wasn't confined to our home at 10 Chapin Street. The war was the hottest topic on campus. Once when I was a freshman, the Students for Democratic Action, the famous, or notorious, agitators, depending on how you looked at them, came to our rather remote university. Thrilled and frightened, I primly gave them a wide berth. Couldn't get too close to that radical contagion. At the same time, I was dying to sample the danger of a conversation with them. Thinking about them now, dressed in suits and ties and standing outside the student center at a folding table with informational materials spread across it, they seem so innocuous.

No matter where you turned, you couldn't get away from the war. It touched everyone in one way or another. Vietnam was the movie *Easy Rider;* it was Elvis Presley putting on the uniform and Muhammad Ali refusing it. It was the Weather Underground, the Black Panthers. Vietnam Veterans Against the War and Vietnam Veterans for Peace. It was Agent Orange, the U.S. incursion into Cambodia, and the carpet-bombing of Laos. It was the My Lai massacre. Vietnam was four dead in Ohio, the reality and the song.

The song was by Neil Young. The reality was National Guard troops called out to quell antiwar protests around the country, and one of them opening fire on college students at Kent State

University in Ohio on May 4, 1970. In a matter of seconds, four students were dead and nine were wounded, one paralyzed for life. Two of the dead had not even been participating in the protest that day. Then eleven days later, two students were killed and twelve others hit by gunfire at Jackson State University in Mississippi. It was like a different take on *Easy Rider* brought to life through college protesters.

Watching *Easy Rider* with a few friends when it came out in 1969 had been unsettling enough. Right up to the end of the movie, none of us believed that the fictionalized rednecks would blow the fictionalized long-haired hippie bikers off their Harley choppers simply because they were different, rebellious. Riding the roads through a pot-induced haze, looking for America.

Even when the rednecks thrust their shotgun barrels through the window of their moving truck, we expected a toothless act of mindless machismo. Surely the bikers would just give them the finger and roar off into their hippy sunset. Instead, the movie ended with gun blasts that knocked the riders head over heels in slow motion to their deaths. It was the rednecks who roared off into the sunset.

We swore we could almost feel the impact of the shotgun blasts. We felt vaguely threatened, and that was just a movie. After Kent State and Jackson State, we walked around campus not understanding how protesting kids exercising their freedom of speech could be shot dead by other kids wearing American uniforms.

America felt threatening then. It was a time of more violence in the country than usual and not just because of the Vietnam War. There was the assassination of President Kennedy. Years and years of fierce and brutal reaction to the civil rights movement led to the assassination of Dr. Martin Luther King Jr., sparking riots around the country. And within weeks, Robert Kennedy was assassinated during his run for the presidency.

The national upheaval had grown beyond the clash between whites and blacks struggling for rights that should have been unassailable. Contention between those who supported and those who opposed the war in Vietnam felt like it could spiral out of control. There were sit-ins and teach-ins, but there were also acts of violence by some opposed to the war.

With the Kent and Jackson State killings, more demonstrations erupted across the country. In my first ever protest, I joined dozens of University of Vermont students who drove from Burlington to the state capital, Montpelier, and entered the legislature building in peaceful protest. We filled the gallery, waving signs and asking our state legislators to pass a resolution calling for an end to the war.

We felt empowered and part of the larger student protest movement that ultimately brought university life to a standstill that May as campuses around the United States closed early to avoid further violence. I went home for the summer. And began dating Claude again in earnest.

·   ·   ·

Not a single friend was excited by the sight of my engagement ring when I returned for my last year at college. Some thought it was a prop for a joke. Once they understood it wasn't, no one thought I was anything but completely mad. What had happened to the emerging feminist who'd proclaimed to anyone who'd listen, and to some who wished she'd shut up, that she was never going to get married?

Everyone but me recognized that marrying Claude was a retrenchment, not a rekindling and maturing of high school love.

As graduation day got closer and closer, my friends were constantly at me to open my eyes to what I was about to do to my life.

I fought back just as relentlessly, trying to convince them that I really, really, *really* was in love. I made great protestations that I'd discovered what I'd always wanted was to get married. It had become crystal clear to me over the summer, and now I was ready for marriage. Why couldn't I be a married feminist? We all knew the person I was trying to convince was myself.

When Claude had given me the ring at the end of summer vacation, it wasn't really what I wanted. As we'd reconnected that summer, I began talking about our living together after college. I don't think my father would have cared one way or the other, but Mom was horrified. At that time, living together wasn't a common practice. She dramatically protested that she'd be humiliated in front of "the whole town." Even worse in her world, living together without benefit of marriage was a mortal sin. I wasn't Catholic anymore, but she was. She said if I wanted to be with Claude, I had to marry him. Living with him was out of the question, and if I tried she'd have my dad fire him.

Our vague scheme for life together included buying Dad's business in some distant future when he decided to retire. That plan made Mom's threat unsettling. I couldn't imagine Claude in any other job. I had no idea what he thought, because we didn't discuss other options. One of the fundamental flaws in our relationship, after the heat that once made deep conversation seem largely irrelevant had died down years earlier, was our inability to talk about anything that really mattered.

It was more than simply the fact that we didn't talk. We didn't think the same way or about the same things. What interested and motivated me was profoundly different from what interested and motivated him. We were both too young and too immature to recognize it, admit it, and move on with our separate lives.

I ignored my friends' entreaties and my own doubts and fears. Immediately upon completing my last exam, I fled the university with my wedding veil between my legs. I didn't even stick around for graduation. Instead, I turned all my attention to planning the August 27, 1972, event.

. . .

The wedding got out of control. The quiet ceremony in front of the fireplace at 10 Chapin Street that I'd had in mind mushroomed. I thought a few flowers here and there would do just fine. A nice little frock for me, Claude in a suit, and a small, relaxed party after. Mom's anxiety about making the house ready for even such a small and informal wedding won out. Instead, I ended up with a smallish ceremony conducted by a justice of the peace at the Unitarian Church, complete with white gown, veil, and hairdo with side curls, immediately followed by a reception that had ballooned to accommodate 250 people.

I'm not sure how many of the guests were taking bets on the longevity of the marriage, but I know Casey, Judy, and Mary Beth were. It lasted just under three years and four months. We started to go off the already fragile track from the very beginning, and we even came home a couple days early from our honeymoon. Bermuda had seemed just too exotic. Why endure more time there when we could be home in comfortable familiarity? Or so our thinking went. The excuse *I* gave was that we wanted to be home for the wedding of close friends who got married five days after we did.

I was twenty-one years old when I got married. We lived in an apartment just around the corner from my parents. Even with my university degree, the only job I could get in Brattleboro was as a surgical assistant to an oral surgeon. No basic training required. Never having seen that much blood in my life, I fainted seven times the first day. To top it off, that day the surgeon's overhead light wasn't working, so I had to shine a flashlight in the patients' mouths so he could work. Every time I went down, so did the lights. For some reason, I wasn't fired. I didn't like the job, but I got used to it.

At home, I was suffocating. It's not that we fought. It was hard to fight, because we never confronted the problems we'd ignored since before we got married. The closest we came to contention was when he and his friends wanted to run screaming into the sunset as I launched into one of my many feminist diatribes. Occasionally they'd egg me on with glee, and I'd rise to the bait every single time.

As I struggled to find my identity as a married woman, I'd started rereading my books on feminism. As soon as I learned that I could have kept my own name when I got married, I took my name back. Claude's parents were appalled, and many people took it as a declaration of independence. I didn't see it that way at the time, but I definitely felt more like myself once I was Williams again.

Claude and I had fun from time to time. But our reality was that we were more like roommates than husband and wife. Not long after the wedding, I started going back up to Burlington on weekends as often as I could to stay with my sister and go partying like we had when I was a student. Mary Beth hadn't deviated in her belief that I took advantage of Claude. But more than most she knew the extent of my disinterest in the marriage, and in being married at all, and we were having too much fun for her to give me much grief.

Claude never asked about the trips or protested at all. Once when I tried to talk with him about it, he stated clearly that he didn't want to hear a word about it. Travel to Burlington came to a screeching halt when Mary Beth graduated, worked to make some money, and went off for a six-month backpacking tour of Europe with a friend. By then, I'd come up with my own plan to leave Vermont.

Somehow I'd managed to convince Claude that we had to reach out and try something new. I felt so stifled I was willing to risk trying for a future that didn't include buying Dad's business someday. I pushed and pushed as I found different training programs he could consider.

I wore him down, and he enrolled in a water management training program in Missouri. I thought it was fantastic. Everyone needed water. The classes would start at the beginning of September 1973. One month before that, we left home, camped our way around the United States, and arrived in Missouri a couple of days before the program was to begin.

We "lived" there less than twenty-four hours. We'd just finished moving into the housing provided by the program when Claude said he wanted to go back home immediately. Although he'd not said a single negative word during our monthlong road trip, he now insisted that he dreaded the idea of living outside of Vermont. He had no interest in water management. He was determined, and I was too frazzled to fight.

We repacked the U-Haul we'd just unpacked and slinked away in the dead of night without a word to anyone. As fast as the overloaded VW wagon would go, we were back in Brattleboro. Claude immediately resumed working for my dad. It was as if we'd never left.

I sank into a deep depression that lasted for months and was only mildly alleviated when we bought a little house that needed a lot of work. We'd qualified for the mortgage only because Claude worked for my dad, and because he'd done a lot of construction work in high school and would be able to make the necessary repairs to the house. At least I could focus my attention on that and a new job I'd started in the accounting department at the School for International Training in Brattleboro. New house and new job aside, I was miserable.

There I was. Twenty-three years old, with a mortgage, a cat and two dogs, a car and a truck, and a husband I couldn't connect with on any level and had long felt no passion for. It wasn't his fault. He was a nice guy. But that didn't change what I was feeling: defeated and miserable.

I stared out the window at the trees surrounding the house and thought, "This is my life? I'm only twenty-three years old! What the hell am I going to do with the next sixty years? Oh my god, *this is my life!*" On some level, I must have started looking for a way out, even if I couldn't admit it to myself. Out of the marriage. Out of Vermont—which just a few years earlier I had thought I'd never want to leave. And out of a life that already felt meaningless as I faced an even bleaker future.

.   .   .

SIT, the School for International Training, slowly became my world, and it was easy to see the place as a world apart. The small and beautiful campus dominates the crest of a hill on the outskirts of Brattleboro, and there's little interaction between the campus community and the people in town. Reached by dirt road, it sits less than a mile from Naulaka, Rudyard Kipling's home when he and his young family lived in the United States. Kipling wrote *The Jungle Book* and some of his other famous works at Naulaka. Long vacant, the Kipling house lent an exotic air to the area.

The school was part of the Experiment in International Living, founded in 1932 to foster international understanding through cross-cultural exchange programs. SIT was started in 1964 to train Peace Corps volunteers, and it later began to offer master's degrees in teaching English as a second language and in international administration. Students also came from around the world to learn English and other languages. The opportunity to mix with them offered me my first taste of the world, and I took it.

Accounting wasn't my forte, and I was no more interested in it than I had been in waitressing or in assisting an oral surgeon. Saving receipts to back up financial reports? Why bother? Those were no more than confusing scraps of paper! I'd simply throw them in the trash. I should have been summarily fired, but the accounting department must have been desperate. When I learned I could qualify for a 50 percent reduction in tuition after working there for eighteen months, I began thinking about studying at SIT.

Listening to the international students had made me think about languages again. My major at the university, which I'd changed five times before finally settling on psychology in order to graduate on time, initially had been Spanish with a minor in Italian. I decided that I'd apply to study for a master's in teaching English as a second language at SIT.

I also wanted to try to qualify for teaching Spanish, which would mean a crash course to revive my dormant abilities in the language. Somehow I managed it and was accepted into the twelve-month Master of Arts in Teaching program for both languages; I started classes in 1975.

The school became more my home than my house was. Between attending classes, working part-time in the accounting department, and hanging out with my new friends there, I went home only to sleep. And sometimes I had to force myself to do even that until Mary Beth came to stay with us.

When my sister came home from her European adventure, she was flat broke and jobless, so we'd invited her to move in with us until she got on her feet. I was thrilled. At last there was some sound in our house, some life. Even Mary Beth was surprised to see that Claude and I had a virtually nonexistent relationship. We still didn't fight about our shell of a relationship; we continued our practice of silence on the subject. It was Mary Beth's separate talks with me and with Claude that helped push the marriage more quickly to its inevitable end.

She badgered me about it endlessly and forced me to the obvious conclusion that the situation couldn't go on forever. I'd whine and cry and manage inane statements like: "I wish he would just somehow disappear." Or: "I don't know what to do. I don't want to hurt him." She snorted and pointed out that my behavior was already demeaning. What additional hurt could I possibly be talking about?

At the same time, she was talking to Claude. When I wasn't around, she started pushing him to stand up for himself. She'd been witness to our nonmarriage for too long and now was living in the middle of it. If the situation had been reversed, I'd have done the same.

One Saturday in December 1975, Mary Beth pushed Claude hard enough that he went to find me and confront me about our marriage. He got in his truck and drove downtown, where I walking down Main Street with some SIT friends. Stopping the truck in the middle of the street, he rolled down the window and politely, if a bit tensely, asked if I'd please meet him back at the house.

When I opened the front door, Claude was standing in the kitchen, leaning against the counter. I stood looking at him from the far side of the kitchen table and waited. The meat of the exchange was essentially two sentences. His ultimatum and my response. "Jody," he said rather calmly under the circumstances, "I need you to act like a wife, or our marriage will have to end." I continued to look at him before answering, "I guess I should leave then." I went into the bedroom, packed a few things in a suitcase, and walked out the door.

Fleeing to Chapin Street, I burst into the house yelling for my mom. She squealed from the bathtub when I walked in on her and threw myself on the floor, crying. Wrestling with a washcloth to cover herself, as if I were paying attention, she said angrily, "Why are you crying? This is what you wanted anyway!"

My family all loved Claude. At one point or another in the years before we got married, each of my parents had asked why I kept stringing him along. Once we were married, they worked hard to ignore the obvious; and when we separated, everyone in the family felt terrible for him.

At the same time, they all knew we weren't meant to be together. Mom's anger came from her fear for my future. She wondered how I'd possibly manage without a husband at my side. Never having been alone in her life, she couldn't imagine that some of us actually wanted to be. She also worried about the stain of divorce.

.   .   .

Years later when I thought about that time, I surmised that Claude had tolerated the facade of our marriage for reasons he himself probably didn't understand. Many of us struggle for years to obtain something we think we can't live without and which always seems just beyond our reach. There's a desire to conquer it, whatever the "it" might be; we tell ourselves that we just have to try a little bit harder. Claude wanted me to love him the way he loved me. And he kept on trying to will it to be so.

And for my part, I had, for years, made Mom and her threat about firing Claude if we just lived together the brunt of jokes about why I got married. She had indeed made the threat, but I'd given in without much of a fight. Probably if I'd pushed back, I could have lived with him and she'd have done nothing. I'd accepted her ultimatum as real because I didn't know what else to do with myself. For reasons that I can't clearly understand, I couldn't see myself getting a job and an apartment by myself or with friends after college. The future felt too big and wide open, and I'd retreated to the familiar and married Claude.

It was Claude who filed for divorce, within weeks of our separating that December. At the hearing, Mary Beth was the only witness, and she testified to the incompatibility that was the legal basis for the end of our marriage. But by then I was already gone. As soon as course work had ended at SIT in May 1976, I'd left for Mexico for the three-month teaching practicum required to complete my degree.

Claude got the house, most everything in it, and custody of the three pets. I got my books, my records, and twenty-five hundred dollars. Not a princely sum, but the house had cost only thirteen thousand dollars and there was still a mortgage. The money was enough for me to return home from Mexico and buy a used white Ford Mustang with a black vinyl top and a sunroof. I packed it full and headed back to Mexico, free to move—blunder?—out into the world and see what I might find.

. . .

Carlos and I had starting hanging out together at SIT, where he was taking intensive English courses. He came from a well-off family who lived in a small town in the state of Veracruz, Mexico, where he had been raised with imported Swiss cows and Arabian horses. At that time in his youth, he valued these animals much more than the peasants who his family paid a pittance to chop down briars and brambles in the pasture so the animals could graze freely. But I didn't see that aspect of him until sometime after we'd started living together in Mexico at the end of August 1976.

By then, my teaching practicum in central Mexico was over. Teaching had been a hellish experience, and moreover, the Mexican family I'd lived with had had no business taking in students. It was so tense in their house—one of the sons acted as if I'd personally stolen half of Mexico after the Alamo—that I lost about twenty pounds over the three seemingly endless months that I was there. When they finally did end, Carlos and I met at the bus station in Mexico City and took an overnight bus to the industrial city of Monterrey, where he was studying engineering.

We arrived with no place to live, I had no job, and I didn't yet have the white Mustang. I walked the streets of that northeastern desert city looking for a teaching job, not considering for a minute that the school year was already beginning and positions had been filled. I left my name and résumé everywhere before I dashed off to Vermont to buy the car and drive it back to Mexico. I returned to a job offer. A teacher had quit after a few weeks at a private bilingual academy, leaving the school as desperate for a teacher as I was for a job. I was going to teach second grade.

It was the worst job of my life. My misery had nothing to do with the staff or the principal, who was a lovely woman. It was because I had no business teaching second grade. It was not much more than glorified babysitting, and I was as unprepared for the second graders as I'd been for taking care of other people's kids when I was just a kid myself. Every single day of that school year, I'd get home to our horrible little rooftop apartment, which wasn't much more than a converted supply room, and cry and cry and cry. During the rainy season, the rain came through the nail holes in the tin roof as I cried, adding insult to my misery.

The next year, we rented a large studio apartment and I found work teaching adults. But by the end of two years in Mexico with Carlos, I'd come to several realizations. First was the fact that being a language teacher, either of English as a second language or of Spanish, would not hold my interest for a lifetime. Even while getting my teaching degree in the two languages, I'd seen it primarily as a vehicle for getting out into the world. I could teach ESL practically anywhere, and I loved Spanish. But I'd not gone to graduate school with the view that I was honing my skills for a new career.

I also saw that spending a lifetime outside of my own country wasn't for me. At least as I'd experienced it in Mexico, being an expatriate felt strange and rarified. Many of the Americans I came in contact with could barely manage in Spanish. One woman I knew had lived in Mexico for twenty years but could say only the most rudimentary sentences. Her speaking ability was less than that of a moderately prepared tourist. But even if I were to become as fluent as a native speaker and live there for years, I'd always be an outsider. I didn't want to live that way. And I didn't want to marry Carlos.

I'd toyed with the thought, but mostly because he kept asking me. Deep in my heart I knew it would be another mistake.

I loved him, but it was a small-*l* kind of love; it wasn't LOVE. He was fun and cute and young, several years younger than I was. He spoke Spanish; we spoke Spanish. Living with him in Mexico was worlds apart from my life with Claude in Vermont. But none of that was a basis for a lifetime together.

I loved his family's ranch in Veracruz. They grew fantastic coffee there. One of my fondest memories was riding horses with Carlos up the mountain where the coffee grew and, later that afternoon, watching him train a young Arabian on a lead rope. Another memory is not pleasant and exemplifies one of the multitudinous reasons why a long-term relationship with Carlos wouldn't work.

We'd gone for the weekend to a lovely lake with a pictur-esque island in the middle. It was a well known tourist area. As we walked the cobbled streets of the village to the top of the island's peak, Carlos kept on making racist remarks about the indigenous people who occupied the village, saying things like: "They are poor because they want to be." And: "They're lazy. They don't like to work." And: "Look, they all have radios or televisions. They should have spent that money on food or shoes for their children." He sounded like an American racist talking about blacks before the civil rights movement changed the dis-course in the United States. I couldn't believe it.

I understood racism and had naively thought it was specific to the United States. I'd never experienced elitism and classism, however. I hadn't known people of wealth before and, while growing up in Vermont, had never seen the dramatic disparity between wealth and poverty that was present in Mexico. On the one hand, Carlos was a kind and generous person; on the other, he was a racist product of his elitist class.

After two years, as I was working toward the decision to leave

Mexico, we had long, complicated, and emotional conversations. He couldn't believe that I honestly had no interest in getting married. I'd not wanted to marry Claude when I married him; why would I marry again? I didn't want to be the señora of his ranch, sitting around all day with nothing to do.

I'd reached the point where I could say that I wanted to do "international work." What that actually might mean, I didn't know. I also had an unclear desire to work to change U.S. foreign policy and believed the best place to try to do that was back home.

I wept all the way from Monterrey, where I'd left Carlos crying on the front step of the apartment, to the U.S. border. The customs official shook his head as if I were crazy to be crying on returning home to the United States. He said it should be an occasion of unbridled joy. But he took pity on me and whisked me and my overloaded car through the stop, and I continued my drive northeast toward my destination: Washington, D.C.

I'd decided on D.C. because it was an international city. I also chose Washington because my friend Casey was now living there with her boyfriend, John Healey, who was also from Brattleboro. At least I wouldn't be friendless in the city. It wasn't part of a plan, but once I got there I moved in with Casey and John and ended up living with them for the next three years.

·   ·   ·

Did I imagine that somehow, simply by living in D.C., I'd be able to do international work? The best idea I had for trying to find such work, whatever that might entail, was to work for a temporary employment agency. That way, in my muddled thinking, I'd be able to try out a variety of work settings and perhaps magically find what I was looking for.

For the most part, I was assigned entry-level secretarial work. I worked at law firms; I worked at professional associations. I worked everywhere but in situations that came even close to fulfilling the amorphous dream I had of work that would somehow tackle American foreign policy. Trying to get a job in the government held no interest for me whatsoever.

One thing that temporary work did provide was flexibility. It didn't pay well, but I didn't care. Having piles of money wasn't important to me; accumulating it wasn't a goal. If money fell on me, I wouldn't throw it away, but getting it wasn't a measure of success or a full life for me. I knew it wouldn't fulfill me or make me happy. It's not that money is irrelevant or unnecessary, but I see it as a means to an end.

My financial needs included being free of debt, being able to pay my meager monthly expenses, and having money left over to go to Vermont to see my family and to Mexico from time to time to see Carlos. (Our long-distance relationship continued, if tenuously.) As a friend of mine once wrote to me, "I've been blessed to have never thought of excess as a necessity that I need to sustain."

Because I had so little money, it helped immensely that I'd learned by osmosis the budgetary skills of my mom. She'd always had the ability to make every single penny of every single dollar stretch beyond what anyone would believe possible. My own frugality made living on the meager pay of a temporary secretary manageable. But it became clear that temporary work was not the road to what I was looking for.

It occurred to me that I might have more options if I had some relevant education. So I applied to graduate school again. The Washington area has any number of good schools, but I chose just one. There was no clear reasoning on my part when

I applied to the prestigious Johns Hopkins School of Advanced International Studies for admission in the fall of 1981. Partly I applied to see if I'd be accepted. And then I was, which left me having to decide if I wanted to go to graduate school at all. It was complicated further by the fact that my life had by then taken a completely unexpected turn, and I'd not been thinking much about graduate school at all. I made a nondecision and deferred admission for a year.

1. Mom at seventeen.

2. Me as a pumpkin-headed infant, Poultney, Vermont, early 1951.

3. Steve, Mary Beth, and
me (from left), Poultney,
Vermont, early 1950s.

4. My First Communion,
1957.

5. Press conference at Los Angeles International Airport upon arrival with the second group of wounded Salvadoran children, Children's Project, Medical Aid for El Salvador, September 27, 1988.

6. A young boy watches a mine clearance operator from the balcony of his semidestroyed home, Sarajevo. Photo by John Rodsted.

7. A mine clearance operator and his mine dog find a landmine.
Photo by John Rodsted.

8. Landmine. Photo by John Rodsted.

9. Unexploded ordnance and mines. Photo by John Rodsted.

10. A landmine survivor, Mozambique. Photo by John Rodsted.

11. Landmine survivors, sisters Mirsada and Farida Dulic. Photo by John Rodsted.

12. *(opposite, above)* Mary Wareham, Bobby Muller, and me at the Third International Conference of the ICBL, Phnom Penh, Cambodia, July 1995.

13. *(opposite, below)* Tun Channareth at the ICBL protest outside the gates of the U.N. in the last days of the failed Convention on Conventional Weapons Review Conference, May 1996. Photo by John Rodsted.

14. Goose, me, and Chris Moon, landmine survivor and former mine clearance operator (from left), during a break at the meeting that launched the Ottawa Process, Ottawa, Canada, October 1996. Photo by Mary Wareham.

15. Bob Lawson, me, and Goose (from left) in Maputo, Mozambique, February 1997, during the 1997 Landmine Ban World Tour. Photo by Mary Wareham.

16. Liz Bernstein at the Mine Ban Treaty negotiations in Oslo, Norway, September 1997. She is holding a thank-you poster from the ICBL to the governments that successfully negotiated the treaty. Photo by John Rodsted.

17. We call this photo "Girls Move the Movement," Oslo, Norway, September 17, 1997. Some of the key women activists from the ICBL and diplomats from Canada and Norway are in this photo. First row, kneeling, from left: Susan Walker, Mette Eliseussen, Anne Cappelle, Mereso Agina. Second, somewhat irregular, row, from left: Judith Majlath, unidentified, Gro Nystuen, Anne Marie Groth, Liz Bernstein, Nicoletta Dentico, me, Anne Hege Simonsen, Dalma Foeldes, Jill Sinclair; two behind me in something of a row of their own: Mary Wareham, Patti Curran. Photo by John Rodsted.

18. Mary Wareham, me, Goose, and Norwegian ambassador Steffan Kongstad strategizing during the suspension of the Mine Ban Treaty negotiations, in Oslo, Norway, September 1997.

19. Me, Song Kosal, and Tun Channareth (from left) signing the "People's Treaty" in Ottawa, Canada, December 3, 1997. Canadian foreign minister Lloyd Axworthy is standing behind me. Photo by Mary Wareham.

20. Me, Dr. Cornelio Sommaruga (president of the ICRC), U.N. secretary general Kofi Annan, and Canadian prime minister Jean Chrétien (from left) watch as Canadian foreign minister Lloyd Axworthy is the first to sign the Mine Ban Treaty, in Ottawa, Canada, December 3, 1997.

21. Me with my white German shepherd, Stella, in the backyard in Virginia not long after the Nobel Peace Prize announcement, 1997. Photo by Micheline Pelletier.

22. Song Kosal and me at the rehearsal of the Nobel Ceremony, Oslo, Norway, December 9, 1997. © Norwegian Nobel Institute, 1997, Arne Knudsen.

23. Tun Channareth and me at the Nobel Peace Prize award ceremony, Oslo, Norway, December 10, 1997. © Norwegian Nobel Institute, 1997, Arne Knudsen.

24. My family just before the formal dinner of the Nobel Ceremony,
Oslo, Norway, December 10, 1997. From left: Uncle Chuck, Aunt Kate,
Dad, Mom, me, Goose, Mary Beth, Janet, and Mary Beth's husband,
Paul. © Norwegian Nobel Institute, 1997, Arne Knudsen.

25. U.S. landmine protest.

26. Speaking at a press conference at the Third Meeting of States Party to the Mine Ban Treaty, Managua, Nicaragua, September 2001.

27. Mark and Dad at a Bertolino family reunion, Poultney, Vermont, summer.

28. First international conference of the Nobel Women's Initiative, Galway, Ireland, May 2007. From left: Wangari Maathai, Betty Williams, Shirin Ebadi, Mairead Maguire, and me. Photo by J. Rand Images, Inc.

PART II

The Making of a Grassroots Activist

CHAPTER FIVE

The Pamphlet

It was a gray, damp-cold February day in 1981, the kind that typifies winter in Washington, D.C. I was walking fast down Connecticut Avenue, my cowboy boots hitting the pavement decisively. I've had a strong gait almost since I could walk. From time to time I'd tried to teach myself to glide, ladylike, across the floor, but it never took. That afternoon I was headed for the nearest Metro stop to catch a train home to Arlington. Getting far away from work as quickly as possible was at the forefront of my mind.

Since the previous September, I'd been teaching remedial English in the Farmworker Paralegal Training Program at the now-defunct Antioch Law School in Washington. The program trained young adults, children of migrant farmworkers, to be paralegals. We hoped they'd use those skills to advocate for farmworkers' rights.

The job started out interesting. By that February, it had gone from something of a challenge in many ways to a nightmare in pretty much every way. We were all stunned that teaching paralegal students had gone so sour so fast. But by the end of the first semester, the students were angry about virtually every requirement of their fully-paid-for year of study. They didn't want to be bound by any rules at all. They weren't being nice about it either.

That day someone had poured sugar into the gas tank of a program administrator's car, freezing up the engine. All I wanted to do was get home and pretend for a few hours that the place didn't exist. Thank God I didn't drive my car to work.

When I reached the escalator descending deeply to the Metro trains, I hesitated in order to adjust my pace to the movement of the stairs. Just then a scruffy-looking guy stepped forward and stuffed a pamphlet into my hand. The first thing I noticed was the mimeograph ink on the cheap paper already staining my skin. I was about to curse it rather foully when the four words on the cover came into focus: "El Salvador: Another Vietnam?" I couldn't imagine a link between Vietnam and a tiny country in Central America that most couldn't find on a map.

That day I still knew nothing of the four U.S. churchwomen who had been raped, murdered, and buried in shallow graves by Salvadoran soldiers on the road to the country's international airport. The Carter administration briefly suspended military aid to the country in response. When U.S. ambassador Robert White denounced the killers, he was threatened by death squads. Within six weeks, the aid was resumed.

That day I'd also not yet learned about Archbishop Romero, hero of El Salvador's poor. When Romero was named archbishop, the country's elite expected him to support the regime as his predecessors had. But attacks on religious workers, including the murder of his close friend, the Jesuit priest Rutilio Grande, whose car had been strafed by machine guns while he was on his way to Mass, produced a profound change in Romero. He became a voice for the voiceless, and his sermons and other actions were calls to conscience.

The archbishop had been greatly perturbed by the United States' role in the perpetuation of violence and repression in his country. Less than a month before his assassination, he'd written a letter to President Carter pleading with him to stop U.S. intervention in El Salvador.

In his final sermon, on March 23, 1980, he called upon Salvadoran soldiers to obey the commandment "Thou shall not kill." Then, speaking directly to the regime, he said, "We want the government to take seriously that reforms are worth nothing when they come about stained with so much blood. In the name of God, and in the name of this suffering people whose laments rise to heaven each day more tumultuously, I beg you, I ask you, I order you in the name of God: Stop the repression!"

The next day Archbishop Romero was assassinated with a single shot through the heart while saying Mass. Major Roberto D'Aubuisson, the founder of Salvador's most vicious death squads, had ordered the murder.

My ignorance wasn't confined to the situation in El Salvador. I knew nothing about the 1979 Sandinista revolution in neighboring Nicaragua that had toppled the dictatorship of General Anastasio Somoza, or that the United States had occupied the country in the 1930s and had been supporting dictators of the Somoza line ever since. Surprisingly, even after Vietnam I was still shocked by the ongoing U.S. interventions throughout the world. But as I would learn through my work on El Salvador and Nicaragua over the years, the United States has always been especially interested in "our own backyard."

Despite knowing little about U.S. intervention in Latin America, beyond our taking more than half of Mexico in the

1800s, I did realize that the linking of El Salvador and Vietnam on the cover of the pamphlet did not bode well. I changed my mind about throwing it away and shoved it in my pocket as the habitually packed rush-hour train arrived at the station to take me over the Potomac River and into Virginia.

·   ·   ·

Nobody was home when I got to the little house on South Quincy Street in Arlington that I shared with Casey and her soon-to-be husband, John Healey. Casey, a nurse then working the evening shift at the Washington Hospital Center, was rarely home in the evenings, and John, an actor-director, was out working on a production.

I liked having the house to myself, especially since John and I were on increasingly rocky terms. This stemmed partly from the tension caused by my friendship with Casey versus their romantic relationship. And partly it was because three people trying to do much of anything together usually isn't easy. Allegiances are always subtly or not so subtly shifting; somebody often feels left out or actively is left out. With Casey working evenings, John and I often danced around each other in the house. Neither of us would have chosen to share housing without the Casey link.

John's quirks didn't mesh with mine. And I wasn't all that easy to live with. Since my first college roommate, I'd been pathetically poor at navigating the normal little conflicts that arise when people live together. Instead of learning how to talk the issues through, I'd withdraw into myself and become quietly hostile. This meant I had unhappy roommates, and more than one of my living arrangements ended with a friendship frayed around the edges.

Sometimes the tension in the Arlington house was palpable.

By the time I moved out in 1981, John and I weren't speaking. We didn't talk again until I called to congratulate him on the birth of their daughter, Drew, five years later. It took a few years, but I became very fond of him. Casey and John became fast and true friends who helped me out immensely in difficult times many years later. But at that point, my living situation was stressful, my social life dismal, and work simply awful. Then I was handed "El Salvador: Another Vietnam?"

When I finally sat down and read the fateful little brochure, the information it outlined in spare bullet points described how my tax dollars were being used to support a war few of us knew about. I was feeling not only frustrated with my life at that moment but also powerless in the face of interventionist U.S. foreign policy—especially after the election of Ronald Reagan. However, instead of giving in to those feelings and doing nothing, I decided to go to the meeting about the war in El Salvador that the pamphlet announced for the coming week. A spokesperson for the Democratic Revolutionary Front of the Farabundo Marti National Liberation Front, more commonly known by the few who'd ever heard of it as the FMLN, would be discussing the situation in his country.

I had little idea what a "Democratic Revolutionary Front" was or how such a thing combined with an "FMLN," but I was agitated enough after reading about U.S. involvement in yet another war to want to learn. I began feverishly scouring newspapers for anything I could find about the war. With the newly minted Reagan administration in power, there was a lot to be found.

Like most people I knew, I'd been afraid of the very thought of a Reagan presidency from the moment the former B-grade actor became a serious contender for office. The Carter administration had left a lot to be desired, and its involvement in Central America had made me angry, but four more years of Carter would have been much more palatable than even four minutes of Ronald Reagan. On Reagan's promises that he could make American pride and power rebound, build a strong economy, and tackle the "evil empire" that was the Soviet Union, he trounced President Carter in the November 1980 elections.

After his inauguration as the fortieth president of the United States, on January 20, 1981, Reagan came into office with guns a-blazing. Some were pointed directly at Central America. His administration launched a fight against communism on every possible front in the world. The Sandinista revolution in Nicaragua and the guerrilla war in El Salvador, in particular, were simply too close to home for Reagan's comfort, and it was there he'd decided to draw the line against communism.

The night of the meeting about El Salvador arrived, and I went—very early. It's a trait carried over from grade school. As a child, I'd arrive in the morning well before the doors were unlocked, for fear of getting a tardy mark on my report card. I wasn't in grade school anymore, but I still didn't want to be late.

As I went down the stairs into the church's basement, I could see a handful of people seated randomly on folding chairs arranged around an empty spot for the speaker. I sat near the exit. If the meeting turned out to be horrible, I could slink out more easily that way. I wasn't particularly comfortable, but I waited. By the time the presentation began, the audience numbered about a dozen.

I imagine I was hoping to see a Salvadoran version of Ernesto "Che" Guevara. But the man who spoke was not a superhot *guerillero* in olive drab wearing a dashing beret. Mario Velasquez was an attractive sophisticate in a three-piece, pinstriped suit. He was charismatic and spoke with a passion and a clarity that might well have rivaled those of the famous revolutionary. He didn't simply spew out facts and figures about U.S. involvement in his country. He wove that information through a personal telling of how attempts at building democracy in El Salvador had been crushed.

Mario brought the story alive, describing the iron hand of the military, the death squads, and the ruthless attacks on any and all forms of dissent, discussion, or peaceful attempts to bring democracy to the country. Union leaders, intellectuals, members of political parties, nuns, priests, the archbishop—they had been raped, disappeared, tortured, murdered, and often their mutilated bodies had been left in plain sight as a warning to others. Mario's father, a colonel who'd earned himself the nickname "the Devil" in a brief war with neighboring Honduras, had been very much a part of the malevolent drama.

Salvador's political history was one of authoritarian rule. Despite coups and countercoups, little changed as the economic power remained in the hands of the relative few who owned most of the land. The land barons were known as the "Fourteen Families," and the alliance between this economic elite and the military and their affiliated death squads kept the structure in place. Civil war was the direct result of the quashing of any attempts at change, of fraudulent elections in 1972 and 1977, and of savage violations of human rights throughout the country.

Mario was the son, grandson, and great-grandson of men who'd become officers in the right-wing army. They'd helped keep the cabal of rich families in power at the expense of the vast majority of the crushingly poor and illiterate population. Mario was supposed to follow in their footsteps, but instead of becoming a soldier he became part of the opposition to military rule and, with that decision, completely estranged from his family.

Listening to Mario talk that night rekindled the anger and confusion I'd felt about the United States during its war in Vietnam. How could this country continue to talk about democracy and self-determination while at the same time supporting dictators and militaries that stopped attempts at democratic change in their countries? But dismay wouldn't accomplish a thing, and anger wasn't a strategy for change. The only thing that might help would be to *do something* to make it different. When a sign-up sheet for volunteers was passed around at the end of the meeting, I added my name.

Even now when I think about that meeting, I can't quite believe I went. It wasn't surprising I'd read the brochure, given its Vietnam hook. Nor was it surprising that I was indignant enough at that moment to think I'd go to the meeting. That I had followed through and attended the meeting a week later is what amazes me. As the fire of indignation or inspiration burns lower and lower, it's too easy to find excuses to settle back into the routine of the familiar and do nothing.

Apart from random protests against the Vietnam War, I'd never been to a political meeting. I'd rarely voted. I'd not been near a church in years, and what I remembered of church basements wasn't inspiring. Linoleum floors, institutional paint on the walls, folding tables and chairs, and—despite the location—an absence of any grace. And attending meant I'd have to be with a group of people I didn't know at all. Each word—*church* and *basement* and *meeting* and *strange people*—left me cold. The combination was almost paralyzing. But against my normal inclinations, I'd gone.

Sometimes I wonder what turns my life might have taken if I'd chosen *not* to act. Which possible future might I have fulfilled? Perhaps I would have remained oblivious to everything going on in Central America. Never a fan of television, instead always opting for a book, I didn't watch nightly news. I read the newspaper sporadically at best. But spending too much time thinking about different possibilities is a futile exercise.

The reality for me was that the impact of the Vietnam War, the protests, and other social unrest during my college years had left an indelible mark. Finally, I needed to *act,* not sit around and fret about things. No matter how much I bitched about Reagan, it wouldn't matter. Complaining in the company of friends doesn't change anything.

Maybe I wouldn't like the people at CISPES, the Committee in Solidarity with the People of El Salvador, the organization that had sponsored the church-basement meeting and with which I'd now be volunteering. Maybe they wouldn't like me. Maybe our working styles would be different. Or what we ultimately wanted for the world would be at odds. I had no idea if handing out mimeographed information about the war in El Salvador in the streets of D.C. would matter either. Maybe I'd never get beyond ink-dyed hands. But I had to give it a try. I wouldn't be paid, but at least I'd be attempting to affect U.S. policy instead of sitting around waiting for the perfect policy-related job.

·   ·   ·

CISPES was on the second floor of a building on Connecticut Avenue, near Dupont Circle. The old walls were plastered with posters about El Salvador and the Sandinista revolution in Nicaragua. And of course Che. They were the brightest things in the dingy office with worn floorboards that creaked when anyone stepped on them. Another office in the building housed the Nicaragua Network, an organization that stood in solidarity with Nicaragua. The floor bustled with activity, and I loved being there.

I began working with two guys at CISPES. Robert was the editor of the organization's newsletter, and his close friend, Stewart, was a volunteer. Doe-eyed Robert was of medium height and had a dark ponytail that went almost to his waist and completely grossed out my family when they finally met him. His father was Greek and Robert looked it. With the hair and semidisheveled look of his clothes, he appeared to be a hippie throwback.

Robert was a favorite of the college kids who came through the office. Particularly the young women, who I viewed as his "harem." He was well aware of his effect on them and used it to full advantage. Stewart, on the other hand, was tall and slender with red-brown hair and a handsome chiseled face. He looked like the preppy he was. Stewart was just Stewart. He didn't try to beguile anyone.

The three of us became close colleagues at CISPES. Together we wrote for the newsletter, plotted, and protested. We protested outside Watergate, where General Jose Guillermo Garcia, the Salvadoran minister of defense, was staying while in Washington to speak to Congress about more military aid. We protested in front of the Inter-American Defense Board on Sixteenth Street to oppose continued U.S. training of Salvadoran troops. The protests were filmed. Not by CISPES people. The emblem of the FBI figured prominently on the cameras.

There also were late-night meetings at the CISPES office with Mario, who'd come and update us about what was happening in Salvador. What he had to say didn't read like a *Washington Post* column on the war. I didn't know for many, many months that he was married to Heidi, the woman in charge of CISPES. Or that the two of them had been significant in establishing the solidarity organization.

Sometime in the fall, Robert asked me out. I politely told him I wasn't interested. At that time I thought he was scraggly myself. His intellect interested me, but nothing else. In fact, Robert and Stewart were the first men I'd spent any amount of time with who challenged my thinking. Not because they knew more about El Salvador than I did, although they did when I first met them, but because of the way they filtered information and produced interesting analysis. Listening to them, working with them, discussing pieces I was writing for the newsletter, I discovered I wasn't so bad at it myself.

At some point while working together and getting to know each other better, Robert asked me out again as we walked home from the office one evening. He had a small apartment in the Adams Morgan neighborhood, and by then I was living in the city, too. Through the Salvador work, I'd met a couple renting out a room in the small house they had overlooking Rock Creek Park in Mount Pleasant, and I'd jumped at the chance.

It had been long past the time for me to move out of the Arlington house where Casey and John lived. Even if John and I had gotten along, I was spending so much time in the city that going to the suburbs simply to sleep made no sense. That night when Robert asked me out, I told him I'd go to Millie and Al's for a pizza with him later in the week. I couldn't see any harm in it. I wish I'd been a seer.

·   ·   ·

While I was at CISPES, the most important activity we worked on was a march on Washington to protest U.S. intervention in El Salvador. It was to be held on March 27, 1982, and we were part of the logistics team for the event. It was a huge undertaking that required a ridiculous number of hours of work. My job at the

Antioch Law School hadn't miraculously disappeared, so I was also still teaching, as I would until starting graduate school at the Johns Hopkins School of Advanced International Studies in September. By then I'd decided that graduate school was decidedly more useful than my teaching job.

With Reagan's anticommunist fervor focused on Salvador and Nicaragua, many people in CISPES became increasingly paranoid about U.S. government harassment, which could take many forms. Naive as I was, and despite the FBI's filming of protesters, I thought my colleagues had an inflated sense of the importance of a small, ragtag group of people in a shabby office with almost no resources. The government would waste its time and taxpayer money worrying about us? It seemed absurd. We were simply exercising our freedom of expression in openly stating our opposition to U.S. policy on Central America. We weren't breaking any laws.

I made fun of Robert, Stewart, and others when they'd insist that we hold "important" meetings at a picnic table at night under some trees in Rock Creek Park. It was a five-minute walk from the house where I was living. There, they argued, it would be impossible for anyone to "spy" on us. As foolish as I thought they were being, I got caught up in the cloak-and-dagger aspect of these nighttime meetings. Our work felt curiously risky and full of weird suspense as the day of the march got closer and closer.

We became overwhelmed at the office. Thousands and thousands of people would be descending on Washington. At least that's what we anxiously expected, given all the groups that had called in from around the country. We wanted to believe that would be the outcome, but we worried that in the end only a few hundred people, or a couple thousand at most, would show up. A poor showing would mean we had overextended and exhausted ourselves for nothing. It also would undercut our ongoing efforts to educate people about America's involvement in the war and would fail to demonstrate the breadth of opposition to it. Thankfully, there was an influx of new volunteers, who helped by stuffing and stamping envelops, making posters to announce the march, and posting them around the city. It was exhausting, exhilarating, and nerve-racking.

One of the many activities in the lead-up to the march was an event at a D.C. university. I'd been asked to be one of the speakers. It would be my first time in front of an audience, and in anticipation I was a complete wreck for days. On the eve of the event I was so worried that I'd make an incoherent mess of it and look like an idiot that I barely slept. It didn't help that Robert was moving into the house that same weekend.

His lease had just expired and the landlord had unexpectedly raised his rent. He couldn't afford the apartment anymore on his meager CISPES pay. He'd asked if he could stay with me "just until he could find a new apartment." My roommates didn't object, so I couldn't see why not. There was no room for him in Stewart's tiny apartment, and I couldn't expect Robert to sleep in the street. Or so I rationalized.

The anxiety I'd already been feeling in the pit of my stomach about seeing Robert spiked. We'd been going out since our first pizza date, but I knew in my heart that being with him was not a good idea. I chose to attribute my feelings then to the fact that I'd be speaking in a couple of hours. I didn't want to acknowledge that letting Robert move in that weekend was a stupid decision that would likely cause a lot of grief. Robert carried his first box into the house not long before I had to take off for the event.

A couple of hours later, it was my turn to speak. When I

stepped in front of the microphone on the stage that afternoon, I literally almost fainted dead on the floor. It was a terrifying moment and one I relived many times during the early years of my activism. But once I managed to open my mouth, adrenaline kicked in and I got through my talk about the war in El Salvador. The anxiety instantly drained from my body. Later people in the audience exclaimed what an "inspiring" speaker I was. I was certain they were being generous. From the minute I'd arrived, all I'd wanted to do was bolt from the auditorium. But I'd done it! I'd spoken before an audience and apparently hadn't sounded like a fool.

The Robert-induced anxiety was another thing, and would persist throughout our painful relationship. He preferred open relationships, and I wanted to convince him of the benefits of monogamy even though I knew he was constitutionally incapable of it. The one who would be feeling the pain was me, and that pain would turn to anger when he left three years later for the second, and final, time. For the moment, though, I kept stuffing the Robert concerns down, which wasn't so difficult then, since we were focused on the rapidly approaching march. And after that there was our move from the overcrowded little house in Mt. Pleasant to our own apartment in Adams Morgan. And then . . .

· · ·

Finally it was March 27. Our logistics team had been down at the Ellipse, part of President's Park next to the White House, building the stage for those who would speak to the throngs we hoped would assemble when the march ended. We'd worked like mad people to get the stage built and everything ready before the march began.

Tens of thousands of people came from all over the country to march together in opposition to U.S. intervention in El Salvador. It was a heady experience and a result of the combined efforts of individuals and organizations around the country pulling together to make it happen. About seventy thousand people completed the march to the stage at the Ellipse that day. One of them was an agent who'd infiltrated the CISPES office by posing as a volunteer to help prepare for the march.

Weeks earlier he'd shown up at the office late one afternoon saying he wanted to help and was willing to do anything that needed doing. He talked like a good ole boy whose intellect wasn't his strong suit, but he was good at stuffing envelopes. He didn't say much except for the occasional lame joke. But we weren't looking for great conversationalists. He came to the office regularly and did whatever was asked of him.

As the day of the event approached, he faded away. Maybe he'd mentioned there was an illness in his family. We didn't see him again until midday at the march. Thousands of people had begun arriving at the stage, and speeches were starting. Robert, Stewart, and I were wandering around the area keeping an eye on things when I spotted a man speaking into a walkie-talkie. There was something odd about him. I couldn't see his full profile, but he was vaguely familiar. I nudged Robert and Stewart, and we moved so we could see his face. It was the good ole boy volunteer.

He was talking intensely while looking through the crowd at somebody. We edged around behind him until we saw the small huddle of uniformed police he was talking with. Our volunteer was a spy. I was outraged. There wasn't anything we were doing that wasn't public and open. Hard to organize a national march on Washington if you didn't communicate openly about it. And this guy was being paid to spy on us.

When we walked up to him to confront him about it, he laughed in our faces and sauntered away to join the police. He was just one part of a massive domestic spying effort carried out by the FBI in the 1980s. Targets of that particular round of spying included U.S. organizations like CISPES and others opposed to U.S. involvement in El Salvador and Nicaragua. It wasn't the first or the last time Americans have been spied upon by our own government. I should have apologized to Robert and Stewart for making fun of them about the late-night talks at the picnic table in Rock Creek Park.

While the government spied on us at home, the Reagan administration was also ramping up support for the CIA-sponsored Nicaraguan counterrevolutionary forces, the "Contra." (Think along the lines of the Bay of Pigs invasion.) The Contra were carrying out attacks on the Sandinista military, and on villages and towns in the countryside, from their bases in Honduras, terrorizing the Nicaraguan people and undercutting their faith in the government.

Reagan's rhetoric against the Sandinista government reached startling levels of fantasy. The American public was being told over and over that if the Sandinista "cancer" in Central America wasn't stopped, we'd find them taking over Harlingen, Texas. From there, the communist disease would spread throughout the United States.

Once we'd recovered from the El Salvador march, Robert, Stewart, and I started discussing the administration's broader Central America policy. Since its policy encompassed the entire region, we thought that solidarity work should have a more coordinated, regional approach in response. No one else in CISPES shared that view.

It was hard for me to understand what appeared to me to

be self-limiting activism. I didn't realize until much later that CISPES's focus was not in fact "self-limiting"; it was purposefully specific. While the goal of the organization was to educate Americans about U.S. involvement in the war in El Salvador, in particular CISPES supported one of the five groups that made up the FMLN. My ignorance notwithstanding, the one-country focus felt too confining. Not long before I started my graduate work at the School of Advanced International Studies in the fall of 1982, I decided it was time to leave CISPES. Robert and Stewart felt the same.

.   .   .

The prestigious Johns Hopkins School of Advanced International Studies. SAIS. Applying to graduate school to see if they'll accept you, and then going because they did and you don't know what else to do with your life, isn't an example of clear thinking about how to further your education. I told myself that having an elitist credential in international relations could be useful given my so-called radical perspective on U.S. interventionism. I intended to specialize in Central America in the Latin America studies program; all students at SAIS were also obligated to study economics.

The economics courses were studies in charts and graphs and supply and demand. All were taught without the tiniest hint that this dry subject matter actually had a huge impact on the lives of real human beings. Once I asked a question about how price fluctuations on the charts and graphs—if we were talking about the global market for coffee beans, for example—might play out in the lives of peasant workers on coffee ranches in El Salvador or Guatemala. The professor looked at me as if I were daft. He almost cringed, as if I were trying to defile the beauty of economic theory by prompting the class to consider the frequently devastating impact of economic theories when linked to reality. He didn't really answer my question, and no one else seemed to care.

SAIS and I were a terrible fit. Many at the school considered me to be far to the left, whatever that meant in a country without an organized political left. But anyone raising any objection to U.S. policy in Central America was considered leftist.

It was not an easy two years. In addition to going to school full-time, I also worked part-time jobs to get by. Sometimes more than one at a time. I felt like my father.

Robert became unsure of his direction after leaving CISPES. At that point, he was working part-time in a bookstore, and that was all he was doing, other than trying to get back together with a previous girlfriend he still fantasized about. I thought of her as his phantom of repressed desire. They could have had a perfect relationship, if only . . . As in many failed romances, including my own with him, the possibility that the "if only" could materialize was mostly a figment of his imagination.

They talked for long hours on the phone, while he told me over and over that they were just rekindling an old friendship. I was turning myself into a neurotic, self-doubting pretzel trying to convince myself that his half-truths weren't really lies, and that my jealousy was my problem. He was more than willing to emphasize the problematic nature of jealousy and its negative impact on relationships. To prove that they were just friends, Robert went to spend a friendly weekend with the woman in the Virginia town she lived in several hours from D.C. As I remember, it also happened to be the New Year holiday.

When he returned, he announced that he'd be giving notice at the bookstore and moving within three weeks to live with her.

Unbelievably, I let him stay in the apartment through that process. What motivated *that* self-torture? My father told me that it was like keeping a dead body in the house instead of burying it.

The only thing that kept me relatively sane then was my part-time work with the Caribbean-Basin Information Project. The project had been set up to provide information to journalists and policy people about what was going on in Central America and the Caribbean that couldn't be found in the mainstream media. It was a small effort to balance the barrage of news that painted the U.S. vision of the battle against communism in the region.

Between classes and work, I didn't have much time to fall apart over Robert's betrayal. Not only that, I avoided admitting to myself that, while he might be a user, the crux of the matter was that I'd allowed myself to be used. And because I'd chosen not to think about that, when Robert came back, suitcase in hand, a few months later, I let him in—for another round of tension, stress, anxiety, and self-doubt.

I guess I wanted to prove that he loved me. I'm not sure if I wanted to prove it to him or to myself or to everyone who knew us. I needed to show I'd not been wrong in letting him into my life in the first place. It took a while to see that I was getting a bit of what I'd treated Claude to for so many years. That didn't happen until Robert finally left the second time—again already involved with another woman—some months after I failed the oral exams that I needed to pass to graduate from SAIS.

.　　.　　.

Passing the orals at the end of the last semester was the final requirement for graduation. Three professors would grill each student for several hours on any material they chose from courses studied during the student's two years at SAIS. Predictably, I was a wreck as the exam approached, and I sought dispensation almost before I'd taken my seat across from the two men and one woman who would carry out this academic inquisition.

I explained to them that my preparation had suffered because I'd spent the past several days dealing with the unexpected death of Robert's father. We'd been unable to get in touch with him over several days. When we went to his apartment, there was no answer when we pounded on his door. Robert managed to get in through a window to find his father dead on the floor. It was shocking. It was awful. Dealing with the aftermath had done nothing to calm either my perpetually fraught relationship with Robert or my mind for the orals.

The professors murmured how sorry they were, reassured me that it would be fine, and started firing questions at me. I'd done well in classes while, at the same time, managing to avoid talking much in many of them. In my self-imposed isolation at SAIS, I'd also decided not to participate in the many study groups practicing for the orals. I concentrated all my mental energy thinking about possible answers for possible questions. Or so I pretended to myself.

In front of the professors and their questions, I was thrown into a fourth-grade, Miss-Larkin-deer-in-the-headlights response. But in this case, the worse it went, the more openly hostile I became. I'd never have dared challenge Miss Larkin. If I'd been able to generate any sympathy about the trauma of Robert's father, I obliterated it with my sarcasm. Nothing could hide the fact that I was not prepared. Finally, Dr. Bagley, my favorite professor during my time at SAIS, took pity on us all, suggested that the exam was over, and told me I'd have to come back better prepared and retake the orals.

I was humiliated. But it was the unvarnished truth. I wasn't prepared. I didn't deserve to pass. When one of my classmates heard I'd failed, she sought me out and offered to help me prepare to take the orals again. This time, I didn't avoid help and was humbled by her willingness to take on the task with me. Without her, I might not have passed the second attempt.

At the same time, life didn't stop because my orals went badly. This time I did go to my graduation, even if I'd only be receiving a blank piece of paper in lieu of my degree. That, I wouldn't receive until after passing the orals later that summer.

My parents had always felt cheated that I'd chosen not to go to my graduation at the University of Vermont. Now they were so proud that I'd gone to Johns Hopkins, and I felt I owed them a graduation. They came to D.C., and we celebrated. It wasn't the most fun weekend of all time, and it would have been much improved had it been just the three of us, but Robert was still in the picture so we made the best of it.

· · ·

Like every other graduate, I needed a full-time job. But I wasn't looking for the kind of work that SAIS grads typically sought—investment banks, think tanks, or work with the government. I wanted a job dealing with Central America. When I saw an announcement for a position at the Nicaragua-Honduras Education Project, I applied immediately.

The young woman who interviewed me was Lisa Veneklasen. Lisa who I'd met with over pizza at Millie and Al's with her boyfriend several years earlier to talk about Central America. At that time they were trying to get as much information as they could about the region before leaving for Nicaragua to carry out projects that were part of their undergraduate work. Lisa had been quiet back then, letting her boyfriend do most of the talking. But Nicaragua had transformed her, and now she was an impressive bundle of self-confident energy.

We absolutely hit it off, and I was offered the job. Despite my twenty-thousand-dollar student loan debt, I accepted. The position paid thirteen thousand dollars a year, with no benefits. I didn't care. SAIS was almost behind me, pending the orals, and I was excited to have a job that would allow me to continue working on Central America. Finally, my activism would take me to the region.

CHAPTER SIX

Boots on the Ground

Sandinista Interlude

My first time in Managua, near the end of 1984, I kept looking
for the city. I could never find it. It was the capital of the country, yet it never felt like a real city. There was no downtown.
What had been the city center of old Managua was destroyed
in a devastating earthquake in 1972. After that, it existed only in
old photographs and the memories of people who knew it before
it crumbled. There was a restaurant in Managua whose walls
were adorned with old photos, and Lisa Veneklasen and I always
took our delegations of Americans there. No matter how many
times I studied those pictures, I couldn't truly envision the city
before '72.

To my knowledge, there was only one elevator in Nicaragua that functioned in the 1980s, and not all the time, at that. It
was in the Intercontinental Hotel, which stood on the edge of
the ruin-inhabited expanse of what might have been downtown
Managua had there been a downtown in Managua.

At the Nicaragua-Honduras Education Project (NHEP), in
Washington, D.C., Lisa and I put together progressive, educa-

tional trips to the region for U.S. citizens. These were attempts to inject some reality into what was being said about Nicaragua. We wanted to provide a tangible, living and breathing context for what delegation members would continue to read about Nicaragua and Honduras in the news once they got back home.

NHEP was the brainchild of Cora Weiss, a longtime activist-philanthropist from New York, and a handful of others. Our delegations were generally made up of local elected officials from towns and cities around the country, journalists from newspapers in smaller U.S. cities, philanthropists, and others well known in their communities. Once and only once, we diverged from the norm and took a group of college students on a trip. It had its eye-opening moments but generally wasn't an enriching experience for any of us.

No one in NHEP suffered the illusion that the people who joined our trips would become instant experts on the complex situation unfolding in Sandinista Nicaragua, let alone on the state of affairs throughout Central America in those years. Nobody would go home detailing the history of U.S. intervention in the region, as particularly enshrined in the Monroe Doctrine of 1823, for example.

What person anywhere, no matter how much of an expert that person might be, could really determine the impact of the multitudinous interventions on centuries of socioeconomic development there and on generations of people in the region? No one would ever be able to say what different histories might have been written in Central America without the enduring, often deadly, interference by the United States. But what Lisa and I did work hard to ensure was that our delegations would have the opportunity to at least get an overview of the political situation in Nicaragua by meeting with people from different parts of the country, from different walks of life, and with differing political views.

We always took our groups outside of the capital. There they'd meet subsistence farmers, whose world was pretty much defined by the land they struggled to cultivate to feed their families and survive. They could tell you everything about corn or other crops. How to plant it, how to grow it. They could tell you how to harvest the crop, how to store it, and how and what to cook with it. I had never heard so much about corn in my entire life, and at times I felt like I'd heard more than enough corn talk for a lifetime.

Essentially, subsistence farming was the world of the campesinos in Nicaragua and served as the basis of "education" for the rural poor. Formal schooling was something for the rich people in the cities. Maybe these families couldn't read well or write, but they could talk about farming and they could talk with you about U.S. intervention in their country and the impact of the counterrevolutionaries on their lives and livelihood.

We also always took our groups to meet the "rich people." The powerful families that had been taking from the land and the Nicaraguan people for centuries. They were used to power, used to controlling the government through the hands of the Somoza dictatorship and the military, and they did not like most of the changes that had come about in the country since the Sandinistas took power in 1979. The rich wanted their power back, even if they wrapped it in more palatable words like *democracy* and *freedom* and *competition and free enterprise* and *free and open elections* when speaking with Americans visiting their country.

Lisa and I hoped the impact of walking the streets of Managua or driving through the often desolate and barren countryside to meet with campesinos or people in the small towns of Nicaragua would stay with the visitors. We also hoped that when they got back home they'd talk about all their experiences and give their friends and colleagues a broader view than what they might get from the U.S. media.

Honduras was on the itinerary because it was the headquarters of the CIA-sponsored Nicaraguan counterrevolutionaries, the Contras. It was also the staging ground for their military attacks on Nicaragua. The United States had built a military base in Honduras, saying it was temporary.

In the United States, we were presented a picture of Sandinista Nicaragua as a seething incubator of revolutionary fervor. The Reagan administration was convinced it would spread wildly if not stamped out inside Nicaragua's borders. Even before I saw the country for myself, I knew it was a ridiculous contention. Once I'd been there, it was utterly laughable. But that story underpinned justifications for U.S. intervention, and there was nothing funny about that at all.

There was no Internet then and no easy access to other sources of information with other perspectives. It's often difficult to recognize how much we really don't know if we hear the same story over and over and over. With dogmatic repetition, half-truths can take on the veneer of history, and reality becomes the lie. Generations later, who cares about it anyway?

Resistance to oppression and dictatorship in Nicaragua, and to U.S. intervention, had been going on in various forms and at different levels seemingly forever. Nothing seemed like it would ever change. The tiny, rich elite population controlled and owned virtually everything; the rest of the Nicaraguan people got by with what was left. And then the 1972 earthquake hit.

It was the Somoza regime's lack of response to the devastating quake that altered the equation—for the regime did nothing other than siphon off international aid sent to help the people and the country rebuild. Support for the Sandinista guerrillas increased throughout the country, and they finally toppled the dictatorship on July 19, 1979. They'd taken their name from Augusto Cesar Sandino, a campesino who'd led a rebellion against the 1927–1933 U.S. occupation of Nicaragua.

The United States had labeled him a bandit, and today he'd be called a terrorist. But he's considered a hero throughout much of Latin America for fighting against U.S. intervention. Although Sandino managed to evade U.S. troops until they withdrew from Nicaragua in 1933, he was assassinated in 1934 by General Anastasio Somoza. Somoza took over in a coup two years later, and his family ran the country like a fiefdom until they were brought down in 1979.

Now, a dozen years after the quake and a revolution later, what had been the center of Managua, the capital of the country, remained a vacant expanse strewn with the rubble and detritus of destroyed buildings. People still gave directions in the city based on physical points of reference that no longer existed. They alone could follow them. For those not from the city, it was another story. If you asked for a map, the best you got was when someone took the time to draw it by hand. Streets had names but there were no street signs. You knew them if you knew them. If you didn't you needed those hand-drawn maps.

If Managua seemed a city that wasn't really a city, Tegucigalpa, the capital of Honduras, felt like a murky cesspool of intrigue, spies, and counterrevolution. This isn't meant as an insult to the Honduran people. The city felt this way because it was the headquarters of the Contras. It was also a focal point of U.S. military operations in the region through Palmerola, the so-called temporary U.S. base.

Located about thirty-five miles from the capital, Palmerola housed the eleven hundred U.S. troops known as Joint Task Force Bravo permanently stationed there. The base operated to support United States military exercises and other activities in the region while also underscoring U.S. resolve against the Sandinista threat.

Periodic American training exercises with the Honduran army involved the short-term influx of thousands of American troops and National Guardsmen to practice joint military operations. With the excuse of the exercises, the United States spent millions of dollars building or upgrading several air facilities, some of which supported the Contras. The United States also built roads in strategic parts of the country. A U.S. military intelligence battalion supported the Salvadoran military with reconnaissance missions against the FMLN. With the end of the wars in Central America, Palmerola was renamed the Enrique Soto Cano Air Base. It's still home to Joint Task Force Bravo.

What we did as part of the Nicaragua-Honduras Education Project didn't feel like work. It was what I was looking for. I was getting paid to do what I believed in. When I first signed on to the project, my parents hadn't exactly shared my excitement. They hadn't understood why their intelligent daughter, now in possession of not one but two master's degrees, and twenty thousand dollars in debt as a result of the second, had taken this extremely low-paying job. They hadn't understood why I didn't want a normal job at this stage of my life—one they could easily understand and explain to their friends.

At the time, Mom and Dad had hoped that, after my El Salvador organizing phase, and with a new, prestigious degree, I'd be a changed woman ready for a real and challenging career. Preferably one in which I made good money so they would not have to worry about my future. What none of us realized at the time was that I *was* on my way to creating a real and extremely challenging way of life. My school-debt-to-income ratio was unsettling, and it took a long time to pay the debt off. But eventually I did. More important, I didn't sacrifice what I believed in to do it.

. . .

The first delegation I helped lead with Lisa that November was huge. There were thirty-two people in the group, when the average numbered twelve. That trip was a cold-turkey immersion into the ups and downs of working with a delegation. With this group, we planned to stop over for a couple of days in El Salvador before continuing on to Nicaragua and Honduras. The bulk of time would be spent in Nicaragua, where we'd observe the first national elections to take place since the overthrow of Somoza. The country was expected to be crawling with people.

First we landed in El Salvador's militarized airport. One of us went through customs with the beginning of the delegation to keep everybody together on the other side. The other brought up the rear, in case anyone was stopped or otherwise hassled. It took time for all of us to get through, but there weren't any problems. Over the years, however, landing at that airport became an increasingly unpleasant experience. Heavily armed soldiers stationed throughout the airport didn't exactly make one feel at ease entering the country.

The thirty-mile drive into San Salvador, the capital, was always unsettling. It was impossible to avoid thinking of the four U.S. churchwomen stopped along that road the night of December 2, 1980. On orders from General Vides Cassanova, then head of the National Guard, and who later became minister of defense, five members of the National Guard took the women to a remote spot off the airport road and beat, raped, and murdered them. Their shallow graves didn't keep the ugly secret for long. Driving that lonely road could make your skin crawl. You always wondered who might be next.

There's one incident I particularly remember from my first time in El Salvador. We were on our way to a meeting in the city. I was riding in the first minivan; we needed a small fleet for that group. Suddenly a military jeep flew past us. In the back, I saw a young man on his knees on the floor. He was blindfolded with his hands tied behind his back. On either side of him stood a soldier. Both had their machine guns trained directly on him.

Three things flashed through my mind as I watched the jeep race away: What happens if it hits a big bump that causes one of the soldiers to accidentally pull the trigger? What's going to happen to that poor guy when they get him wherever it is they are taking him? Where the hell is my camera and why don't I always have it ready?

Welcome to El Salvador? I felt safer when we landed in Managua a couple of days later. I always felt safer in Nicaragua than in Salvador. Always.

·　　·　　·

Until I went to Nicaragua, I couldn't understand why it was so difficult to schedule meetings without being in the country. After that first trip, I couldn't understand how we ever managed *any* meetings by phone from Washington. It made Reagan's arguments about the Sandinista threat even more ridiculous.

Infrastructure and services in Managua were a disaster. Telephones weren't ubiquitous or, where they did exist, always working. The best way to even tentatively arrange a meeting was in person. Once a group arrived in country, we often had to rush about reconfirming the tentatively confirmed meetings. Despite that, things worked out more or less as planned.

The itineraries—where we'd go, who we'd meet, what we'd see—were always packed. In Nicaragua, we'd meet with representatives of the Sandinista government, including President Daniel Ortega or Vice President Sergio Ramirez; and with the military, including Comandante Tomas Borge or Comandante Dora Maria Tellez. We saw opposition figures, political parties, businessmen, and Violeta Chamorro, owner of the famous anti-Sandinista newspaper *La Prensa Libre*. (Later, in the 1990 elections when the Sandinistas were crushingly defeated, Chamorro was elected president.)

Our delegations met with priests and nuns who'd supported the insurrection and with human rights organizations. We also visited prisons. Once in Honduras, we'd see government officials, human rights organizations, leaders of the Contra, and U.S. Embassy officials. Delegations always made a trip out to Palmerola, where we'd be given a briefing by the U.S. military about its perspective of the situation in the region.

Sometimes in Managua, we felt as if we were witnessing an ideological fight between the biting rhetoric of the Sandinistas and that of the opposition, whose beliefs were often best captured by Chamorro and *La Prensa*. Outside the capital, the war could feel very different. We took one group quite far into the countryside, toward the Honduran border. Traveling the main roads was rough; then we turned off and started bouncing down a deeply rutted dirt road, leaving clouds of dust in our wake. Finally, we crested a rise and saw the little village below, where we were going to meet with members of a farming cooperative.

From the rise, we saw not only the village but also a Sandinista tank squatting beside a short, spindly tree. It was camouflaged with branches that were only sparsely populated with leaves and which had been attached here and there to the tank. Somehow in that setting it looked almost ridiculous, like a twisted scene from a Monty Python movie. But it was anything but amusing. The farmers told us that the soldiers were there because Contra raids in the area were on the rise. With that bit of information, the delegation's only focus was on getting back to Managua as quickly as possible.

.   .   .

The attacks were grinding away at the early gains of the Sandinista government. When they'd first taken power, the Sandinistas had launched a massive literacy campaign and made economic reforms to benefit the majority of people in Nicaragua. International financial institutions had praised these early efforts. How the country might have continued to develop if left alone is something we'll never know.

In addition to creating the Contras, the United States took other steps to undermine and isolate the Sandinista government. The war of attrition affected the economic, political, and social fabric of the country. The Sandinistas became increasingly entrenched and hardened. Corruption among the power elite also grew. But even as many Nicaraguans became disillusioned, some Westerners working there seemed to become more Sandinista than the Sandinistas.

These Westerners' unquestioning revolutionary fervor earned them the nickname "Sandalistas," a play on the name of the favored footwear of the activists. Even though the gap between what might have been, and what actually was, got worse, these Sandalistas believed that open discussion of the problems would be seen as supporting U.S. intervention. I marveled at their purity. Unlike most of the Nicaraguans, they had plane tickets out of the country to use whenever they chose; and yet they argued most vociferously for the government, in particular the revolutionary commanders at its head—no matter what many Nicaraguan people might have to say about things. In commenting about this period, one observer wrote, "There are a lot of needs being met here and some of them are Nicaraguan."

Commander Omar Cabezas had gained international recognition not only for being a member of the Sandinista military and the government but also for his book *Fire from the Mountain*. In this autobiography, published in 1985, he recounted his development from student activist to Sandinista guerrilla. The book was popular at the time, and Cabezas often spoke to promote it and the Sandinista government. But our one and only delegation of college students got to see a different side of him.

The students had met with him outside Managua near the end of their trip and had been as taken with him as he was with one of them. It was disconcerting to see Cabezas, a leader of the revolutionary movement, flirt with her unabashedly. The object of his attention was a tall, well-built redhead, the captain of the college cheerleading team. Her boyfriend, also on the trip, was captain of the football team. The other students fawned over the two of them. Their professor was too easygoing, and the students viewed the trip too much like a vacation, and not enough like a serious political learning experience, for our taste.

Once we got back to the capital, there was one more day of meetings, followed by an informal dinner around the swimming pool on the group's last night in the country. Over dinner we had wrap-up discussions and then toasted our trip and each other. The adults began to peel away and head to our rooms. Our flights back home were scheduled for very early in the morning, and Lisa and I had to be up particularly early to make sure everyone got on the bus to the airport.

Everyone did make it, but just barely. The students had partied at the pool until about three or four in the morning. The hotel staff had tried to get them to wind down hours earlier, but they'd been cajoled into letting the students stay there "just a little bit longer." An hour later, at their second attempt, the staff had found not only the students still in the pool chugging beer but also a fully uniformed Cabezas in the water with them, beer in hand.

The behavior was all too human, but I didn't have the patience for it. *Inappropriate* didn't adequately describe it.

·   ·   ·

I usually had mixed feelings when our trips ended. Once on the plane back home, I'd feel light and liberated. No more people trailing behind me no matter where I went. No more talking with or for them. At the same time, I often felt like a mother duck who'd lost her ducklings. But the delegations were also taxing because I'm an introvert.

Many think *introvert* means someone who's inarticulate in public and unable to interact with others. I'm neither, but I need lots of space. Physical as well as mental and emotional space. Central American culture doesn't lend itself to space. Nor does leading a delegation. Being an introvert, I found it took all my energy to interact with everyone on the delegations, as well as all those we met with, and to translate when necessary. To activate my public self, then and now, I have to work myself into a different frame of mind, which isn't role playing or even like role playing. It's simply a different way of being.

On the trips, I'd struggle to find time for myself, which was usually impossible until the end. Then, despite the luxurious pleasure of being alone again, I was generally so drained that, for a few days, I wasn't good for more than lying around and reading. The longer and more complicated the trip, the longer it took to get my energy back. Too many trips in too short a period was debilitating. The political work wasn't easy, either.

Trying to organize support to stop U.S. intervention in Central American countries was different from the waves of activism to end the Vietnam War. Then, it was our own who were fighting and killing and dying. Because the sons of American families could be drafted into that war, everyone in some way had a stake in the national discussion about Vietnam.

That wasn't the case in Central America. Badly bruised from the Vietnam experience, the United States wanted at that time to avoid major overt military involvement in conflicts in other countries. So our nation didn't send U.S. troops to fight in Nicaragua or in El Salvador. Instead we sent millions and millions in military aid, military trainers, and other types of support. That made it much easier to avoid national debate back home about U.S. intervention in those wars.

The Nicaragua-Honduras Education Project's situation was even more difficult because it operated on a shoestring. Delegations weren't moneymaking enterprises. The trips barely covered their own costs, and often the project was on the edge of financial disaster. At one point right before payday, we had a grand total of $106 in the bank. Being unsure from month to month whether we'd continue to exist frayed nerves already stretched by the nature of the work itself. The board became less and less enthusiastic about continuing to bail the project out.

Finally, at a meeting at the beginning of the summer in 1986, the board decided NHEP would close its doors as a stand-alone operation that August. A peace and justice organization at a small college was going to absorb the work of NHEP, and Lisa would stay through the end of the year to help with the transition.

Despite the strains and pressures I'd experienced at NHEP, I was glad I'd had the chance to work with Lisa. She is one of the best and most creative activist-organizers I know. She's also irreverent, funny as hell, and great to work with. We had fun and were equally adept at black humor as a safety valve in difficult circumstances—time at the bar at the Intercontinental lent itself to such amusement. I learned a tremendous amount during those years as we worked to mitigate the impact of Reagan policies on Nicaragua and Honduras. We didn't change that world, but we tried.

My heart wasn't broken with the demise of NHEP as we knew it and, with it, the end of that phase of my work. It was time to look for another job. Serendipitously, Mario Velasquez, who I'd first met in February 1981 at the meeting in the church basement where he'd spoken about El Salvador, showed up again on my doorstep. Mario wanted me to come back to the Salvador work. It almost felt like I was going back where I belonged.

Working with Mario and Medical Aid for El Salvador would consume the next five and a half years of my life. Nothing I'd done up to that point in my life could compare with the work I did during those years. If Vietnam opened my eyes to the world, it was El Salvador that would change the course of my life and my activism.

·   ·   ·

I hadn't seen Mario since long before starting work at NHEP. He'd disappeared from CISPES. The last I'd heard, he and Heidi had gotten divorced and he was living in California. When he showed up in D.C. and offered me a job, he was working for the Los Angeles–based Medical Aid for El Salvador. The organization had been founded by Bill Zimmerman, Ed Asner, Lee Grant, and others to provide humanitarian relief to civilians in El Salvador. It counted on the support of celebrities Jackson Browne, Darryl Hannah, Bianca Jagger, Kris and Lisa Kristofferson, Oliver Stone, and Bonnie Raitt, among others.

My first task with Medical Aid was to help with a delegation that would take medical supplies to El Salvador in November 1984. The supplies were being sent not only in response to the war but also because of a serious earthquake that had hit the country on October 10 that year. In the earthquake and aftershocks, about fifteen hundred people had died, ten thousand were wounded, and two hundred thousand were left homeless. The epicenter was directly under San Salvador, the capital.

At first, I agreed only to a consulting contract that would last long enough for me to accompany the delegation. In addition to feeling some burnout from the Nicaragua work, I was cautious about jumping into an organization that I didn't know and which was based in L.A. Mario's charisma was unparalleled. He's a man of huge vision. But sometimes vision can prove challenging in the execution.

The November trip was complicated, especially because Mario couldn't go himself. He'd not been in El Salvador since the end of the 1970s. Because he had been a spokesperson for the Democratic Revolutionary Front of the FMLN, was a founder of CISPES, and had in other ways opposed the military government in Salvador, it was considered too dangerous for him to go there.

His intense frustration at that painful reality was completely understandable. And if you were one of the people trying to communicate with him from El Salvador about what was happening with the delegation and with the medical supplies, that wasn't always easy either. Today, with the Internet, the challenges would be greatly diminished. In 1986 it was another story.

Before my contract with Medical Aid expired, and despite my trepidations, I was talked into working full-time for the organization. A key selling point was that I didn't have to move to L.A. for the job. I'd be able to do some of the work from my home, and there would be support from L.A. I'd spend time in D.C. and Salvador, as well as in the office on Wilshire Boulevard. There was no set formula, but I was in Salvador and L.A. much more than in D.C.

My task was to create and direct the Children's Project. We'd bring kids wounded in the war to the United States to receive donated medical care, but the effort wasn't only humanitarian. It was also a way to build awareness in the United States about the war and its impact on civilians, primarily the rural poor.

Each child would be accompanied by a family member, usually a parent, who'd help care for the child and also speak with community organizations in the host cities about why they were there. About the war. About U.S. involvement in the war. And why it was so important for Americans not to passively condone U.S. policies by their inaction.

Even during that November trip, before I'd signed on to the project, I'd been asked to meet three wounded kids who'd be possible candidates for participating in the project, once there was a project to participate in. One was five-year-old Norma. She'd lost her hearing during an attack on her village when a bomb explosion perforated her eardrums. Her hearing had been greatly diminished immediately, and she'd had repeated ear infections. With each one, she lost more of her hearing. If her condition wasn't treated, ultimately she'd be completely deaf. Also, as a result of the trauma of the attack, Norma had stopped speaking. The only person she might say a few words to was her mother. And then not often.

To make the project work, I had to find hospitals and doctors who'd donate treatment for the kids. We were supported by an order of nuns, whose superior had signed a letter addressed to hospitals run by religious orders. Dozens across the United States responded, and over the course of the project, we placed kids in twenty-one hospitals.

In each city, I worked with local Central America solidarity groups to recruit families to host the kids and their parents while they were in the United States. The groups also helped arrange interviews and speaking events for the accompanying parents. In one case, the family of the doctor who performed the surgery on the child also hosted her and her mother. The mom herself had lost a hand in an attack on their village, but she had no interest in a prosthesis. Her concern was for her daughter, who carried shrapnel in her skull from that same attack, which affected her life on a daily basis.

In El Salvador, we worked primarily with the Archdiocese of San Salvador to find wounded kids from the parts of the country that bore the brunt of the war. I spent lots of time in and out of the U.S. Embassy getting visas for the kids and their parents. Pan American Airlines, now defunct, donated round-trip tickets to get the children and their parents to the United States; United donated domestic tickets.

Twelve kids, each with a parent, made up the first group who came to the States. I'd been back and forth between Salvador and Los Angeles over the course of a few weeks to make the final arrangements before families departed for Los Angeles. From L.A., they would go to cities across the United States, where they'd be treated. A small delegation, including Bianca Jagger and Lynne Cutler, then head of the Democratic National Committee, went to Salvador with me to help accompany the children on the first leg of their trip, to L.A.

The first time we all met as a group—the kids and their parents and those who'd be taking them to the United States—was for two days of orientation. A Salvadoran psychologist specializing in war trauma in the civilian population worked with the families. All were subsistence campesinos barely eking out an existence in the war-ravaged countryside. The orientation was designed to prepare them for what they'd experience over the next months.

Pretty much everything would be new to them once they got to the United States—electricity, toilets, and washing machines, not to mention the high-tech hospitals and the medical treatment they would undergo. In many ways it was as hard for the American hosts to understand as it was for the Salvadorans. How hard is it to flip a switch to turn on a light? Or to press the handle to flush a toilet? My dad would have understood immediately and completely. But host families, whose houses the Salvadorans could barely comprehend, didn't get it at all. It was nobody's fault. It was just the way it was.

One of the mothers was so embarrassed and traumatized by being unable to operate the washing machine and having no river to wash her clothes in that she longed to be back home from the moment she arrived in Boston. The picture of a washing machine she'd seen in orientation, and the subsequent two-minute overview of how to use it when she'd first arrived at her host family's house, didn't begin to suffice. She was afraid to ask for another lesson, and her hosts didn't have a clue that she had no idea what to do with a washing machine.

Other objects that seem benign to us had a very different meaning for these families. One of the first orientation sessions began with pictures of passenger jets. They'd all seen planes before. The Salvadoran military flew planes that bombed their villages. Some of the kids had been wounded by them. They had no lack of understanding about attack helicopters. But passenger planes? They'd never heard of them.

The psychologist worked hard to explain that the planes they would fly in were for people. They didn't have bombs or guns or soldiers who would hurt them. It was hard to imagine if you weren't there with the kids. Or didn't know their stories.

Most of the news about El Salvador that people heard in the United States indicated that it was a fragile, emerging democracy. That the various transformations of the government, including "elections," were signs of a peaceful future as it struggled to "put down the insurgency." You might even see it that way if you lived in San Salvador. The fighting rarely touched the capital. However, that's not how people who lived in the countryside where the war was being fought described their lives.

In the war, the Salvadoran military killed thousands and thousands of people and disappeared thousands more. They carried out bombing raids on villages in areas of the country where rebel groups might be. They designed scorched-earth policies to drive from their villages the people they believed might support the FMLN. The children and their families had lived through such experiences and would tell their stories across the United States. The families, hospitals, and cities that took them in received them with open arms. The doctors healed their physical wounds. But who could predict what would come of the other wounds of war that people carry in their spirits?

.   .   .

While trying to flesh out and manage the Children's Project, I also took delegations to Salvador who supported, or who might support, the work of Medical Aid. Those delegations weren't always easy, but I made fast friends in the process. Trips in El Salvador were always more difficult than those in Nicaragua, where there was a relative sense of safety, something no one experienced in Salvador. One of the 1988 delegations was a case in point.

I'd gone to Salvador a week before the delegation arrived to firm up the itinerary for the group and make sure the hotel and other logistics were in order. I'd be meeting up with Eileen Rosin, a staff member from the L.A. office who'd moved to San Salvador earlier that year to help with our programs from inside the country. In addition to working on the Children's Project, she also helped out with the Prosthetics Project, which was run by Dave Evans, a wild and colorful Vietnam vet who was a double-amputee himself.

Eileen shared a small house with Corinne Dufka, a human-rights-activist-turned-fantastic-photojournalist. Everyone on the delegation would be staying at the Camino Real Hotel. I was at an inexpensive, small, but quite decent hotel about five minutes away from the Camino.

As on all such trips for Medical Aid, and as had been the case with delegations I'd led to Nicaragua and Honduras, meetings in El Salvador would be almost back to back, and days were long and full. We always tried to make sure that our groups met with as many people and organizations as possible. They met with government officials, but more important they also met with the Salvadoran high command. It was the military that actually ran the country.

We had meetings with human rights organizations; the Catholic archdiocese, headed by Archbishop Rivera y Damas since the assassination of Romero; and representatives of the Lutheran and Episcopal Churches. We saw journalists, officials at the U.S. Embassy, and political opposition leaders, such as Ruben Zamora. Delegations also had discussions with the Jesuits who ran the University of Central America.

One of our meetings on that trip was scheduled for the end of the day at the military's high command. We met with General Adolfo Blandon, head of the Salvadoran Joint Chiefs of Staff. Such meetings were never pleasant, and this one with Blandon in particular was more unpleasant than most. He started by giving the official line on the fight against the "terrorist" rebels while downplaying human rights abuses by the military and its affiliated death squads. He insisted that the Salvadoran military had nothing to do with the death squads.

One member of the delegation asked him to explain civilian casualties during counterinsurgency campaigns. In a moment of startling candor, Blandon said it was necessary to get rid of potential future rebels, and that this meant dealing with the civilian population in the areas where the rebels operated. We all stopped breathing for a second when he said that. Kill the young so they can't grow up to be rebels? He said it as easily as if he were saying, "When a mosquito lands on my arm, I smack it dead."

Once we piled back in the minivan, we started discussing what we'd just heard. As I drove out of the military headquarters, the lights in the city went dead. We later learned that the

FMLN had attacked a power station. In the blackened city, I quickly became disoriented and drove in circles trying to find the Camino Real. At one intersection, we saw a body draped over the curb, surrounded by soldiers. People were very tense by the time I found the hotel. They quickly jumped out of the van and hurried into the brightly lit hotel. The Camino had its own generators.

I left the van, jumped into the Jeep Cherokee I was driving, and headed back up the hill to my hotel, the only car in the streets. As I made a brief stop at a corner before turning left, a BMW appeared out of nowhere, racing down the hill in my direction. I made my turn as the BMW whipped around in the middle of the intersection and began speeding after me.

I didn't think. Adrenaline pumping, I drove like a fiend. I took a right off the main road, which the other driver wasn't expecting, and got a fair lead on the other car. I had to make only a quick right after that, and then another, to get to the hotel, where I came to a screeching stop, bolted out of the car, and grabbed the iron gate protecting the entrance. It was locked. I was slamming on the bell and shaking the gate as the BMW rounded the corner.

The desk clerk let me in as the other car whipped around the cul-de-sac in front of the hotel. As the car sped by me and back up the street, the man in the passenger seat yelled, "You got away from us this time . . ."

·　　·　　·

Whether it was working on the Children's Project or taking people to El Salvador, my time during those five and a half years was spent in constant motion as I traveled between D.C., the Medical Aid office in L.A., and El Salvador, where I spent weeks and weeks on the ground. Occasionally I'd make it to Vermont to see my family. One year I spent a total of eleven weeks in D.C.

Vermont trips weren't always restful. Sometimes they were full of tension and denial. I was always wound tight and wanted everyone to feel as intensely as I did about what was happening in Salvador. Sometimes my family would listen, but mostly they didn't want to hear too much about my work. I got angry that the only thing they seemed to want to talk about was Mark's, Mary Beth's, and Janet's kids or other benign topics. I'd become irritable and estranged.

They weren't avoiding the subject of El Salvador out of disinterest; mainly they were afraid of what they might hear. I didn't tell them the more unpleasant things, and eventually I didn't talk about it much at all. When the situation really began to heat up in El Salvador in 1989, it became a more difficult topic to ignore. I experienced a taste of the violence myself.

CHAPTER SEVEN

Dinner with the Death Squad

San Salvador was a city of menace. This despite the fact that the Salvadoran military's counterinsurgency campaign in 1988 continued to ravage campesino villages in the countryside far from the capital. If you hung out in San Salvador too long, you learned to sit with your back against the wall. You also began to walk facing the oncoming traffic. If somebody were to jump out of a car and try to snatch you, it would be better to see him first. When we looked for a hotel for Medical Aid staff to stay in, we looked for security.

The hotel we found was centrally located and sat at the end of a short, dead-end street. It was just far enough off one of the main thoroughfares of the city to avoid the sounds and smells of the battered, pollution-spewing buses and other vehicles, many of them in an indescribable state of disrepair, that trundled up and down the road from dawn to dark. It was not possible to escape the *chop-chop-chop* of the military helicopters flying low over the city, however.

The hotel was enclosed by a high wall, and you could not

enter it after dark unless a security guard admitted you through the locked gate. Only hotel guests were allowed access to the rooms. If you had visitors, the clerk at the front desk would call to let you know, and you had to come down and meet them in the lobby. With its wall around the perimeter, the locked and guarded gate, and the type of clientele it served, the place offered a reasonably secure environment in a country of fairly complete insecurity.

The rooms were not great, but the hotel had redeeming features beyond the security: it was relatively cheap, and the other guests who tended to stay there were very quiet and kept to themselves. Short-term contract employees of the U.S. government frequently stayed there. The hotel's interior garden area, which surrounded a pretty little swimming pool, was very pleasant; with the quiet and the relative seclusion, it was almost soothing.

My favorite part was the "workout room" located toward the rear of the garden, near a hotel work area. At one time it must have been an open-fronted storage shed of some sort. The rough cement floor apparently was impossible to clean, and mastering the rudimentary equipment, including free weights, required imagination coupled with stoicism. Despite its condition, I was thrilled it was there and used it as often as I could.

I also had my trusty jump rope, which I took everywhere. I was good at jumping rope, having started back when I lived in Mexico. I could manage it even in extremely confined spaces and often would start a workout with about twenty minutes of jumping; when I really needed a release, I could go for twice as long. Years later I had to give it up because my knees would no longer cooperate; I still resent the hell out of them for that.

The hotel staff always made me laugh, because no matter how

many times they saw me working out, they were stunned at the sight of a woman lifting weights. I could never convince them that it was fantastic exercise for women. They'd just walk away shaking their heads and chuckling. The only time I didn't mind the heat of El Salvador was when I was working out. You're supposed to sweat when you work out. Anyway, then I could dive into the hotel swimming pool.

Salvador was always hot, and the hotel didn't have air conditioning. The smothering humidity made the aqua-blue water of the pool more than just inviting—it was beguiling. I learned to swim when I was four, thanks to my mom's brother, Chuck, who'd taught me at Lake St. Catherine in Vermont. He must have been a good teacher, because I'm a good, strong swimmer. It was hard not to jump in the pool at every opportunity, but there was always too much work and too little time. I usually managed only after I'd carved out time to use the workout room first.

Everything took longer to accomplish than you'd expect in Salvador. It wasn't as bad as in Nicaragua, but inexperienced people from the north could be easily defeated there. Little could be arranged by phone; business was best conducted face to face. This wasn't only because the phones weren't great in El Salvador; it was mostly because of security. Surveillance was everywhere.

But managing to find the people you needed to conduct your face-to-face business with was an enormous challenge. Often circumstances beyond everyone's control made it impossible to meet at an appointed time. Sometimes people just pretended that circumstances beyond their control had made it impossible to meet at an appointed time. In either case, you'd have to try to arrange another time to try to meet.

It was a constant struggle that often left you running in sweat-lathered circles. Given all the time and effort wasted, it was hard not to get totally frustrated and decide to give up and spend time sitting beside the swimming pool instead of continuing to run in circles.

One Sunday, when most everyone was either at church or at home with their families, I was sitting in the shade of a palm tree at the edge of the pool, lost in the pages of a book. When I'd get too hot, I'd take a swim, then return to my book and air dry until the heat overtook me again. The pool was mine. It was a luxurious treat to be alone there.

My idyll was shattered when three men in their late twenties or early thirties cannonballed into the water. My reflector sunglasses shielded them from my withering look, but the set of my jaw more than likely sent them the desired signal. They stayed at the far end of the pool as they fooled around in the water and tossed a ball back and forth. Boys being boys, they cast glances toward the girl from time to time to see if the girl was responding to their boyish charm.

My book was much more interesting than them and their antics, and I buried my nose as far into it as I could, ignoring them until the sweat ran down my forehead and into my eyes, blurring the words on the pages. Surrendering, I closed the book and quietly slid into the water, keeping to my end. But it was inevitable that they'd make their way to the middle of the pool, their ball would somehow end up almost hitting me in the head, and they would all clamor about, each trying to apologize more loudly than the others.

Of course it had been a ploy, but I ended up laughing at them and with them from the side of the pool as they continued playing with the ball. Nothing of substance was said, but it was clear to me that these three guys were not exactly the kind of people I'd normally mingle with. The way they walked—like they owned the world. The way they talked—like they were used to being listened to. They did ask me in passing what I was doing there, but I artfully (or so I thought) gave a nonanswer. They didn't bring it up again, and I was pretty sure they'd assumed that I was another of the many State-Department-contractor types doing my time in Salvador.

Of the three, one was clearly dominant, and he asked what I was doing for dinner. I said I'd not given it much thought, so he suggested that he'd make it easy for me and take me to dinner at a very nice restaurant. The invitation wasn't really surprising, but it didn't feel right. "No" was on the tip of my tongue, but I heard myself say yes as I was already convincing myself it was harmless. What could be wrong with a nice dinner someplace I'd never go on my own or with any of my friends or colleagues? Why not spend a couple of hours engaging in mindless chatter on a boring Sunday evening while eating a nice dinner in an air-conditioned restaurant?

I have no memory of where we dined. I have no memory of what we ate or what we drank with our meal. I do remember that there was little mindless chatter. Instead my date ended up spilling his guts across the elegant table when I asked him what he did. It has always amazed me how much people will say about themselves when given the chance, and how little interest they will show in hearing anything about the person they are talking at. At the time, I didn't realize there was more going on in this case and a purpose behind telling me his story.

When I asked him what he did, I knew he wasn't going to be describing his work in a refugee camp or anything of the sort. I thought he probably did something like manage his father's coffee ranches or a bank or a business, but I never expected what I was about to hear. Now, I wouldn't remember his name if my life depended on it. I'd never be able to pick him out of a lineup. But I'll never forget his line of work.

The long and short of it is that he was, or had been, a member of one of the most notorious of Salvador's notorious death squads, those soulless individuals who made it their business to torture and kill people who didn't agree with or otherwise support the military dictatorship in his country. He said he'd left the group—although of course he was morally committed to totally supporting its aims and objectives. He'd left, he said, because the stress had gotten to him.

Apparently he didn't mean the stress of a conscience burdened by memories of innocents dragged from their homes in the night and never seen again. It was the stress of worrying about "the enemy." It had gotten so bad, he said, that he sweated and trembled through the night worrying that all the guns under, around, and in his bed wouldn't keep him safe. He lay awake night after night, wondering if and when they'd come for him. "They're everywhere, you know," he said, looking at me now through half-crazed eyes. It's hard to believe that eyes can spin in their sockets and blaze red, but I swear I saw it myself. And I knew his enemies weren't mine. *He* was the enemy.

But before his nerves had gotten the best of him, he said, it had been exhilarating and all-consuming. One of the nights he remembered most fondly was one he'd spent in Roberto D'Aubuisson's car. D'Aubuisson was a killer's killer, legendary "patriot," and death squad founder. (No one I knew shed a tear when he died after the end of the war, very painfully, of throat cancer.) That was the night when D'Aubuisson's "people" had gone in their weapon-laden vehicles and surrounded the residence of the U.S. ambassador, Robert White, salivating over the prospects of doing him bodily harm if they thought they could get away with it.

White had denounced D'Aubuisson, who he'd called a "pathological killer," for planning and ordering the assassination of Archbishop Oscar Romero. Romero had been conservative when appointed archbishop. But witnessing the death and oppression in his country, including the assassination of his close friend the Jesuit priest Rutilio Grande, made Romero radically change course and choose to "walk with the poor." Increasingly revered in his country and recognized around the world, the archbishop lost his life as a result of this decision.

Describing that night with D'Aubuisson, my dinner partner seemed transported as he poured out his hate. Somehow I managed to keep myself together, enduring his diatribe throughout dinner while trying to will it to end as quickly as possible. How I wished I could just disappear from the table, teleport myself back to my room or, better, back in time just a few hours so I could revisit the dinner invitation and this time sensibly refuse.

If he smelled my fear or sensed my revulsion on the drive back to the hotel, he gave no indication. With the end of dinner, his rant too had ended, and now he was pointing out landmarks of the city like a tour guide. Having been on automatic pilot throughout dinner, I was able to rouse my inner tourist and respond appropriately to his comments about the capital.

The ride was short, although it didn't feel like it at the time. I didn't bolt from the car before it came to a complete stop at the front gate as I dearly wished to. Instead I thanked Mr. Death Squad for the nice meal, got out of the car, and calmly waited for the guard to let me in. Robotically, I turned and waved good-bye as my dinner companion wheeled his car around and drove away.

Back in my room, I didn't shake or tremble. I picked up my book and tried to read, but all I could think about was what an idiot I'd been. It seemed impossible that I'd actually had dinner with such scum of the earth.

Self-accusations played over and over in my head: What had I been thinking, going to dinner with a man like that? Even though I hadn't known how much "like that" he was, I'd recognized that he wasn't out there defending the powerless. Where had I put my political judgment? Although I didn't quite realize it yet, I'd been more than just bored and was on the verge of burning out again.

My reverie of self-flagellation was interrupted by a soft tapping at my door, irritating the hell out of me. Why was the security guard or the desk clerk bothering me at this hour? Nothing could be that urgent, and why hadn't someone just called me from reception? I opened the door to neither of them. Instead, I was face to face with Mr. Death Squad.

Instinctively I stepped back from him. His menace filled the room even before he stepped inside, took the door from my hand, and closed and locked it behind him. He backed me to the edge of the bed and said I'd not fooled him at all. It didn't matter that I'd not said a word about myself or what I was doing in his country. He knew.

He spit out the words that people like me weren't welcome in El Salvador, and smiled malevolently as he noted that I didn't seem to understand how careful I should be. As his hot breath and hotter words seared my brain, he started to touch me and the bile rose in my throat at the vile certainty of what would happen next. There was no love in those death squad hands. There was no lust in them either—unless you count the blood lust for threat, intimidation, and violence.

I lay there, a rigid slab, wondering if I should scream out loud or just scream inside. What difference would it make, I wondered, but somehow I believed screaming out loud would fuel his hate and make him more violent. Deciding without deciding, I silently endured the mechanical act, which had nothing to do with sex and everything to do with delivering a political threat in the form he and his colleagues believed most likely to devastate any woman and make her flee. They could get rid of me without having to bury another American body and risk another cutoff, however brief, of U.S. funds for their war.

The art of emotional dissociation, honed over so many years of dealing with the out-of-control, schizophrenic violence of my brother Steve, was my salvation. As that man and his hate penetrated me, I numbed all feeling, not exactly by choice; it just happened. I even reasoned that there was no one I knew who hadn't had to put up with sex when they weren't particularly in the mood. I could just consider this to be a more extreme circumstance of "not being in the mood."

He likely assumed, like an experienced torturer, that I was frozen in terror. Terror was not what was going on for me. I knew he wasn't going to hurt me. I knew he wasn't going to disappear me. I knew I wasn't going to die.

My spirit retreated and waited for him to exit what I now understood was his uncle's hotel. When he left, I couldn't tell if it had been a minute or an eternity. I did note that there was no smirk of the sexual predator on his face as he quietly hissed his parting shot, "Watch out. I know who you are."

The door closed softly, and I forced myself to keep my breathing as shallow as possible until the noxious vapors of his presence dissipated. I rolled over and resumed my self-flagellation, this time with even more intensity. That couldn't have just happened. But of course it had happened, and I couldn't make it go away. I could do the next best thing and think of it as a very, very bad date with a very, very bad ending.

I could also resolve never to talk about it, because talking about things makes them real. If I never spoke about it, no one could ever question my political judgment. Even thinking about trying to explain to any of my colleagues how I'd made such a stupid choice, in a country where stupid choices can be fatal, seemed like deciding to dig my own political grave. If I'd made such a serious miscalculation, what else might I be capable of? Already starting to put the experience into a little box to be filed away in some remote part of my mind, I managed to fall asleep, get up the next morning, take a shower, and go about my work as if it were any other day in El Salvador.

I had an appointment in a part of the city I'd not been to before. It was a bit far but I wanted to walk. I needed the exercise and it was a nice morning. I added extra time because I knew I'd probably not easily find the little side street I was looking for.

I'd been walking for about thirty minutes when I heard a car pull up beside me. I turned to look, and there was Mr. Death Squad staring dead at me. With a twisted smile he said, "Want a ride?" I jumped away from the curb as he sped off into the heavy traffic. That was almost more frightening than the previous night. How could he possibly know where I was going to be?

Just like in the movies, where scenes you're not supposed to see fade to black, the death squad date faded too—if not completely to black, then to a very obscure brown-black. I didn't talk about it, and if I ever thought about it at all, I only marveled at having sat through a whole dinner listening to the stories of a mass murderer. And marveled that he'd known where I was going to be the next day. But after that, I didn't see him again. At least not that I know of.

I didn't pull that story out of its little box and tell it to anyone until after I'd fallen in love with Goose. But that was long after we'd met. I knew he'd understand it exactly as I described it to him. That he'd really get the dissociation response and how and why it worked for me. Goose would know I wasn't hiding great emotional trauma from that specific act, and that what had happened had been a political threat. And I wasn't wrong.

A few years after I told my story to Goose, Eve Ensler, actor, activist, author of *The Vagina Monologues,* among many other works, and creator of V-Day to stop violence against women, asked if I wanted to contribute a monologue for a V-Day event in New York. She suggested that maybe a piece about the violence of landmines against women, or against a particular woman, would fit the theme. I asked her instead how she'd feel about a story about my dinner with the death squad man. It took a few minutes to explain, to make it clear that it was me I was talking about. My only request was that I read it myself—I didn't want anyone else to try to be me in my monologue.

I did read the monologue before an audience of two thousand people in New York City in June of 2006. I felt it was time to use the example to tell women they didn't have to let horrible experiences ruin their lives. I didn't let it ruin mine.

·   ·   ·

Roberto D'Aubuisson ran more than just death squads. In September 1981, he'd also formed a political party, the Nationalist Republican Alliance, known as ARENA after its name in Spanish, to oppose the so-called reformist junta in power at the time. In 1984 he ran for president and lost. Jose Napoleon Duarte won, in no small part because of the infusion of U.S. money and support for his campaign.

But in March 1989, the ARENA candidate Alfredo Cristiani, who served as the public face of the party and was more palatable than D'Aubuisson, did win. The elections were marked by violence. At different times and in different places during the elections, three journalists, including a Dutch television reporter, were killed—all by the military.

The deaths of the journalists were just the tip of the iceberg. With the ARENA victory, violence in the country accelerated. Everyone I knew had predicted it. The U.S. government, however, touted the results as the first successful transition of power from one "democratically elected" president to another in El Salvador. All the while, the death squad assassinations continued, as did the military's counterinsurgency operations in the countryside. The FMLN also continued fighting, and it sporadically attacked government officials and infrastructure in the capital. It was untenable.

On November 11, 1989, all hell broke loose in San Salvador. Catching the Salvadoran military and the U.S. Embassy completely off guard, the FMLN launched a military offensive that captured major cities in the country and, for the first time, hit the capital hard. Their fighters occupied areas of the capital city, even taking over some homes in the elite neighborhoods.

The military's response was immediate and predictably brutal. They began bombarding the FMLN-occupied parts of the city and raiding the offices of national and international nongovernmental organizations. During their frenzy, a decision was made at a meeting at the high command to kill Father Ignacio Ellacuria, the Jesuit priest who ran the University of Central America in San Salvador.

The military and far right saw Ellacuria as aligned with the FMLN, and the university as a hotbed of subversion. Many had wanted Ellacuria dead for a long time. The members of the Atlacatl Battalion, an elite counterinsurgency unit of the Salvadoran army, had been assigned the task and were told to leave no witnesses when they murdered the priest. The battalion had been created at the School of the Americas, located at Fort Benning, Georgia, which was a training ground for military from throughout Latin America.

On November 14, soldiers searched the university rectory where the priests lived. It was really a reconnaissance mission. Then in the early morning hours of November 16, they entered the rectory again. The six priests they found asleep in their beds were dragged outside, along with their cook and her daughter. There they all were murdered in cold blood. The Jesuits weren't the only ones on the military's hit list, but many of the others had gone into hiding when the offensive began. The shock at the brutality reverberated around the world. And the offensive continued.

During the fighting, Medical Aid flew two planeloads of medical supplies into the country. I was on the plane full of supplies accompanied by the Archbishop of Los Angeles, Roger Mahoney, whose brief visit was a show of solidarity with the beleaguered churches in the country. After the archbishop left, I stayed behind to help facilitate entry of the medical supplies into the country. If and when they cleared customs, they would be administered through the Church.

After a meeting about the supplies, Eileen Rosin, our in-country program officer, and I came out of the church offices and got into Medical Aid's small truck to head back to the Medical Aid office. As we were driving, I told her about an unsettling incident a few nights before. I'd been on the phone with a Salvadoran journalist friend talking about the Medical Aid shipments.

I'd told him we were insisting on their being received by the church and not the government. When I saw my friend the next day, he told me that he'd barely hung up the receiver when the phone rang again. When he'd answered, a man had said, "Why do they want to give it to the church and not to the government?" Click. The man had hung up. Intimidation. Veiled threats.

When we pulled up in front of our office, a young girl from next door ran up to us. She said that while we were gone she'd seen three members of the National Police unlock our door and go into the office. They hadn't stayed long, and when they came out it didn't look as if they were carrying anything with them.

We went into the office and didn't see anything out of place. But we knew the police had been there for a reason, even if we didn't know what the reason was. It felt threatening. We had boxes of materials in the office that, especially during the offensive, could be problematic. As hard as it was to imagine, these informational materials included booklets explaining a national dialogue in Salvador to end the war and bring about peace.

We had to do something with all of it. If police came once, they likely would come again. Many foreigners were being captured and deported. Others were leaving of their own volition. One Salvadoran friend had said to me, "If they'll do this to you internationals, I'm afraid to think about what they will do to us." So many Salvadorans we knew had been arrested; some tortured.

Eileen and I decided to burn the "incriminating" material. We spent hours late that afternoon at a barrel in the office courtyard slowly feeding the fire we'd built. We were tense and anxious, worried that if we burned things too quickly we'd create such a plume of smoke that it would draw firemen—or worse, the police. Also there were only so many hours during which we could burn, because we couldn't be out after the curfew put in place when the offensive began.

We burned as much as we could, but it was impossible to finish it all in time. We decided to take whatever was left with us and dump it in the trash at the Camino Real. Many people had taken refuge at the hotel. If the police decided to go through the trash at the Camino and found the material, they couldn't arrest an entire hotel, could they? It was November 25.

That same day, President Cristiani issued an order to the police to stop ransacking the offices of nongovernmental organizations without the express order of the high command. I left for L.A. a few days later. One week after Cristiani's order, our office was ransacked. Everything but the kitchen sink was taken— including a crate of empty soda bottles (which could be turned in for a few cents each). They took a biofeedback machine and several dozen TENS units, small portable devices used to treat pain. They pulled wooden panels off the walls, smashed through the ceiling, and broke through the concrete patio to dig around underneath it. Since they believed every international organization in the country worked with the FMLN, they were probably looking for weapons. Two days later Eileen left for Los Angeles. The offensive continued.

·   ·   ·

My parents and family were very, very unhappy that I continued to go to El Salvador during the intense fighting. It was rough on them. I was rough on them. I'm not sure how many times I tried to reassure them. Probably not as many times as I lashed out at them as a result of my stress. Recently, I found a letter I wrote to them about it. It reads:

12-6-89 Continental flight
to LA 3:40 PST

Dear Mom & Dad,

I write to apologize for being sharp last night. I appreciate your concern for me, but I would ask you to please direct it toward the people I care deeply about in El Salvador, who are suffering and who do not have the luxury to leave as I do.

My work is not "work." It is born of a commitment to stand with the poor. I know that sounds strange coming from an "elitist" ex-Catholic like myself. But I guess I have to blame you two for your beautiful faith that is not oppressive but is an example of how it should be. And Stephen John. And Michael in 4th grade.

I know what I do and why I do it and am happy with the choices I have made in my life. I do not take irresponsible actions—I'm no John Wayne.

But I ask you to trust me and support me. It is hard when I have to reassure you and explain myself. I need your support so I can give mine to those who really need it in El Salvador.

Yesterday I was getting aggravated with a woman that I have been working with in Iowa. Perhaps I was being a bit overzealous—hard to imagine, I know—when she said, "Jody, I understand what you are talking about. My brother is in Zacamil. I have asked him to come home. I worry about him. He told me he would stand with the people as witness until he was deported. He asked me to pray for those who cannot leave."

Gwen is a nun. Her brother is a priest. Needless to say, it brought me back down to earth *very* quickly. (By the way, Zacamil is one of the hardest hit areas of the capital—aerial bombardments, army raids, etc.)

All of this to say, I love you. I understand your concern. But I am no fool. Trust me. Pray for others who have no hope. No escape.

On that cheery note, I end. See you at Christmas.

P.S.: It is a beautiful sunset on the plane. The world is so beautiful. Why do we humans make it so ugly?

•   •   •

It was two in the afternoon on April 5, 1990. I'd called the office of Colonel Innocente Orlando Montano, the vice minister of public security, earlier that day to try to arrange a meeting to talk about the still unresolved issue of the ransacking of our office during the offensive. I said the U.S. Embassy had advised me that he was the man to talk to. And there we were. That same day. Almost as soon as Eileen and I arrived, we were ushered in to see Montano.

We were shocked that he wasn't alone as we'd expected. Montano introduced us to the heads of the National Guard, the National Police, Hacienda (Treasury), and Bomberos (the firemen). All were dressed in camouflage uniforms. We sat directly in front of them. There was no "general discussion." It was a dialogue between me and Montano. Eileen carefully took notes.

I briefly summarized the humanitarian work of Medical Aid to help the people of El Salvador since 1982. I noted that one of our relief shipments sent during the offensive, which also included a mobile hospital for the Salvadoran Green Cross, was still being held in customs and thus wasn't benefiting the people. I hoped he could help get it released. Finally, I asked why our office had been ransacked a week after President Cristiani's order of November 25, who had been responsible, and where all the things taken from the office were.

Montano acknowledged Cristiani's order and said that after that date only the high command could authorize the ransacking of the offices of churches, unions, human rights groups, and other such organizations. It was hard to keep a straight face when he said that sometimes, however, "mistakes" were made. He said it was impossible to know who might have ransacked the offices, because only communist regimes would have such control over a situation. Not democracies like El Salvador.

I didn't laugh, but I did interrupt Montano to point out that on the very day of the order, three uniformed members of the National Police *had* entered our office. All they had done that day was search the office. But someone had come back a week later and trashed it and stolen the contents. We believed that it was either elements of the National Police or, if not them, the First Brigade of the Army.

Montano asked if we had a list of the contents. I handed it to him, and he had his secretary make copies for all the men in the room. He then ordered the head of the National Police to "investigate" the situation with the First Brigade to see if they knew anything about it and to get back to him. The meeting was over.

I thanked them all, told them we'd be providing them with the address of our new office shortly, and that we'd like to be able to avoid such problems in the future. Any one of them should feel free to call us if they felt there were any problems with our work. After all, everything we did was public.

Eileen and I stood to leave, and I told them we'd be sure to tell the U.S. embassy how helpful they'd been. As we walked out of the office neither one of us doubted for a second that each one of those men would have gladly put a bullet in our backs if they'd thought they could get away with it. But they'd already made a few "mistakes" too many. Montano, it turns out, had been one of those at the meeting where it was decided to order the murder of the Jesuits.

We never did see any of the contents of our former office again (although months later we heard that the TENS units were being sold out of the military hospital). But we did get something much more valuable. A couple of months after our meeting with Montano and his cronies, a letter arrived at Medical Aid in Los Angeles. It was signed by the minister of defense and acknowledged all the humanitarian work our organization had done for the people of El Salvador. It also said that our work had the full support of the military.

Mario called it the "golden letter." It gave us relatively easy access to places we might otherwise not have been able to go. At a military roadblock, for example, all we'd have to do was flash that letter and the guns would go down, and we'd sail on through. We used it—unsuccessfully—to pressure the customs office to release the medicines and mobile hospital they were holding up. It was an interview about the hospital in the *L.A. Times* that finally ratcheted up the pressure enough to persuade them let the hospital and supplies out of customs. We learned that it wasn't the Salvadoran military who had held up our shipment, but the U.S. Embassy.

CHAPTER EIGHT

I Thought I Wanted a Straight Job—Instead I Got Landmines

It was 1991. I didn't want to think about war in Central America, scorched earth campaigns against peasant villages, tortured and murdered civilians, or the military and death squads who murdered them. My work had left me drained, even as the political situation in Central America grew more complex.

In February of the previous year, and to the shock of many, the Sandinistas had lost the general elections in Nicaragua, and Violeta Chamorro, head of the opposition newspaper *La Prensa Libre,* became president of the country. It wasn't close. The Sandinista president, Daniel Ortega, received 40 percent of the vote to Chamorro's 54 percent. Then, that April, in the aftermath of the fierce fighting in Salvador that began with the November 1989 offensive, the government and the FMLN resumed peace negotiations.

I began to fantasize about losing myself in a regular nine-to-five job. I even bought a black pantsuit at Casual Corner and made a doomed attempt to find work through a professional job counselor. My colorful résumé left her speechless, except to say that it would be a challenge to "mainstream" me. I was saved from that questionable enterprise by an unexpected call in November 1991.

Thomas Gebauer headed up Medico International, a German humanitarian relief organization that supported some of Medical Aid's projects. I knew him from the times our paths crossed in Salvador, but outside of that we had never communicated directly. I was surprised to hear him on the phone. He said he was calling because he needed a ride from the airport and a place to stay for a night. On his way to Frankfurt from Salvador, he had a couple of meetings in Washington and wondered if I could help him out.

It struck me as odd, but I picked Thomas up and brought him to my always-under-construction apartment in my always-needing-construction house that I'd bought a few years earlier. It was located in a dicey neighborhood, one with crack dealers working the corner one street over. Rumor had it that the area would soon be experiencing revitalization. (*Soon* didn't happen for more than fifteen years, and by then I was long gone from the neighborhood.)

When I bought the house, it was the only thing I could afford. My theory was that I'd live in one of the apartments, and the rent from the other three would help pay the mortgage. Instead I became a one-woman social service agency for my needy tenants. I inherited Mrs. Parker, for example, who'd lived in the basement apartment since the 1940s. The house was much more hers than it ever was mine. Her apartment wasn't a palace, but she'd been paying $222 a month rent for decades. And that included utilities. She was still living there when I sold the house, still paying $222 a month.

To make matters more unpleasant, I was struggling with a

lot of the renovating myself. Charles, a guy I'd started going out with in Vermont, would help when he came to visit. I stripped layers of paint off of fantastically carved, beautiful old wood-work; I plastered walls (self-taught and far from perfect); I painted; I put tile in bathrooms (taught by Charles). First I lived in the third-floor apartment. Once it was refinished, I rented it and moved to the first-floor apartment to start all over again there. The whole thing was a nightmare. I began to think of it as the house from hell. It was no soothing sanctuary between my trips to Salvador.

Which is all to say that Gebauer's accommodations at my place were rudimentary. All I could offer was the futon sofa in the living room amid plaster dust, the chemical smell of wood stripper, and the occasional stray hairs of my two cats, Maxim and Uzi.

The next morning Thomas asked if I'd drive him to a meeting he had scheduled with Bobby Muller, the executive director of the Vietnam Veterans of America Foundation. Any marginally good excuse to avoid working on the house was good enough for me. I'd met Muller once a few years earlier when Dave Evans, a Vietnam vet and the director of Medical Aid for El Salvador's Prosthetics Project, asked me to talk to people at VVAF about the war in El Salvador. Despite Bobby's reputation for charis-matic leadership, I remembered little about him except his head of white hair and his wheelchair. He'd been a marine lieutenant in Vietnam and had been shot in the upper spine about a month before his tour of duty ended. He never walked again.

Gebauer promised it would be a short meeting, so I brought a book for the wait. Instead of letting me read in peace, how-ever, they insisted that I join them. I was beginning to feel put upon, but didn't want to make a big deal about it. Maybe I'd learn something about their work together in Cambodia, a part of the world I'd not yet been to.

While they discussed prosthetics and amputees in Cambodia, they kept trying to draw me into the conversation. Bobby and Thomas were animated and enthusiastic while talking about their project training landmine survivors, all former soldiers from the various armed factions in Cambodia, to make prosthetic limbs for other amputees. They also said that, over the six-month life of the young project, they'd come to the conclusion that making prosthetics alone, without going to the root of the problem, was like trying to stop a hemorrhage without even a Band-Aid on hand. Landmines were contaminating areas throughout about half of Cambodia, taking lives and limbs every day.

It was interesting enough, but I couldn't see where their conversation was going or why they were bothering me with it. I was familiar with prosthetics work through Dave's work at Medical Aid. But it wasn't what I worked on directly, nor was it something I envisioned working on in my future. So why did I have to sit here and listen to them?

They were getting so fired up that Muller was practically bouncing in his wheelchair, and he concluded by saying that the only solution to the problem was to ban landmines. With a bit of a dramatic pause, he then said that he and Gebauer thought I was just the right person to tackle building a political movement to ban landmines. They just *knew* I'd be able to bring together nongovernmental organizations, NGOs, to put sustained pressure on governments to make them get rid of the weapon forever. So what if virtually every fighting force in the world had been using landmines for most of the century.

I rolled my eyes, looked at them like they were completely

mad, and laughed out loud. Why me? I knew nothing about landmines, and I'd never given any thought at all to a global campaign about anything. Yes, I'd been the main force behind the success of the Children's Project, which did involve work with the hospitals and NGOs across the United States that had become part of the effort. I'd had to travel to many of the sites before the children arrived, and had visited some once the kids had reached them. But that couldn't be compared to trying to bring organizations and individuals around the world together in a coherent, coordinated effort to ban a widely used weapon. Just thinking about the linguistic and cultural challenges alone was daunting.

What's more, I couldn't see what was so special about land-mines in particular, why they merited a campaign to ban them. What about all the guns flooding the world? Why not deal with them? Or serious weapons like nukes?

In the 1980s, millions of people had marched against nuclear weapons; I'd participated in a million-person march in New York City in the summer of 1982. Where were all those protest-ers now? With the collapse of the Soviet Union, it seemed more appropriate to get people fired up again to tackle nuclear weap-ons rather than landmines. Wasn't anything possible now in our post-Cold-War world? (I didn't believe that for a minute, but a lot of people wanted to.)

Muller was ready with his answer, and his argument was con-vincing. In fact, it didn't take long for me to understand the dis-tinction between landmines and other conventional weapons. From there it was a tiny leap to recognizing the need to ban them.

Bobby talked about his own transformation in thinking about landmines. When he was a soldier, he'd considered them just another weapon available to fight the war. But he pointed out that most guys were more unnerved by them than by other weapons. No young, fit soldier wants to be mutilated in an anti-personnel landmine blast.

When someone stepped on a mine and set it off, often everyone around him would freeze for fear of stepping on landmines themselves. Also, it's harder to get mine victims off the battlefield, and they generally need more blood, more surgery, and more resources than those with other types of combat injuries, which can overwhelm military medical teams.

Bobby said it wasn't until he took a delegation of vets back to the region years after the Vietnam War that he began to understand the horrific reality of antipersonnel landmines. The war was over, but landmines hadn't gone home with the soldiers like guns and other weapons. Once in the ground, they waited in deadly silence until the unsuspecting stepped on them or picked them up. Then the mine exploded, shattering not only the individual but also the victim's family and community. And with the end of a war, the victims were all civilians. Children playing or going to school. Kids gathering firewood. Mothers and grandmothers getting water in the river or washing the family's clothes there. Farmers working in their rice paddies.

When Bobby and the other vets got to dirt-scrabble-poor Cambodia, they saw amputees on too many corners in Phnom Penh, the capital. The country was a shambles from decades of war and had almost no medical infrastructure for responding to all the landmine victims—or to all the other health issues plaguing the country. The social and economic strains on mine survivors and their families often plunged them more deeply into poverty. With huge swaths of the country full of mines, the resulting challenges were overwhelming, and the impact on postwar redevelopment devastating. All this from the lowly little antipersonnel landmine—an inherently indiscriminate weapon that can't tell the difference between a soldier and a grandmother.

Listening to Bobby, my mind began racing excitedly. Understanding the immediate and long-term impact of landmines was pretty easy. Almost immediately, I thought about the possibility that maybe, once people understood the postwar problems caused by landmines, they would see the weapon as a metaphor for the less tangible consequences of war long after the guns fall silent.

I also recognized how the work would affect me personally. If I *were* to work on landmines, I'd learn more about international law, specifically the laws of war, an issue I'd been dealing with only peripherally in my Central America work. I liked the promise of being intellectually challenged again and the thought of tackling an issue with global impact. Achieving a ban on landmines would likely be a decades-long exercise, if it were successful at all. But if an effort to deal with the weapon had any positive impact on the lives of people living in the middle of minefields, it surely would be worth it.

It was pretty clear that Gebauer, and maybe Evans, had talked with Muller about me and my work. Thomas knew that, once I committed myself to something, I'd work as hard as I could to reach a goal. For me, "no" isn't necessarily the end of possibilities; it's an obstacle to be overcome.

He also had to know that, while I relish the power of words, what really matters are the actions people take to fulfill the promise of those words. Calls for change without actions to back them up are largely irrelevant to me. I want to see what you do. Gebauer knew, too, that I really needed to do something new and different. No doubt he and Bobby saw a strong possibility that I'd at least consider the proposition.

After sparring over it for a while, mostly with Bobby, I found myself telling him I'd do it. I said I'd work for three months as a consultant to VVAF to explore the possibility of starting a campaign to ban landmines, and then would let him know if I thought it would be feasible to pursue it. Although skeptical, I was intrigued by the possibilities and wanted to at least check it out. Bobby wanted a bigger, longer-term commitment. I wouldn't give it. No more tilting at windmills.

Muller, now really pumped, pushed for specifics. I looked at him blankly, wondering what the hell he was thinking. Until the last forty-five minutes, I'd never thought about this in my life. But Bobby wouldn't let go of it. I said I'd start by meeting with individuals and groups already working on landmines in some way. A serious campaign would ultimately have to engage NGOs from countries that produced and exported landmines, as well as organizations from mine-contaminated countries. Their voices would be important parts of a campaign that would have to exert enough pressure on governments at the national, regional, and international levels to make them act. It would also be important to see if there were any existing laws dealing with landmines, and if so, how they might be relevant in a ban campaign. Those were my immediate thoughts on the subject; more would take some reflection.

·   ·   ·

It was the pre-Google era. No web surfing to make my quest easier. I needed to get my hands on materials as quickly as possible to begin to educate myself about the weapons. Who produced them? Who used them? Where, how, and why? Why weren't minefields being cleared? Most huge World War II minefields in western Europe had been tackled at the end of the war and cleaned up relatively quickly. (Those in northern Africa had not.) Why wasn't that happening in other parts of the world now?

I also started making lists of NGOs and individuals to meet with to see if there might be any interest in a campaign to ban landmines. Among the first I met with were Susannah Sirkin and Jonathan Fine at Physicians for Human Rights (PHR) in Boston and Eric Stover, who then was doing work for Human Rights Watch (HRW), which is based in New York. PHR and Asia Watch, a part of HRW, recently had jointly produced *The Coward's War: Landmines in Cambodia,* a seminal work on the impact of landmines. One of the report's recommendations was to consider a ban on landmines, but so far nothing had been done about it.

Rae McGrath had also been involved in the research for *The Coward's War* and was currently engaged in producing another Human Rights Watch report on landmines in Iraqi Kurdistan. I wouldn't meet him for many months, and would spar with him often once I did. Rae, a former member of the British military, had been involved in the first efforts, under the auspices of the U.N., to begin mine clearance in Afghanistan. He stuck it out for a while but then left to form his own mine clearance organization, the Mines Advisory Group. Rae's group dealt frequently with Handicap International, a French NGO providing prostheses to amputees, but I didn't meet people from the latter until later.

I also scheduled a meeting with Tim Rieser, a key aide for Senator Patrick Leahy of Vermont. Leahy had traveled to Central America with his wife, Marcelle, a nurse, where they'd met child survivors of landmines. Moved by their plight, he'd returned to Washington and persuaded Congress to appropriate funds in 1989 to create the Leahy War Victims Fund. It wasn't inconceivable that the senator and Tim would be willing to support a ban campaign.

Once I started thinking about landmines, the subject, like so many other things in life, suddenly appeared to be everywhere. I began to see news articles about the weapons and startling pictures of landmine survivors, along with the stories of the horrors they'd lived through and continued to live with in the aftermath of landmine encounters. Everyone I met with suggested others I should meet, and the circle kept widening. The landmine issue was beginning to bubble just beneath the surface of general awareness; it simply needed a determined catalyst to galvanize the public.

It turned out that there *was* existing international law dealing with landmines. In shorthand it's called the Convention on Conventional Weapons, the CCW. To this day I can't remember its proper name. Its more apt, if less used, moniker is the Inhumane Weapons Convention. It was the child of global outrage over weapons used during the war in Vietnam: napalm, incendiary weapons, landmines, and booby traps. The CCW also looked at weapons that left fragments in the body that couldn't be detected with x-rays. If you couldn't find them, how could you safely remove them?

The treaty's purported goal was to ban or restrict the use of specific weapons that cause unnecessary or unjustifiable suffering to combatants or are indiscriminate. The part of it dealing with landmines, Protocol II, was supposed to restrict how those weapons are used. In polite terms, the treaty was an abject failure. At that point only a few dozen countries had even signed it; fewer had gone on to ratify it. The biggest problem of all was that no one actually obeyed it.

While essentially worthless in terms of its impact on the ground, it did provide a hook for campaigning. After ten years, the CCW could be amended through a treaty review conference. Importantly, it would take only one government to request the review at the U.N., and the treaty's ten-year anniversary was coming up in 1993, which was two years away. Going after the Convention on Conventional Weapons could be a key part of international work on a campaign to ban landmines.

Landmines and their use proliferated dramatically after World War II, especially antipersonnel landmines. Antitank mines were designed to explode when a tank or other heavy vehicle came in contact with them. Antipersonnel landmines explode when a person steps on, handles, or otherwise comes in contact with them. Mass-produced much like any other commodity, they could be had for as little as fifty cents in arms bazaars in conflict zones around the world.

Antipersonnel landmines were contaminating more than eighty countries in the world. In some places, the numbers of mines in the ground were small. But in others, like Cambodia, Afghanistan, Angola, Mozambique, Iraqi Kurdistan, and Somalia, they were horrific in their numbers and their impact. At that point, at least fifty-four countries produced and sold landmines. Sometimes they just gave them away, toxic rewards for buying other, more significant and expensive weapons. Going after landmine producers could be another avenue of work in banning landmines.

By the end of my self-induced three-month contract, I didn't want to stop. Essentially everyone I'd talked with over those weeks thought the idea of a ban campaign was great—as long as someone else started it. So I began working half-time for VVAF on what was promising to evolve into a campaign to ban landmines.

• • •

Increasingly I was talking about the "International Campaign to Ban Landmines." The name sounded convincing even if at that point we were still really just VVAF and Medico, barely united under that banner. Medico didn't have a hierarchical structure; decisions were made by consensus. That often resulted in inordinate amounts of time passing without reaching agreement with them or even getting Medico's input on issues, because they couldn't agree on things internally themselves.

Consensus can have its place, but it's often romanticized as a panacea for alleviating potential conflict instead of recognized as the powerful means of blocking action that it can be. I'm comfortable with a clear chain of responsibility. However, for the purpose of creating momentum, our landmine effort, with one American organization and a German one, was "international." With an international staff of one. Me.

I focused on making that international campaign a real force. Given the seeming fragility of the effort and lack of clarity about how things would ultimately play out, I thought it would be useful to pull together a campaign advisory committee that could add some heft to the undertaking. I managed to convince people known for their concern about landmines, and who also had a broader audience, to sit on this committee. They included, among others, Senator Patrick Leahy; Congressman Lane Evans; Bishop Walter Sullivan, of the Diocese of Richmond, Virginia, and president of Pax Christi USA; U.S. ambassador Charles Floweree, who had worked on the Convention on Conventional Weapons; and Aryeh Neier of Human Rights Watch. The advisory committee itself never really took off, but it was very useful in lending credibility in that first year.

By June 1992, I was no longer at Medical Aid for El Salvador.

I'd been working with Mario for a long time, which made my departure neither fun nor easy. It was the right thing for me and for Medical Aid by then, but I felt sad and at loose ends in many ways, especially with the raggedy closure of such an important part of my life, even if it meant I could now fully embrace the landmine campaign.

Bobby offered the support of Tom, a young guy at VVAF. I was wary. When I'd started the Children's Project, I'd inherited two young and inexperienced kids to help with the work. It was awful and more so when I had to fire them. Especially since I'd not hired them in the first place. Most important, though, I lacked the skills to successfully manage other people's work day in and day out in an office setting.

It sounds odd, because in some respects that's what I did as landmine campaign coordinator, but the nature of that work was very different. It required staying on top of an increasing number of independent organizations around the world that were members of the campaign. My job was to make sure they followed through on commitments to the campaign overall and to pressure them when they seemed to be faltering. But I couldn't fire them or put them on probation to focus their attention. Maybe it could be likened to a global chess match. I had the ability to mobilize peer pressure and had no reluctance to use it. But it wasn't like working in an office.

Predictably, and probably because of my office ineptitude, things didn't go very smoothly with Tom. Thankfully, he got married later that summer and, after his honeymoon, decided to move on to other work. With that peaceful resolution, I thanked Bobby for the support but asked to be spared more. If I felt like I needed it, I'd come to him.

Everyone at VVAF was already stretched thin while working

on the foundation's many projects. Bobby was focused on complicated issues concerning the Cambodia office and staff. The country had barely emerged from decades of war, and sorting everything out in the chaos of Phnom Penh would consume his time and energy for more years than anyone expected. It wasn't until the end of 1995 that he was able to fully throw himself into the work—and he focused almost exclusively on the U.S. Campaign to Ban Landmines. But then, Gebauer didn't get involved much beyond the German campaign, either. Bobby made it only to the big, annual international conferences of the ICBL in Geneva in 1994 and Cambodia in 1995, although we did see Thomas a bit more.

Sometimes it still strikes me as odd, but as the ICBL grew quickly, exponentially, and globally, few in the international campaign knew Bobby. But I kept him and VVAF inundated with information about campaign activities and progress in moving it forward. Everybody was happy in those years.

· · ·

Bremen, Germany, via Frankfurt, in May 1992, was my first international trip after starting my work on landmines. I'd be attending a meeting of the European Network Against the Arms Trade, a natural constituency. After Medico International's prodding, and on short notice, they were giving me time to make a pitch about the landmine campaign and invite the many organizations in the network to join.

Gebauer picked me up in Frankfurt, where I met with him and Angelika Beer. Medico had hired her to build up a national German Campaign to Ban Landmines. After we discussed landmine work in Germany and internationally, they dropped me off at the office of a small German organization that worked on the arms trade. They'd be giving me a ride to Bremen.

Going up the stairs to the organization's office was a walk back in time. The open door revealed a couple of disheveled guys, one lounging on a torn and broken-down couch and the other in a chair even more dilapidated. By comparison, the old CIS-PES office looked almost palatial. I didn't openly roll my eyes or shake my head, but I was glad they couldn't read my mind.

I already was feeling anxious at the prospect of spending a couple of days in Bremen with people working on conventional weapons. They were coming from all over Europe, and I didn't know any of them or anything meaningful about the arms trade. So the office and the guys in it didn't inspire confidence in me. After being there, I imagined we'd be meeting in a place something like it, only bigger. I had visions of sleeping in some kind of dormitory with a communal bathroom. What was I getting myself into?

The five-hour car ride to Bremen offered too much time to think about it. But we arrived at the meeting site, and to my blessed relief the Lutheran conference center was lovely, and the sleeping accommodations clean and pleasant. I had my own room and bathroom, and the furniture throughout the place was intact.

I spoke to the meeting the next day. The arms trade people listened closely when I described the nature of landmines and their generations-long aftermath, the scale of the problem, and the basic thinking about the International Campaign to Ban Landmines. We came away from Bremen with some new support, including that of the UK's Campaign Against Arms Trade.

Ann Feltham ran that NGO and became a staunch ally. She

housed me at her flat on my many trips to London for the campaign and was a key partner when it came time to organize the first international conference of the ICBL in London, in May 1993. But there was still much to do before we got to that point.

I was in regular communication with Human Rights Watch as well as Physicians for Human Rights, the Mines Advisory Group, and Handicap International. Handicap International, joined by Physicians for Human Rights and the Mines Advisory Group, had just issued a call: "Stop the Killing in the 'Coward's War.'" As they stated at the time, they were calling primarily on "the UN and those governments who supply mines to make the clearance and destruction of mines an urgent humanitarian priority in Cambodia and other countries [and] to respect international law and to control the production, sale, and use of these weapons that kill and maim even in times of peace." The rest of us—HRW, Medico International, and VVAF—wanted a ban.

So in June 1992, I started pushing the six organizations to meet in late September or early October in order to reach a common position on landmines and begin strategizing together on how to get rid of the weapons. Human Rights Watch offered meeting space, and finally a date was fixed for October 6 in New York.

• • •

Even in the earliest days, landmine ban synergies could be simply awesome. Almost like the work of a stealth team, Senator Leahy in the Senate, working with Congressman Evans in the House, managed to speed landmine legislation through Congress, which was signed into law in October 1992. They were supported in the legislative effort mostly by VVAF and the other Washington-based NGOs that made up the Arms Trade Working Group, which met regularly at the Mott House on Capitol

Hill. I'd been going to the working group meetings from time to time to keep them updated on progress in building the landmine campaign, and they wanted to help in any way they could.

The new law mandated a one-year moratorium on the export of U.S. landmines and carried importance way beyond the language of the law. The fact that the sole remaining superpower would voluntarily stop the export of a weapon that most considered legal was startling in its implications. It helped establish the fact that antipersonnel landmines were *not* just another weapon. The ripple effect was tremendous. Probably most important, the moratorium made people believe that banning landmines might actually be possible.

By then, I'd also started meeting with people at the U.N.'s Office of Humanitarian Affairs, in New York, who were working on landmines. And for a while I joined their cross-department meetings on landmines that were meant to coordinate what the different departments were doing or might do related to landmines. I didn't last long there, because nothing seemed to get beyond the talking stage, and those meetings faded into obscurity.

But to get more recruits for the landmine cause, I had started meeting with NGOs in New York that were working on disarmament and the arms trade overall. From there it was a small step to start meeting with government representatives at the various countries' missions to the U.N. Mostly I was granted meetings with lower-level officials, and I used to joke that I'd get to see the second cousin of the mission's janitor. No matter who I met with, they looked at me as if I were nuts. Completely nuts. The only one who began to really listen to what I had to say was the diplomat Max Gevers of the Netherlands, who became one of my first allies.

•   •   •

The offices of Human Rights Watch in New York were a far cry from the one I'd visited in Frankfurt not many months earlier. It was October 6, 1992, and people from four of the six organizations that would become the first steering committee of the ICBL were there. We were seated around a table in a comfortable conference room with a fantastic view of Central Park.

The purpose of the meeting was to cement a partnership among the six organizations and together launch the International Campaign to Ban Landmines. The people who attended included Aryeh Neier, Ken Anderson, Andrew Whitley, and Sydney Jones from Human Rights Watch. Angelika Beer and Ronald Ofteringer had come on behalf of Medico International, and Bobby Muller and I were there on behalf of VVAF. Tim Carstairs and Dr. Philippe Chabasse, one of the founders of Handicap International, represented that organization. The two there in spirit if not in person were Eric Stover of Physicians for Human Rights and Rae McGrath of the Mines Advisory Group.

Human Rights Watch was among the first NGOs in the world to systematically document the impact of landmines on civilians. Their first report, published in 1985, dealt with landmines in Nicaragua and El Salvador. Their ongoing research and reporting provided important data which established that landmines violate two important provisions of international law: proportionality and distinction.

The effect of landmines is disproportionate, which means the long-term impact of the weapon on civilians outweighs the benefit to the military of using it. Any weapon that continues to affect civilian populations for generations after conflict can't be considered anything but a total assault on that principle. The violation of distinction is obvious because, by landmines' very

nature, they are indiscriminate. No landmine can tell the difference between a soldier and civilian. They kill and maim people
with the misfortune of coming in contact with them and with
ruthless impunity. For many of us, these facts made landmines
already illegal under existing law, even if most of the world
hadn't recognized it yet.

Physicians for Human Rights also looked at the landmine
issue from the perspective of the humanitarian impact. As I
mentioned earlier, PHR had collaborated with Human Rights
Watch on the most important early report on landmines: *The
Coward's War: Landmines in Cambodia,* released in September 1991.
The report's recommendations about banning landmines were
among the first to be made.

In 1993, the two organizations would also cooperate to produce *Landmines: A Deadly Legacy,* a seminal work on the global
scope of the problem and one that would serve as a baseline
of information on landmines and their impact for many years.
Amazingly, the Arms Division of Human Rights Watch and
PHR would manage to put together a draft of the report in less
than four months, in time for the ICBL's London conference in
May 1993. The final report would be released that November.

Handicap International provided prostheses to landmine survivors in dozens of countries, and the Mines Advisory Group
was a major demining NGO. Not only did the organization take
mines out of the ground, but it also trained teams of local demin-
ers in the countries where the organization worked. Ultimately,
it would fall to such teams to carry out the long-term removal of
landmines from the soil of their own countries.

Each of the six organizations would be important to the partnership; and at our meeting in New York on October 6, 1992,
our mix demonstrated our approach of bringing a wide range

of organizations into the campaign. Each NGO brought differ-ent expertise to the table, and this helped forge a strong core of credibility for the landmine campaign. Combined, we were working on virtually all aspects of the problem—legal, humani-tarian, and military, as well as with landmine survivors and on mine clearance.

I kept my anxiety under wraps at the meeting. By that October I'd already put nearly a year of work into laying the groundwork for the campaign. I was fully engaged and excited about what we might accomplish together. If we walked out of the offices of Human Rights Watch without concrete commitments, I couldn't quite imagine what would happen next. I didn't even want to try.

To provide background for our meeting, we'd invited two legal representatives from the International Committee of the Red Cross (ICRC) to speak with us about the organization's view of the weapon and the current status of the Convention on Conventional Weapons. The ICRC had played a pivotal role in preparatory meetings for the negotiation of the CCW in the late 1970s, and its medical people in the field dealt with landmine victims with appalling regularity.

In fact, ICRC field staff and doctors had long pushed the orga-nization's Geneva headquarters hard to advocate a ban. Although the ICRC later changed its position and became a fervent ally in the ban movement, at that point it still considered antipersonnel landmines to be legal weapons and was not calling for a ban, as its representatives explained to us in New York.

The ICRC lawyers left, and we began our discussions about working together on the International Campaign to Ban Land-mines. Despite my worries, there were no serious obstacles. The conversation flowed for the rest of the day as we discussed how we'd work together to advance the campaign. By the end, we'd agreed to serve as an ad hoc steering committee to host the first international NGO conference on landmines in London in May 1993. It was also agreed that I'd continue coordinating the work of the campaign, as well as take the lead in putting the conference together and in drafting a campaign call.

By the time the call was drafted about a month later, Handicap International, which had been thinking about it, finally embraced a total ban on landmines. That New York meeting marked what we came to call the "official launch" of the International Campaign to Ban Landmines.

Obviously, an international campaign to ban landmines is about getting rid of the weapon. But we had to be perfectly clear about what were we calling for. The campaign's call had to be brief and simple. It was also an organizing tool. If it were too long and complicated, the audience would be lost before we could win them over. Once people's attention is captured, there's plenty of time to provide all the information anyone might want. But overwhelming possible newcomers before they even know what you're talking about is not a good starting point.

Our one-page Landmine Campaign Call started with a brief description of the problem. Then we specified three things necessary to solve the problem: The first was a complete ban on the use, production, trade, and stockpiling of antipersonnel landmines. The second was increased resources for mine clearance. And the third was increased resources for landmine victim assistance. It was short. It was clear. It left little room for confusion about the goals of the ICBL.

．　　．　　．

Already by the time of the ICBL's London conference in May 1993, the landmine issue and the International Campaign to Ban

Landmines were gaining traction. Once we'd agreed on the campaign call, I'd mailed it out to numerous NGOs, inviting them either to join the campaign or, if they couldn't join, to endorse it. Dozens had answered the call. In fact, the first individual to endorse the campaign was former president Jimmy Carter.

By the end of 1992, Angelika Beer and Medico International had held a series of meetings with German NGOs to coordinate the German Campaign to Ban Landmines, and NGOs in Sweden had begun public hearings on the weapon. I'd learned that, back in February, Australian NGOs had gathered signatures on petitions calling for aid for landmine victims and for the government to support banning landmines, which they'd presented to Parliament. Finally, that December, the European Parliament had passed a resolution demanding that all member states declare, "as an emergency measure," a five-year moratorium on the export of landmines and on training in their use.

France had followed the 1992 U.S. landmine export moratorium with its own three-year moratorium in February 1993. The French Landmine Campaign had also convinced its government to request a review conference on the Convention on Conventional Weapons. In February, the French Foreign Ministry sent the official request to the secretary general of the U.N., which would be approved by the U.N. General Assembly in December 1993, when it also passed a resolution calling on all countries to enact moratoriums on the export of landmines.

As we were busy preparing for the May 1993 ICBL conference in London, the ICRC announced it would hold a three-day symposium on landmines in Montreux, outside Geneva, that April. It would still take almost another year for the ICRC's president, Cornelio Sommaruga, to declare that from a "humanitarian point of view," the only "truly effective solution" was a global ban on landmines. But even before that, the work that the ICRC started to do again on landmines was important.

Many campaigners participated in and spoke at that April ICRC meeting, including me. I took advantage of being in Switzerland and also set up a meeting with the executive director of UNICEF Geneva. He was very interested in the landmine issue, recognizing early the significant impact that the weapons had on the children and families that the agency dealt with. I wanted to talk with him about the International Campaign to Ban Landmines and convince him to make UNICEF Geneva a partner in our effort.

I was down at the Montreux station waiting to catch a train to Geneva for my meeting with the UNICEF director—which did prove successful—when I ran into a jet-lagged Steve Goose, who was just arriving for the ICRC symposium. He'd started working at the Arms Division of Human Rights Watch a couple of months earlier and would be presenting at the meeting some of the data from the still-being-put-together report *Landmines: A Deadly Legacy*. I'd met him only once before, briefly and in passing, and had no idea what close partners we'd become in the ICBL.

ICBL was on a roll as we opened the conference in London one month later. Although not huge in size, the London conference was huge in its significance. About fifty people representing forty organizations that we'd invited to the conference participated; we'd also allowed people from the U.S. State Department and Pentagon to come as observers. London put the ICBL firmly on the political map and helped generate additional momentum that would push the campaign forward. We hammered out a basic campaigning strategy for the next year. It was broad yet also had concrete actions for campaigners to take, critical to building an ongoing sense of positive action in the effort to get rid of landmines.

The ad hoc steering committee was affirmed in London as the first steering committee of the International Campaign to Ban Landmines, and I was affirmed as the campaign's coordinator. Participants also recognized the need to move immediately to establish campaigns in countries outside the United States and Europe. The West was the home of major landmine producers in the world, and it was easiest for us to start with the political systems that we knew how to influence. But no global effort could succeed without involving NGOs in countries contaminated by landmines.

.   .   .

For me the role of coordinator was clear and reflected pretty much what the word implied. It meant keeping track of what we'd all agreed to in the strategy outlined in London and pushing NGOs to fulfill their commitments. Because parts of the strategy were interlocking, if one organization didn't follow through, it could affect the work of others. Coordinating also meant keeping track of the many NGOs joining the coalition, reaching out to bring new organizations on board, and making sure everyone knew what was going on in the campaign.

Information is power. For the whole campaign to move forward together, we all had to operate with the same information. I'd also been thinking about ways to make sure the diverse NGOs, already working on a variety of issues in their own organizations, would take their involvement in the ICBL seriously. Key to that was ensuring that all felt ownership of the campaign and understood that everyone was important to our common success. Otherwise, interest could quickly wane and we'd lose campaigners. That meant involving as many as possible in campaign discussions as regularly and quickly as possible, especially as the young and increasingly dynamic campaign continued to unfold.

I couldn't rely on regular mail; it could take forever if it arrived at all, especially in countries like Afghanistan or Cambodia. I didn't have time for stuffing and stamping envelopes. I had no assistant to help. So early on I got a fax machine and began to write regular summaries of what was going on in the ICBL, about new organizations joining the campaign, or about questions that needed feedback, all of which I sent off by fax. Most days I was up before dawn faxing key information about our work as it evolved to NGOs in different parts of the world.

I also recognized that, because the fax was new then, it was "techno-sexy," so to speak. If you got a fax, it meant you'd received something important that needed immediate attention. It also meant you had to think about it and write back; I loved the paper trail it created. What I sent rarely went unanswered. In relative terms, that machine helped move things through the campaign smoothly and quickly, even if faxing could be extremely expensive in some cases and tedious on my end.

The technology helped me, it helped NGOs and campaigners, and it facilitated the work of the ICBL itself. But technology wasn't then, and isn't today, the goal in and of itself. It was a tool that helped activists work together better while taking concrete action to change our world with respect to landmines. Email was an even more efficient tool. We made the switch to using it while organizing our landmine conference in Cambodia in July 1995. The Cambodia campaign was the first to push us to use email, because communication was easy, phenomenally fast, and fantastically cheap. They went from spending hundreds of dollars a month on faxes to about twenty dollars a month for email.

Coordinating the ICBL also meant overseeing campaign meetings and activities. After the French campaign succeeded in getting its government to call upon the U.N. to start the process for reviewing the Convention on Conventional Weapons, I oversaw ICBL activity at those meetings as well. Initially, there were to be four meetings of so-called experts in Geneva in 1994 and 1995 to prepare for the three-week-long CCW treaty review conference itself. That conference would take place in Vienna in September–October 1995. There was never time to be bored while working on the Landmine Campaign.

As it happened, our Second International NGO Conference on Landmines coincided with the first CCW expert session in Geneva in May 1994. An important element of our landmine conference was that it was cohosted by UNICEF, the first U.N. agency to fully embrace the ICBL. More than 110 people, representing seventy-five organizations, participated in the Geneva meeting, resulting in more strategizing, more momentum, and new national campaigns. Being in Geneva, where campaigners would end up spending lots of time over the next two and a half years, also gave us our first taste of the expert sessions. It's also where I fell in love.

. . .

Goose. Stephen Douglas Goose. He's the person I worked with most closely and consistently throughout the Landmine Campaign. Goose started at Human Rights Watch, in the D.C. office, in February 1993. He'd been hired to help develop the work of the organization's new Arms Division, which Ken Anderson was heading at the time. Ken was dealing with the ICBL as a representative of Human Rights Watch, and Goose was supposed to focus on the arms trade and other conventional weapons.

With the rapid development of the campaign, however, Goose was quickly drawn into the work, which was fantastic even if I didn't recognize it immediately. I was used to Ken by then and thought he'd remain HRW's point person on landmines. Instead, he left the organization not too long after, and it was Goose who became fully dedicated to ICBL work on behalf of Human Rights Watch.

He knew how to wear a suit. Before him, I'd never worked with anybody who wore a suit every day. He was so totally comfortable in one that I couldn't imagine him in jeans and a T-shirt. Ever, under any circumstances. When we first started working together, I called him Mr. Goose; he seemed like such a real adult. Later he became just "Goose." Everyone else called him Steve. I couldn't. Steve is my brother.

Before Human Rights Watch, Goose had worked on the Hill in D.C. for six years and, before that, with a Washington think tank for seven years. In addition to possessing sartorial splendor, Goose was adept at talking with policy makers. It wasn't my forte or my desire, but I talked with them, too, in my own way. Goose and I became an effective Geneva lobbying team. By personality, not design, he was the good cop and I the bad.

Despite my purchase of the Casual Corner suit, I didn't wear business attire. That suit had stayed in my closet since my simulated job quest. I didn't wander around in jeans, but my style had little resemblance to diplo-normal. I didn't care if the policy makers liked what I wore or not. My purpose wasn't a display of fashion.

Nor was I particularly interested in learning diplo-speak. I was there to talk about what needed to be done to solve the landmine problem. Period. As far as I was concerned, the only way to do that was with straight talk that would challenge the government types to respond in kind. I wanted them to shed their diplomatic armor and talk like human beings, or at least try sometimes.

Often Goose and I worked together when attempting to change someone's point of view. But sometimes he'd go alone, if his particular skills were necessary. Likewise, I'd do the same if we felt that a bit more overt pressure would be useful. I had little problem getting in peoples' faces when getting in their faces was what was needed to help them focus. I wasn't particularly impressed by titles either. Strip everything away and they were just other people, not so different from me.

On the surface, Goose and I appeared to be very different. Given his style, some of the hard-liners in the campaign thought he might waffle on issues of substance. What these campaigners didn't understand for a long time was that Goose was solid on substance and wouldn't back down. While I didn't waffle, I could get frustrated and want to leave the discussion table. Goose taught me that leaving was sometimes exactly the wrong thing to do. It was often the last people at the negotiating table who came away with most of what they wanted. He walked softly; I was the big stick. Fundamentally, however, we pretty much agreed on everything.

CHAPTER NINE

Landmines and Love

Imagine a bunch of men in suits and military uniforms in meeting rooms and coffee bars at the U.N. overlooking the splendid lake in Geneva framed by the Alps. In glorious isolation, they conveniently divorce themselves from the fact that landmines kill or maim a woman, a child, or a man somewhere in the world every twenty minutes. They content themselves with tinkering with words in the Convention on Conventional Weapons and its Protocol II, the landmine protocol, without seriously thinking about or making a dent in the problem itself.

The diplomats and military strove to focus narrowly on military doctrine. Inside the U.N., the sterile hows and whys of landmine use on the battlefield could seem so clear-cut and logical. It didn't matter that doctrine and tactics had almost nothing in common with how landmines were really deployed and no relevance to their long-term impact. The diplomats and military provided clean and easy justification for the weapons, as well as rationalizations in which they alleged that landmines weren't the problem. It was how people used them that could be a problem.

We'd been watching government delegations in Geneva do nothing meaningful on landmines since the first expert meeting in May 1994. But little happens quickly in the U.N. We pushed hard to get delegates to seriously assess the impact of landmines. If they did, the logical result could only be to ban them. However, from beginning to end, most governments were assessing how to appear like they were doing a lot while actually accomplishing very little. From their perspective, it would suffice to simply play around with treaty language. We knew long before the Vienna review conference that nothing of substance was going to happen there.

Sometimes I'd get livid and scoff that the high point of a day's work would be if they managed to negotiate changing a comma to a semicolon in the treaty. The best way to get the diplomats and military to focus, I'd say, would be to put the negotiating table in the middle of a vast minefield in Cambodia or Angola or Afghanistan. That would surely sharpen their minds. We wouldn't show them the safe lane out until they banned the damn weapons.

Diplomats could avoid us once they got to the U.N. conference rooms. We weren't allowed inside, even to observe their deliberations. But we refused to let them off that easily and were committed to hanging around the halls to grab them when they came out for the inevitable coffee and cigarette breaks that punctuated their workdays. Those generally began very late, ended very early, and were broken up with lunches that lasted two hours at a minimum.

Despite our limited access, we dominated information on all aspects of the landmine crisis. Governments needed our expertise to be able to formulate their own arguments. That, coupled with our tenacity, slowly strengthened relationships between the campaigners and representatives of the governments that were becoming increasingly pro-ban. These interactions paved the way for the open cooperation between the ICBL and those governments, which would mark the Mine Ban Treaty negotiations that took place outside the U.N. that ultimately became known as the Ottawa Process. But first, the CCW review process would fail. Not because we wanted it to, necessarily, but because this was inevitable.

.   .   .

Receptions in Geneva were never-ending. We couldn't go to government meetings, but campaigners were invited to the receptions hosted by governments involved in the treaty review process. I didn't go often, because I couldn't stand seeing the same people over and over during the day and then again in the evening. When there weren't receptions, there'd be campaign dinners to revisit the day, perhaps plan, and mostly just hang out and decompress. I didn't go to those either, still preferring books and my solitude anytime.

But now we were getting closer to the endgame of the CCW review, which was still going nowhere. The Big Powers hadn't budged; they considered banning landmines as giving in to the whims of ordinary citizens. The U.S. military in particular viewed this as a potentially dangerous and slippery slope, a concern they openly expressed. If they gave up their landmines, who knew what weapons people might go after next.

The United States was a major stumbling block. While the military was willing to take some steps to get rid of some of the worst landmines in use, it wanted to protect and promote high-tech U.S. landmines, also known as "smart mines." These mines supposedly would become harmless after a relatively short period of time and thus pose no threat to civilians after the end of armed conflict, unlike "dumb mines," which could go on killing and maiming for generations.

The ardently pro-ban countries wouldn't accept a technological solution to the problem, believing that such a solution didn't really exist. After all, the self-destructing landmines that the United States used in the first Gulf War in 1991 didn't prove to be fail-safe. They were still killing and maiming people. Many governments and campaigners alike believed the United States really wanted to make the world safe for U.S. landmines after everyone else's low-tech dumb mines were banned and destroyed.

Tension was high. Members of the U.S. delegation were claiming that, in order to "win," we campaigners were willing to sacrifice their "real" solution to the landmine problem. They were trying to establish an imaginary moral high ground in promoting their smart landmines while painting campaigners as extremists or purists or utopian dreamers. They believed that if they held out long enough, sooner or later we'd have to recognize their reality: landmines were here to stay, so better to support U.S. smart mines and focus on getting rid of the dumb mines used by almost everyone else in the world.

One particular evening in 1995, Goose and I were at a reception at an elegant restaurant close to the U.N. As at all such events, wine was flowing freely and few were turning it down. Goose and I were in a "lively" discussion with a U.S. colonel we'd been sparring with since first meeting him in early 1993. As usual, he was elaborating on the military's love affair with high-tech landmines, and we were telling him that his high-tech solution was a nonsolution that wouldn't fly.

As he kept on trying to convince us of the virtue of his argument and his weapons, the discussion began to get heated. We'd been having the same back-and-forth for more than two years, and nobody in this debate was about to relent. As far as we were concerned, it was past time for President Clinton to consider more than just the military point of view. As both commander in chief of our armed forces and president, he bore the obligation to weigh *all* the political and humanitarian factors involved, and to make a political decision to override the military's determination to keep a weapon it didn't really need.

The colonel began to switch gears and slid into a genial "Come on, we're all Americans" mode. As if just because we were born in the same country we'd share the government's view on anything and everything. He was now saying that actually we were "all on the same page," that all of us "really wanted to help the victims," and we were "all in this together." With each "we are" and "all of us," I got more and more incensed until I couldn't listen anymore.

At that point I didn't employ Mr. Goose's diplomatic skills. Instead I was in the colonel's face, trying hard not to choke him as I told him that "no fucking way" were we on the "same page." We wanted to ban everybody's landmines, while he wanted to promote U.S. landmines. We wanted to protect civilians, and he wanted to protect his landmines.

At that point Goose intervened with something like, "Well, Colonel, what Jody really means is . . ." and started to do a diplomatic rendering of my comments. In no mood for diplomacy, I cut him off. "No. I said no fucking way because it's exactly what I meant. No . . . fucking . . . way!" The colonel and I glared at each other while Goose maneuvered me to another part of the room, where I fumed until we left shortly after.

$\cdot \quad \cdot \quad \cdot$

Sometimes it might have appeared that Geneva was the epicenter of efforts to get rid of landmines, but it wasn't. The four expert sessions of the Convention on Conventional Weapons totaled only seven weeks spread out over two years. They might have seemed like a waste of our time and resources, but we used the meetings as tools to steadily lay the groundwork for a ban. We had an impact not only on the thinking of some governments represented there but also in capitals around the world.

While the diplomatic ballet proceeded in Geneva, sometimes with a bit of the boxing ring thrown in, it was the work of the ICBL's national campaigns that was key to change. The campaigns in the various countries carried out a variety of activities that worked in their own cultures to educate their governments and militaries as well as the general public about the need to ban landmines. As we racked up successes, more organizations joined the ICBL.

National campaigns pushed hard, and some governments began to respond. It didn't take long for those governments to begin vying with each other to be the most progressive on landmine policy. First had been the United States, French, and Belgian governments with their export moratoriums. After that, the export moratorium initiative quickly gathered momentum and more than a dozen countries followed suit.

In what seemed a surprising development given his administration's lack of enthusiasm for a ban, President Clinton was the first world leader to call for the "eventual elimination" of antipersonnel landmines, in his address before the U.N. General Assembly in September 1994. But his real focus was on "eventual"; ours was on "elimination." That distinction was reinforced almost immediately by the release of the State Department's "landmine *control* regime" policy just one month later. The ICBL bashed the administration for the quick step backward from Clinton's purported goal of eliminating landmines.

We used Clinton's statement to hammer him, the U.S. military, and his administration—which was increasingly divided over the issue—to eliminate landmines now, not eventually. We wanted Clinton to show real global leadership on solving the problem, as Senator Patrick Leahy kept pressing the president to do. Soaring rhetoric does nothing to save lives.

Governments began taking steps more radical than export moratoriums. In March 1995, Belgium became the first country in the world to unilaterally ban the use, production, trade, and stockpiling of antipersonnel landmines. Norway followed in June 1995, and almost immediately, Austria. The tide was turning, although it was sometimes hard to feel it inside the U.N. bubble. I never forgot for a moment that not one single thing would have been done to tackle the global landmine problem without the work of all of the individuals who made up the organizations that together were the International Campaign to Ban Landmines.

. . .

Brescia, Italy. There were so many moments during the campaign when we experienced awe and inspiration, but some really stand out for me. One was an action by the Italian Campaign to Ban Landmines, in Brescia, Italy, the home of Italian landmine production. The experience was made more meaningful because of the inauspicious start of the Italian campaign.

We were all anxious to see an Italian landmine campaign take off. Italy was one of the biggest producers and exporters of landmines in the world. When I picture a mine, Italy's Valmara 69 is always one of the two or three that come to mind. It was a modern version of the German "Bouncing Betty" used during World War II.

The relatively big body of the Italian mine is buried so that a few prongs on the smaller top barely emerge from the ground. When a person steps on a prong, the mine bounds up out of the ground to about waist high. Then, it blows up, and the eviscerating results are not pretty. If Italy stopped producing and exporting its landmines, it would be a huge step.

So when Nicoletta Dentico asked me to come to Rome in December 1993 to support the launch of the Italian campaign, I couldn't say no. Even though that was really what I wanted to say. I'd already been traveling a lot. That, coupled with a strong sense that the Rome launch would be a flop, made me want to offer compelling reasons not to go. Instead, precisely because it might be a less-than-inspiring beginning, I knew it was important to go. We had to send a signal that a strong Italian landmine campaign was important to everyone in the ICBL.

It was as tragic an attempt to get things going as I'd imagined. Of the few people who showed up for the Rome meeting, most were *not* from Italy. It was disheartening and didn't bode well for getting the Italian government to move anytime soon on landmines. Six months later, in June 1994, in a burst of creative activism, the Italian campaign gained steam and blasted into the Italian public's consciousness.

They managed to convince the most popular Italian television talk show to devote time every day to the issue of landmines. The several-week-long series culminated with members of the Italian campaign and the Italian minister of defense appearing together on a show. There, the minister made the surprising declaration that Italy should ban the use of antipersonnel landmines and end their production.

Italian campaigners didn't stop there. They also managed to convince representatives of workers at Valsella Meccanotecnica, one of the world's biggest mine producers, along with the trade unions of Brescia, where Valsella was located, to issue a press statement stating they "agree with and support the campaign to ban landmines. It is mandatory to eliminate the production of every type of antipersonnel mine, including the so-called self-destructing and self-neutralizing mines." Trade unionists asked the Italian government "to take immediate initiatives to stop landmine production and trade, and support all the humanitarian actions in favor of the victims."

We were in complete awe of that work. And more so when the defense minister quickly followed through on his public declaration. In a letter to a pro-ban Italian senator, the minister said he'd given the "necessary instructions to start the procedure that will bring Italy to the unilateral commitment not to produce and export antipersonnel landmines." Then on August 2, the government said it would "observe a unilateral moratorium on the sale of antipersonnel mines to other countries" and was readying "the necessary instruments for stopping production of such devices by Italian companies or companies operating on Italian territory." It was positively outstanding.

The Italian campaign wouldn't rest with this unexpected and tremendous success. Pressing its advantage, it was planning three days of activities in Brescia in late September. There'd be a concert to raise money for the Italian campaign, a daylong seminar on landmines, and finally a march to Castenedolo, the town where Valsella's production facility was actually located. Again Nicoletta asked me to come. Again I wasn't excited about it.

Not that they weren't doing fabulous work, but I'd just been there. There were many other campaigners in lots of countries asking me to come and support their national campaigning efforts. I couldn't be everywhere at once. And frankly, the thought of marching to a place where landmines were produced didn't inspire me much. Despite what the Italian campaign had accomplished, I imagined that only a handful of people would turn out for the march, especially because their government was moving forward so quickly. Again, however, I caved in and went back to Italy.

The concert was standing room only, and the seminar was solid, full of people, and informative. But what moved me to tears was the march. The march, to this day, remains a high point in my memories of activities by national campaigns to get their governments to ban landmines.

We started out at the town square in the early morning fog. "We" were as few as I'd imagined we'd be. I anticipated a reprieve, with a blessedly short march route, and that the whole thing would be over quickly. No one had bothered to mention it was seventeen kilometers to where we were going. Ill prepared, I was wearing cowboy boots that definitely weren't designed for a 17K march.

We'd not gone far when I began to notice that people kept appearing, seemingly out of nowhere, to join as we continued to walk. At some point when I turned to look, the line of marchers was so long I couldn't see the end of it. It continued to grow all the way to Castenedolo, where we joined up with thousands more already in its town square. There were speakers, there was music, there was joy in taking action to support the positive change the Italian government was making on landmines. And there were four heroic women from the landmine factory.

As the rally continued, a hush began to settle over the crowd. Everybody was turning toward the water fountain in the middle of the square. Standing there, in front of the fountain and facing the church, were four women. They didn't say a word. The long banner they were holding said it all: "We will not feed our children by making landmines that kill other people's children." The cheers in support of the women's action reverberated through the square. I cried. Not a single man from the production line at Valsella joined them.

In a special session a few nights before the march, the town council of Castenedolo had voted unanimously to join the Landmine campaign. The Italian campaign had been working with municipal governments throughout the country, and more than 160 city councils passed resolutions in support of banning antipersonnel landmines.

From their weak showing just nine months earlier, the Italian campaign was working the landmine issue at all levels. They involved the media, moved the federal government, worked with local governments, went after the producers, and involved the workers and trade unions. Their example inspired a lot of other campaigns to expand their thinking about the work to ban landmines. Italian people had come together in a short period of time and had accomplished the extraordinary.

·   ·   ·

The Cambodia Campaign to Ban Landmines had been launched in August 1994 with a letter written by four landmine survivors, and it quickly became a strong and important national campaign. The letter, which became the call of the Cambodia campaign, read:

We are amputees.
Before, we were soldiers,
members of four different armies
that laid landmines that blew the legs,
arms, and eyes off one another.

Now we teach and learn together at the Center of the Dove.

We beg the world to stop making mines.
We beg the world to stop laying mines.
We beg the world for funds for clearing mines so that we can
    rebuild
our families, our villages and our country again.

Hem Phang, Klieng Vann, Tun Channareth, Suon Creuk

The Center of the Dove was a vocational training center for people with disabilities built in 1991 by the Jesuit Refugee Service, one of the founders of the Cambodia campaign. Apparently, the area had been the site of an arms storage facility, a killing field, and a prison. As the training center was being built, many landmines and cluster bombs were found on and around the site.

Tun Channareth, known as Reth and one of the signers of the call, was one of the earliest and most vocal landmine survivors in the campaign. Another was a young girl named Song Kosal. Their stories were horrible and even more so because they were representative of the stories of tens of thousands of others who'd lived through the terror of stepping on landmines in Cambodia and other countries around the world. Their ban advocacy was powerful even if they didn't always feel all that powerful themselves.

In early 2012, in a booklet titled *Ambassadors before They Knew It*, which includes reflections by Reth and Kosal from the first seventeen years of the Cambodia campaign, Kosal wrote, "I went to the CCW in Vienna in September 1995 to try to tell them, 'Please ban landmines so that children can run safely in the fields,' but I was so afraid of all those men in their suits I forgot what I wanted to say." At that time, little Kosal had been only about ten years old. She'd been six when she lost a leg to a landmine. When working in a rice paddy alongside her mother, she'd stepped on a landmine submerged in the water of the paddy.

Reth, on the other hand, lost both legs to a mine when he was a soldier in one of the four factions fighting in Cambodia. Afterward, he'd wanted to commit suicide because he felt worthless to his family and himself. But Reth fought through the pain, the horror, and the depression. And when the landmine campaign started, he knew he wanted to be part of it.

Both of them, helped by the Jesuit Refugee Service, had come to the campaign because they wanted to work so that someday people everywhere could walk without fear of stepping on landmines. Neither was acting as anybody's poster child for a landmine ban. Reth, Kosal, and many other landmine survivors became fearless advocates of banning landmines and, later, cluster bombs.

Among the Cambodia campaign's first actions was a massive signature campaign calling for a ban in order to build public awareness about the campaign and mobilize support throughout the country. Buddhist monks helped gather names and thumbprints—many people couldn't write—at temples, markets, and schools throughout the country. At every public event, and any time or place people gathered, the Cambodia campaign was there. Signatures were also collected along the annual peace walk, held in late spring every year, when thousands would walk the length of the country to symbolize their cry for a peaceful, united Cambodia.

Other important members of the Cambodia campaign were Sister Denise Coghlan of the Jesuit Refugee Service and Liz Bernstein. Denise is an Australian nun who has lived in Cambodia for more than thirty years. She's one of the most human, humane, and awesome nuns I've ever met. Sr. Denise and the Jesuit Refugee Service's support have ensured that Reth, Kosal, and many other Cambodian landmine survivors have been able to fully participate in the ICBL.

Liz had worked in the region for a decade, including in the Cambodian refugee camps on the Thai-Cambodian border. She is fluent in Khmer. (She also speaks Thai and French and some Portuguese and Spanish.) When I met her on my first trip to Cambodia near the end of 1993, she was sharing a Buddhist temple, a *wat*, with a Jesuit who was morphing into something of a Jesuit-Buddhist. Her willingness to subsist and sleep on the floor of the *wat* was intimidating, even if I masked my feelings by telling myself that she was "weird."

When I'd been preparing for that long campaign outreach trip in '93 that would include Cambodia, Australia, and New Zealand, everyone said I had to be sure to meet Liz Bernstein. But it wasn't until we worked closely while preparing for the July 1995 Cambodia conference that I recognized what an organizing genius she is. Australia and New Zealand provided some campaign stalwarts as well, including Kiwi wunderkind Mary Wareham and two Aussies: Sr. Patricia Pak Poy and campaigner-photographer extraordinaire John Rodsted.

The Cambodia conference in 1995 was first meant to be a regional campaign meeting. We didn't believe it was possible to hold an international ICBL conference in Phnom Penh. There was little infrastructure in the city, and the electricity failed constantly. What facilities could house a conference, and where would people stay? War hadn't been kind to the city. But the ICBL steering committee believed it could work for a regional meeting, even with the sorry state of the infrastructure, and we pitched in to help develop the agenda for the conference.

The more we worked with Denise, Liz, and others, the clearer it became that the conference was growing beyond the regional scope we'd imagined. There were so many new organizations joining the ICBL, and it seemed that everyone wanted to come to the Cambodia conference. So it became our third international ICBL conference, following London in May 1993 and Geneva in May 1994.

The creativity and excitement generated by the Cambodia campaign, in addition to the fact that it would be the ICBL's first conference in a severely mine-contaminated country, helped result in its wild success. This time more than four hundred people from forty-two countries participated, representing NGOs, governments, the U.N., and the ICRC.

In fact, it was at a panel discussion by government representatives that China quietly announced it was stopping the production of antipersonnel landmines for export, in recognition of the mines' human toll. That might not sound like much, but it was of great significance as China was one of the biggest producers and exporters in the world and held no love for a complete ban on antipersonnel landmines.

We emerged from Phnom Penh with new action plans. And, importantly, six new national campaigns, mostly in developing regions, were launched as a direct result of the conference. These included campaigns in Afghanistan, Kenya, the Philippines, South Africa, Spain, and Thailand.

By the end of that conference, 340,000 Cambodian citizens, including King Sihanouk himself at a meeting during the conference, had added their names to the Cambodian petition calling for an immediate ban of landmines. Their initiative sparked new and renewed signature drives by other national campaigns, ultimately resulting in 1.7 million people around the world calling upon governments to amend the Convention on Conventional Weapons and ban landmines. Landmine survivors would present the signatures to government delegations at the Vienna review conference, which would open three months after our ICBL conference in Cambodia.

·   ·   ·

The ICBL descended on Vienna for the review conference in late September 1995. From the outcomes of the expert sessions, we believed that little of substance would happen in the Vienna negotiations. The United States was still fighting hard for its smart mines, and other countries didn't want to see any change at all to the CCW's landmine protocol, while at the same time the number of pro-ban countries was increasing.

The Vienna negotiations ended in deadlock. Governments didn't want to be blamed for doing nothing about landmines, but they couldn't find a way to go forward either. Kosal and Reth, joined by landmine survivors from Afghanistan, Mozambique, and the United States, among others, had together presented the 1.7 million signatures, collected in fifty-three countries, to the review conference's president, calling for a ban on antipersonnel landmines. The most the governments could muster was to call for two more meetings in Geneva. They would convene for one week in January 1996 to work on technical issues related to Protocol II, which really meant trying to find a way to deal with the United States' instance on keeping its smart mines. Then there would be a two-week negotiating session in April and May to finally bring to a close the seemingly never-ending CCW review process.

As the Vienna deadlock was developing, campaigners began discussing strategies to undertake after the review conference. We made what turned out to be a pivotal decision. The ICBL prioritized getting avowedly pro-ban governments to work together as a bloc to push the ban agenda forward. There was an increasing number to work with. When the Vienna conference opened, only fourteen countries avowedly supported an immediate ban on landmines. By the end of the negotiations six months later in Geneva, the number had grown to forty-one.

.   .   .

About 150 campaigners from twenty countries participated in the final two weeks of the review conference in Geneva in April and May 1996. More than ever, I wished we could put the diplomats in a minefield for the negotiations' endgame, because it was clear that nothing was going to happen in Geneva that would have any impact on the landmine problem. But since that wasn't possible, the more creative members of the ICBL worked hard to bring the experience of the landmine survivors and minefields to them.

Of course Reth and Kosal were there. And Ken Rutherford and Jerry White from the United States, who had both joined the ICBL in 1995. Ken had lost both legs to a landmine while doing humanitarian work in Somalia. Jerry's leg had been blown off by an Israeli mine while he was hiking in the Golan Heights on vacation. The two became so active in the landmine campaign that later, in 1997, they cofounded the Landmine Survivors Network to link survivors in their efforts to advocate for survivor rights.

Campaigners managed to have the sound of a landmine explosion go off near the review conference meeting room every twenty minutes, underscoring the fact that every twenty minutes, somewhere in the world, a person was killed or maimed by a landmine. A counter in the hall outside the meeting room continued registering a new victim every twenty minutes as the review conference droned on. Campaigners put up a "Wall of Remembrance" composed of pictures of mine victims, as well as holding other landmine-related photo exhibitions. There were ban posters on Geneva buses and "Ban Mines" stickers throughout the city.

We were also catching government representatives at their diplomatic games. While pro-ban governments had been sharing information for a long time, it was much easier when they decided to include campaigners on their official delegations. Even the United States invited Goose and me to join its delegation. The catch was that we wouldn't be allowed to speak inside the conference room or to publicly disagree with the U.S. landmine position anytime during the conference. Of course we refused the invitation, which was nothing more than an attempt to muffle us as well as possibly discredit us for joining the delegation of a country opposed to banning landmines.

Two times a week, the ICBL produced the *CCW News,* our newsletter on happenings at the review conference. We exposed governments that publicly proclaimed they held pro-ban positions, but which made statements behind the closed doors of the conference room that didn't match up. They weren't the least bit happy to see their real negotiating stances in print. In particular, this news was conveyed in the newsletter column "The Good, the Bad and the Ugly." It not only roused their ire but also forced them to try to bring their public statements in line with the realities of their negotiating positions, or vice versa.

The *CCW News* wasn't meant simply for consumption in Vienna and Geneva. As we were distributing it at the conferences, we were also sending it out to our national campaigns so they could use the information to pressure their governments at home to take action. We hit governments coming and going.

National campaigns also carried out other activities to keep up the visibility and the pressure. For example, the Austrian campaign delivered six tons of shoes to the Austrian Parliament. These symbolized shoes that countless past, present, and future mine survivors could never wear. A similar event was carried out the same weekend in Paris; Handicap International had originated the "shoe pyramid" idea with a huge pile of shoes in front of the Eiffel Tower some years previously.

The ICBL forcefully argued that negotiations were *not* moving toward a ban but actually were making the already horribly weak landmine protocol even weaker. Our successful media strategy was keeping the international community informed of proceedings at the conference. We were making governments squirm at the thought that they'd be bearing the brunt of the bad press, followed by a public backlash, because of the nonresults of the CCW review process. Who could accept that the process was dragging out for more than two and a half years, it would accomplish nothing, and taxpayers were paying for it?

The ICBL continued working hard to develop a campaigning strategy for use after the review conference. Goose convinced me to go to dinner to discuss possible ways forward. If receptions and campaign group dinners were infrequent activities for me in Geneva, going to dinner with an individual was even more rare. When Goose managed to convince me, it felt a little strange.

His vision of where to go, which he didn't confess for a long time, was an expensive and elegant restaurant in Geneva's Old

Town. When he mentioned the restaurant's name, which I'd never heard of and so wasn't impressed by, my first question was whether it was within quick walking distance of the hotel. I wasn't interested in any big production involving taxis that might leave me feeling trapped if I couldn't easily walk home. His plan dashed, we walked down the street to an informal Italian restaurant frequented by campaigners and even a few pro-ban government-types.

When we met in the hotel lobby to walk to the restaurant, I almost didn't recognize him. He wasn't in a suit. Goose was wearing jeans and a polo shirt. The slightly open neck revealed a bit of hair on his chest. The night was chilly, and he had on a sports jacket as well. But he wasn't wearing a suit and tie!

It was startling. Suddenly everything seemed the tiniest bit out of kilter. Not that it felt like anything approximating a date; nor had I thought it was intended to be. To all appearances, and in his own mind, Goose was a happily married family man who adored his wife and three kids. I was still involved with Charles and had moved to Vermont in 1992—since I worked out of my home, I could coordinate the ICBL from anywhere.

We were going out for dinner to strategize, to try to determine how the major change in the Canadian government's position that January, and its proposal, might affect the outcome of the review conference. It's not like we were talking about anything personal. We'd worked together for well over a year before I'd even asked him why he wore a hearing aid every day. It was work and, after all, people did have to eat.

When we walked into the restaurant, there were landmine people everywhere, and a big table full of our colleagues asked us to join them. We declined and sat at a distance from the somewhat rowdy group so we could actually talk. It was no big deal.

Everyone in the campaign knew Goose and I were close political allies, agreeing on virtually everything, even though some couldn't understand how or why. We were always intense about planning and plotting campaign moves.

We immediately started talking about the committed pro-ban governments that the campaign had been working to bring together since January through quiet, informal meetings at the Quaker U.N. Office in Geneva—its office for advocacy on peace and disarmament—on the sidelines of the CCW meetings. It was the strategy we'd come up with during the Vienna conference in order to form a bloc to push the ban agenda forward, and it was working. We were also trying to figure out the likely impact of an unexpected proposal by the Canadians for continuing work to ban landmines after the Geneva meeting ended.

The Canadian government had been such a staunch ally of the United States that it had been hard to believe the Canadians had changed their views on landmines virtually overnight in January and announced an immediate moratorium on the use, production, trade, and export of antipersonnel mines. And Canada wasn't the only country to take concrete action on landmines.

In March, the Dutch minister of defense had announced a ban on the use of the mines and, in a joint operation with Belgium, the destruction of landmine stockpiles. And in April, Germany announced that it would no longer use, produce, or export landmines, and Austria shifted its policy toward a total ban and suspended use of landmines.

The CCW review conference might not accomplish anything, but individual governments were responding to the pressure to ban landmines. And now Canada was offering to host a conference of pro-ban states, some months after Geneva, to plot out concrete steps that would lead to a landmine ban treaty.

They were going to announce the meeting at the closing session of the review conference.

At first, I'd thought the new guy they'd sent to the January meeting, Bob Lawson—in his not-so-great sport jacket that didn't really go with his pants and tie, and his brown suede shoes that didn't go with anything he or any other diplomat in Geneva was wearing—couldn't be trusted. What if, I'd asked Goose then, Lawson was some sort of infiltrator whose real purpose was to derail efforts to ban landmines in the wake of the imminent failure of the review conference?

Goose wasn't all that convinced by Canada's initiative either. But what if, he responded, this is all we've got right now? We didn't have too many options, and even if the Canadians had been playing a game of deceit, going along with them could buy us time and open new avenues for action.

Goose tends to want to give people the benefit of the doubt. By nature, I'm an optimistic pessimist who believes in doing the best I can do for humankind while not being all that convinced about human beings themselves. That and too many bad experiences with Central American governments made it difficult for me to believe much that a government representative might say. But the Canadian proposal proved to be real, with the full backing of the government. And Bob proved to be one of our most important allies in the effort to ban landmines.

·   ·   ·

After that Italian dinner, everything with Goose and me was the same yet somehow slightly not the same. All we'd done was discuss work. There was nothing to speculate about, yet now we had a heightened sense of each other's presence. A couple of days later he simply touched my arm to signal he was going to a media interview and would be back. Even though we both felt something different, not only in that touch but also when our eyes met as I nodded at him and returned to my conversation with another campaigner, there was too much going on to think about it.

The two weeks were dragging to a close, and the review conference was finally sputtering to its death. On the last day, the ICBL held a vigil at the gates of the U.N. It was sad and rainy, and some of the landmine survivors decided to take off their prosthetic limbs and hold them in the air as the diplomats were driven through the gates and dropped off for the meeting. At our request, the closing plenary session of the review conference began with a minute of silence in remembrance of mine victims past and those yet to come.

Two and a half years of tinkering with language and moving commas and semicolons had resulted only in weakening the Convention on Conventional Weapons. On a more positive note, in their final statements to the conference, government after government expressed dismay at the outcome and spoke out for a ban. As planned, the Canadians announced the pro-ban strategy meeting it would hold later in the year in Ottawa and invited everyone to attend.

While we welcomed pro-ban statements and the Canadian announcement, the ICBL was scathing in our denunciation of the review conference farce and the countries that had devoted their strongest efforts to blocking change. We immediately held a press conference with the Canadians, which clearly symbolized our growing partnership with pro-ban governments. For both governments and NGOs, our basic message was the same: only a ban will do.

After the press conference, Goose and I trudged back to the

campaign office to help finish packing up ICBL documents, banners, books, and other materials to use again in the next round of the fight against landmines. By ten that night only a handful of us were still there. Many had long since headed down to the Pickwick, a British-style pub with greasy food, beer, and lots of cigarette smoke that campaigners frequented. Goose and the others were planning on joining them when we finished. I was even considering going, which would be my first time in the place.

Between the grease, the beer and the smoke, it had always seemed like a gross place. I'd never been tempted to go there. But that night was different, with the culmination of two and a half years in and out of the U.N. trying to get rid of landmines. Maybe a farewell to Geneva at the Pickwick was just the right way to exit the town.

I didn't like the place any more than I imagined I would. Their wine was barely palatable, but better bad wine than beer anytime. I tolerated the Pickwick longer than I'd anticipated I would before deciding to make one of my trademark put-on-my-coat-and-slip-out-the-door-without-a-word-to-anybody exits. It was so much easier to just leave than to go through the good-bye, good-bye, good-bye business or, worse, the why-don't-you-stay routine. With decades of practice I'd pretty much perfected the art of the unnoticed escape. When it was properly executed, I could be gone for a long time before anyone was aware I'd left.

This time, I was barely out the door before Goose showed up at my side, and we walked back to the hotel together. As we approached the entrance, we heard our names from somewhere above us. It was our good friend and veteran campaigner Susan Walker standing on the small balcony of her room, waving a bottle of wine. It could only be French; she'd worked for Handicap

International in the field and was representing the organization on the ICBL steering committee. The temptation was too good to ignore, and up to her room we went.

The three of us drank, laughed, complained, and commiserated over the end of all the work in Geneva. Susan had been sitting on the end of her bed when suddenly she was down and "gently snoring." Just as suddenly, without premeditation, Goose and I kissed. The whole day had been a surreal, almost anticlimactic end to years of work. And now Mr. Goose and I were kissing? It was startling, disconcerting, and ended in a flash.

I looked at my watch. It was so late that if I didn't immediately dash out the door, get to my room, and pack, I'd miss my disgustingly early plane home to Vermont. Even with the wine and no sleep, I managed to stuff everything into my suitcase and get myself to the airport in time to catch my flight. Too exhausted to think about why Goose and I had kissed, I fell asleep on the plane. I woke up deciding it was just one of those stupid and potentially embarrassing things that sometimes happen.

First, there'd been the heightened emotion prompted by the end of the review conference—heightened and deflated at the same time, actually. There was uncertainty about the campaign's way forward, coupled with the unpredictable potential of the Canadian meeting. Throw in a little wine, and the mix was volatile. By the time I was back at home—after sleeping on the plane and starting to feel like myself again—I'd already put the events of that night in Geneva in a little box in my head, where I had every intention of keeping them.

But life doesn't always work that way. Goose called me at home the next day, on a Sunday. He'd never called me at home on a weekend. And we'd just left Geneva. It was too weird, and the call itself was weird. We mumbled through some awkward

"just wanted to make sure you made it home okay" ridiculous-
ness and just as awkwardly hung up.

Why did he call me? It was unsettling. That strange little
phone call on May 5 was what confused me. The kissing incident two days earlier I could have easily kept in its compartment
and never have mentioned again. But the phone call? What did
that mean?

As Goose and I spent the next five months preparing for the
Canadian meeting, it became clear that the kiss wasn't just a kiss
and the call wasn't just a call. The issue at hand turned out to be
love. It was every bit as thorny and painful for everyone as one
could imagine, and it got much more complicated and difficult
before it finally got better several years later.

Love became the wondrous and torturous backdrop to everything connected to the Canadian meeting held that October
in Ottawa and all that followed from it. The Ottawa meeting
turned out to be the place where a ban phoenix rose much more
spectacularly from the ashes of the CCW review process than
we'd ever expected, even if Goose and I recognized its potential
then and are still in awe of it now. We rode that phoenix, our
love-entangled emotions probably heightened initially by our
political exhilaration. But not long after Ottawa, as the end of
1996 approached, his wife asked him if he was in love with me.
When he answered yes, she told him to leave.

If Goose had moved into the basement of their house for a
while and they'd faced their issues head on, that might have been
the end of the story. She could have kept him there until they'd
worked out what, in their lives together, had let them grow so
far apart, and had created so much space, that a "me" could happen. I certainly was no saint. But I was a symptom, not the cause,
and I'd not pursued him. Instead he was thrown out of the house,

and he and his wife legally separated. In July 1997, Goose and I rented a house together in Virginia, but that wasn't the end of the story either.

Goose remained deeply, deeply shaken. At first, he couldn't make sense of how a couple so in love, together since they were about fifteen, had moved so far apart. He also tortured himself wondering what had happened to the family man he believed himself to be. He worried about his kids and whether he'd be able to continue his close relationship with them.

While he'd worked on the Hill, he'd been responsible for getting his children, Jimmy and Sarah, to and from day care every day when his wife, a nurse, had decided to go to medical school. He'd gotten the kids up in the morning, made them meals, and put them to bed at night. Emily was born a few years later, just before they moved to Fredericksburg, south of D.C., so his wife could join a medical practice there.

Emotionally, Goose was now twisted into an unhappy pretzel. As painful as it was to confront the issues, they couldn't be ignored, for anybody's sake. Over time I helped, and sometimes forced, him to face his demons, and slowly Goose began to work through them. Several times, he tried to go back home. I never tried to stop him.

Finally in July 1999, it was unbearable. We agreed I'd move back to Vermont, and he could give it another try back home if he wanted. I told him there could be no communication between us at all. If he really wanted his relationship with his wife to work out, he'd have to focus all his attention on that.

My sister Mary Beth flew down to help me pack and drive back to Vermont. My old friend Casey came down from Silver Spring, where she and John and their daughter, Drew, were living. I didn't take much with me, because I was determined to leave our Alexandria house largely intact so Goose wouldn't feel deprived of a comfortable, safe space when I was gone. When our beautiful white German shepherd, Stella, Mary Beth, and I pulled out of the driveway, the U-Haul we were towing was ridiculously packed and so unstable that it's a miracle we arrived in Vermont unscathed.

Goose became an even bigger wreck than before. Not that I was any better. When I arrived in Vermont, I threw myself on the floor and wept and wept and wept. I think I stayed in my pajamas for ten days. But when I'd left our life together in Virginia I'd been resolved. Things could only work out the way they had to work out. And that would be that.

Finally I was sick of crying in my pajamas and decided to visit a friend in L.A. Susan Whittaker, who I'd shared many delegation experiences with in Salvador, had lost her husband to lung cancer about a year and a half before and was still deeply mourning his loss. We were a somewhat dismal pair but a good fit in our grief.

After a couple of weeks, we started talking about the possibility of my moving out to stay with her for a longer term. Hollywood was just about as far away from landmines as I could get, in every way possible. Unlike many who are not from there, I like L.A. and had quite a few friends there, mostly from the days of my work with Medical Aid for El Salvador. Moving there was starting to feel like a very good idea. Then I got an email from Goose. I wanted to smack him. Instead I answered:

> Email—to what end? My soul is in shreds—the warp that was the weave of my spirit has been torn out. Now, fragile threads barely hold my soul's cloth together.
>
> I am soul lost. And our modern world has taken away the trappings of grief public. If I could but shave my head bald, rend my

garments, keen, and wail at a public wailing wall so all would know the depth of my distress and would cut me a wide, wide berth and know I am grieving the loss of part of my soul, and thus know not to ask questions that I do not want to entertain until I might be ready to take off the mourning weeds, if ever, and try to feel like part of this planet again.

I am soul lost, but what is my pain cannot be my consolation. Do you seek assurance of my anguish?

I am soul lost ...

My answer lacerated him, and I can't say I didn't want him to feel my pain. But we continued to communicate. He called and said he'd never moved out of our Alexandria house. It now felt more like home to him than the one he'd been grieving for. Yet so tenuous. And I told him I was thinking about moving to L.A. I felt his heart clench.

I went back East after my visit with Susan, and Goose and I saw each other a month later. Then followed a few months of stressful, unpleasant ping-pong, but by the end of the year, we were back together in our house in Virginia. We "fondly" refer to that time as the "glitch period," but it was over. But before the glitch came to pass, there was Ottawa, the Ottawa Process, the Mine Ban Treaty, and the Nobel Peace Prize.

CHAPTER TEN

The Ottawa Process and the 1997 Landmine Ban World Tour

Bob Lawson of the bad outfits and brown suede shoes was our primary link with the Canadian government. His experience in the worlds of both government and NGOs made him a natural partner. We communicated feverishly while preparing for the October meeting. Bob and Goose worked particularly closely together, then and for the next few years.

Some of us did come to poke fun at them, calling them the "dynamic duo." But the reality was that they were. Something about the way their brains worked individually and together got their creative sides going, and they produced some amazing and truly groundbreaking work.

Canada's foreign minister, Lloyd Axworthy, would host the conference, which was supposed to produce a concrete action plan leading to the elimination of landmines. Any government could participate by signing the Ottawa Declaration, a public declaration of their commitment to banning landmines. Governments unwilling to sign could attend as observers. The International Campaign to Ban Landmines, U.N. agencies, and the

International Committee of the Red Cross were full participants as well.

This time, conference room doors wouldn't close us out and it would be the observer governments who sat at the back of the room. Not all diplomats were excited by the egalitarian nature of the meeting. But it helped underscore the fact that business as usual at the U.N. in Geneva had failed, and that this was going to be a very different scenario. We weren't at the U.N. anymore, Toto.

The 1996 Ottawa Conference was open and free flowing. By the end of the three days, we'd produced a solid action plan that we knew could very well lead to a world free of landmines— but that would happen only with serious follow-through on the commitments all the conference participants had made there. Communications between Goose and me and the Canadians was tight in Ottawa, not only with Bob Lawson but also with Jill Sinclair, who was Bob's superior, Mark Gwozdecky, and others.

NGOs could—and, more important, would —say things that many others in the room were thinking but couldn't say without offending diplomatic sensibilities. Some loved it and some hated it. At one point, near the end of a ridiculous statement by the French, the Canadians subtly signaled for me to respond. I was happy to oblige.

The French diplomat had taken the floor, indicating he had an important announcement to make. After his lengthy, circuitous statement that few could follow in any language, he concluded with an absurdity he was trying to portray as a dramatic development in French policy. He declared that France had decided to ban landmines—except, and only, when they actually needed to use them. I was already signaling to speak even as I quickly conferred with Goose to make sure I'd heard what I thought I'd just heard.

Wasting no time, I condemned the so-called new French ban policy. What exactly did that mean? France would "ban" landmines in peacetime and then "un-ban" them if it decided to use them again in war? It was a ludicrously specious policy. The diplomat was already squirming in his chair when I concluded that the "new development" was only slightly better than "getting a stick in the eye." The Canadians and ICBL campaigners loved it. The diplomat in question never stopped holding me in ill regard. But there were differing opinions on that point.

During the CCW days, a member of the Finnish delegation had approached me once during a coffee break to defend yet again Finland's determination to keep its landmines. The Finns were somehow convinced that antipersonnel landmines would help save them from a Russian invasion, should one ever occur. As too often happens in military thinking, they were planning for the last war, not for the changing world. The fact that the Soviet Union had collapsed and the Berlin Wall had come down made little impact on their strategic planning.

At one point in the conversation the Finn confessed that, often when it was time to come to a CCW meeting, I'd start appearing in his nightmares. I thought it a strange admission. Maybe he thought if he said it out loud to me directly, I'd be exorcised at least from his dream world.

Conversely, at a different landmine meeting, a U.S. general surprised me by saying that, while he didn't agree with my position on landmines, he had a lot of respect for me and how I worked. It was all sort of curious, but I've never forgotten either of them, or the French diplomat.

During the Canada conference, we were involved in drafting both the final declaration and the action plan, but I can't remember the details of either. Axworthy, the foreign minister, overshadowed everything when he came back to the conference room to close the meeting. Goose and I could hardly wait for him to speak.

A few hours earlier, Bob had pulled us aside to tell us Axworthy would be making a real, and completely unexpected, announcement. He was going to issue a challenge to the governments there to negotiate a treaty completely banning landmines within one year and to return to Ottawa at the end of 1997 to sign it. It was an astounding act of diplomatic courage and true leadership. If it failed, it would be one hell of a failure. Not only would it be an embarrassment to the Canadian government, but it would also be a huge setback for our effort to ban landmines.

The Canadians wanted the ICBL to be ready to support Axworthy's challenge. They'd also informed our close ally Peter Herby, of the International Committee of the Red Cross, in order to ensure their support too, but that was it. Only a handful of us in the room knew what was coming. The Canadians hadn't even broached the topic with other key pro-ban governments, such as Norway, Austria, Mexico, and Belgium, among others. They feared that, even among them, there'd be too much resistance amid cries from some that it was "premature" to actually negotiate a treaty, even if they allegedly all supported the notion.

The room was quiet as Axworthy came to the podium. Everyone was expecting a pro forma thank-you, so many were quietly filling their briefcases in order to leave as quickly as possible after he closed the conference. Some were already gone. For example, the head of the U.S. delegation had left, figuring that anything that was going to happen already had. Other members of his team could handle the requisite handshakes and good-byes. Instead, however, the room was turned on its head when the foreign minister spoke.

Axworthy thanked everyone for the work over the past few days, but almost immediately moved to issue the challenge. Anyone who hadn't been paying close attention when he started speaking was now riveted by his words. Essentially, he told the governments it was time to put up or shut up. Since they'd all pledged to ban landmines, there was no better time than now to get started. He concluded by saying Canada was prepared to sign a mine ban treaty in Ottawa in December 1997 even if only one other country signed it with them.

The Canadian challenge was also a shunning of the U.N. It meant governments would come together in a series of meetings completely outside the normal U.N. process to negotiate the treaty. It was a total shock to the system on multiple levels. But the reality is that treaties can be negotiated anywhere. It's not the setting itself that matters. If I invited a group of government representatives to my house to negotiate an agreement, and they did so and then signed and ratified it, it would be law just as if it had been accomplished in the hallowed halls in Geneva.

The government representatives didn't know how to react. They were caught with their diplomatic pants on the floor. The ease of lofty ban rhetoric is one thing, but the hard reality of a public challenge to act on it is quite another. All were stunned and most were outraged by the diplomatically incorrect "stunt." Governments that had been extremely active in promoting the ban long before Canada stopped mirroring the U.S. position felt they'd been upstaged by a political Johnny-come-lately. There weren't very many happy government types in that room—or back in their capitals once the diplomats relayed this breaking news back home.

On the other hand, we campaigners were euphoric. There was clapping; there was cheering; and there was crying. Goose and I and other campaigners quickly took the floor to congratulate Canada on its bold leadership, as did the ICRC. It was a monumental moment in our effort to get rid of landmines. I imagined a lot of governments were now ruing the outcome of the CCW review process. Other choices they could have made over those two and a half years could have ensured that nothing like Ottawa would ever have taken place.

While the ICBL was ecstatic, we were also worried. The political fallout might be fiercely negative and might kill this non-U.N. negotiating process before it even got started. If enough of the pro-ban governments were sufficiently angry about Canada's unilateral move, they could and would find multitudinous ways to slow down the process or derail it completely. On top of all those possibilities sat the biggest elephant of all, the United States.

The United States hadn't gone to Ottawa to get rid of landmines. The government was there to make sure nothing dramatic happened to speed up the "eventual elimination" of landmines. To the United States, that meant at least a decade. It most definitely did *not* mean one year. It was going to be a pissing match every step of the way, between everyone in the world who wanted to end the scourge of landmines as quickly as possible and the world's greatest military power, supported by its allies, which wanted to hang on to every weapon in its deadly arsenal. Thus began one of the most intense years of my life.

.   .   .

The relentless pressure was on. We had to create unstoppable momentum that would give us a mine ban treaty to sign in Ottawa at the end of 1997. The ICBL met immediately after that October Ottawa meeting and then again in Brussels in December that year to plan our way forward in the aftermath of the ban challenge.

In an unexpected aside at our Brussels ICBL meeting, Carl von Essen, a politically astute and absolutely fantastic Swedish campaigner, wanted to add the Nobel Peace Prize to the meeting's agenda. Way back in 1992, someone had said that banning landmines could earn whoever accomplished the seemingly impossible goal the Peace Prize. It had seemed so ridiculous then and still so presumptuous now that all I could do was roll my eyes at Carl's suggestion. And who knew how that whole Nobel process worked anyway? We had so many important issues to cover in the meeting that it seemed an absurd waste of time.

When we got to the Nobel Prize on the agenda, Carl said that a Swedish parliamentarian, head of their foreign affairs committee, was going to nominate the ICBL for the Nobel Peace Prize and was hoping the ICBL could get some letters of support for the nomination from elected officials in other countries. Carl told us that the letters had to arrive at the Nobel Institute in Oslo by midnight, January 31. Several of us said we'd try.

When I got back home, I got in touch with Cindy Buhl, who I'd worked with on Central America and who now was an aide to Congressman Jim McGovern from Massachusetts, to see if he might be willing to send a letter of support for the nomination. I knew Jim, too, from when I worked on El Salvador. Jim and Congressman Joe Moakley, who he'd worked for at the time, had saved my butt more than once back then.

When Cindy spoke with Jim about it, he wanted to send a nomination himself, not just a letter of support, which he did. Over the months of the Ottawa Process, we learned that the ICBL had been nominated multiple times by various individuals. Other organizations and individuals important to the ban movement had also been nominated. But no one in the campaign focused on it; all our energy was directed toward seeing a treaty banning landmines within a year.

. . .

Immediately after the October Ottawa meeting, the Canadian government went on a political offensive. It sent diplomats to meet with all the key pro-ban governments, smooth ruffled diplomatic feathers, and pull together a core group to push the process forward. The initial group included Canada, Norway, Austria, South Africa, Belgium, Mexico, the Philippines, and Germany. Our national campaigns were also working hard on their governments to get them to fully embrace the challenge and publicly support the Ottawa Process. Once that support was shored up, the momentum appeared to build continuously.

But there were many times when Goose and I talked about the whole thing being really only smoke and mirrors, especially in the months immediately following the Ottawa Conference. We knew that, under the right circumstances, it could come to a screeching halt. But the Ottawa Process, even if many of us recognized its fragility, was real, and it was moving forward.

There would be a series of governmental meetings to develop and negotiate the Mine Ban Treaty itself, as well as events and activities around the world to put maximum pressure on governments to participate and then sign the resulting treaty. The Austrians, led by diplomat Thomas Hajnoczi, prepared a draft treaty for the core group that was the basis for discussion and preliminary negotiations at government-sponsored conferences in Vienna, Bonn, and Brussels. Those meetings would culminate in a final three-week negotiating session in Oslo in September 1997.

An ICBL ad hoc working group drafted our version of a ban treaty. Beginning in January 1997, we took our draft to New York several times to discuss it with representatives of different governments at the U.N. We wanted everyone to be clear about what campaigners saw as essential elements of any ban treaty.

· · ·

Most anyone who travels constantly for work would say life in airports, airplanes, and strange beds is not wondrous and exotic. But sometimes, despite the unpleasantness, the outcome can trump the sense of perpetual jet lag, of never quite being sure where you are or even what date it is. That describes the year after Ottawa. We called it the "1997 Landmine Ban World Tour" as we jumped from country to country and continent to continent. The ICBL even made up World Tour T-shirts to remember it all.

In addition to ICBL meetings in Ottawa and Brussels in 1996, we held campaign conferences in Tokyo, Mozambique, Stockholm, Sydney, New Delhi, Senegal, and Yemen in 1997. There were also trips to New York, Oslo, and Helsinki. The ICRC held meetings in Zimbabwe in April and the Philippines in July 1997. We were all back in Africa in May for an Africa-wide conference cosponsored by the Organization of African Unity and the South African government. The government of Turkmenistan held a meeting in Ashgabat in June. No matter who was the sponsor, all the conferences were characterized by open cooperation among the partners in the ban movement—the ICBL, the ICRC, and pro-ban governments.

Despite what many think, a string of meetings and conferences isn't necessarily just a string of trips to exciting places punctuated by talks. But some complained that conferences wasted precious resources that could better be spent directly on mine clearance. They somehow managed to avoid understanding that, without the pressure generated by meetings, there would have been little interest in putting up money for mine clearance at all. Without the ICBL and the treaty process, few in the world would have had any idea about landmines and the impact they were having on ordinary people in countries around the world. Dealing with the landmine problem was never something that governments would have taken on without pressure.

So first we were in Vienna in mid-February. It was the starting point where the essential components of a treaty to ban antipersonnel landmines were laid out. No one had expected 111 countries to attend the February meeting, joined by official delegations of the ICBL, the ICRC, and U.N. agencies. Even though half the governments there weren't yet ready to ban the weapon, the wide participation was evidence of the seriousness with which the Ottawa Process was being taken globally.

Drawing on the solid work by Judith Majlath and the Austrian Campaign to Ban Landmines, the ICBL held press conferences in Vienna at the opening and closing of the meeting. But it wasn't just the campaigners doing all the talking. The Austrian chairman of the conference, as well as representatives from the German and Belgian governments, who would be hosting the next two ban treaty meetings, and the ICRC were also there. Governments didn't hold separate media events at the conferences anymore.

In early March, the Japanese had hosted a small meeting on mine clearance and victim assistance attended by 27 countries, the European Union, and ten international organizations. Then it was on to Bonn in April to discuss treaty verification and compliance measures. Just like in Vienna, no one expected high attendance, but 120 countries showed up in Bonn. Goose and I, as the ICBL's official delegation, were full participants in that meeting too. Somewhat surprisingly, the German campaign didn't care to be on the ICBL delegation. They didn't send anyone to Bonn at all.

·   ·   ·

By mid-1996, the ICBL managed to "steal" Liz Bernstein from the Cambodia Campaign to Ban Landmines. It helped that she was excited by the ICBL and had already been thinking about leaving Cambodia after a decade in that region.

Liz was no stranger to landmines herself. During one of the annual Cambodia peace marches, she and a couple of others had been captured by the Khmer Rouge, who'd decided to take them to their commander far away from the march route. Pattie, a tall and strapping young woman, was made to carry their rocket launcher. Liz was ordered to walk the point position— through the minefields. Hours later and still intact, they reached the commander, who was sitting alone under a tree. After some tense discussion via Liz, he decided to let them go. The Khmer Rouge soldiers all disappeared into the jungle, leaving her and the others to find their way back to the march on their own through the jungle and the landmines. I worked with Liz for years before she ever mentioned it.

But it wasn't her fear of Cambodia's mines that led her to Africa for the campaign; it was a desire to work on landmines everywhere. In August she was in southern Africa to help figure out the best place to hold our fourth ICBL conference. Although Africa was the most mine-infested continent, campaign activity was slow to build there. Campaigners needed shoring up, and we believed a landmine conference in the region was key to making that happen.

Before we asked Liz if she'd go to Africa, the ICBL had decided to focus some of our work on helping create "mine-free zones." Central America had declared itself the world's first such zone in September 1996, signaling the commitment to become mine-free. Caribbean nations forming the Caribbean Community and Common Market (CARICOM) regional group followed two months later. The Organization of American States called for making the entire Western Hemisphere a mine-free zone. Even today that remains an elusive goal, since neither the United States nor Cuba has banned landmines, even though all other countries in the hemisphere have.

We recognized such zones as an important way to build strong regional blocs to support a ban treaty. The campaign wanted to target the twelve states that then formed SADC, the Southern African Development Community. They made up the most heavily mined region in the world, so a mine-free southern Africa would be especially important.

The entire ban movement—ICBL, ICRC, and pro-ban governments—saw African involvement as crucial to the success of the Ottawa treaty. A key failure of the CCW review process had been the lack of participation by mine-affected countries in particular and the developing world in general. We wanted to help turn that around in the Ottawa Process.

Liz first went to Zimbabwe, but not much landmine campaigning was happening there. Mozambique offered stronger possibilities. A national campaign had made a modest beginning there in November 1995, with activists beginning to gather signatures in support of a ban. People in that extremely poor country were weary after decades of war, and wary because of it. Many were reluctant to promote a campaign that their young government hadn't yet embraced.

What happened in Mozambique is a prime example of how being part of the landmine campaign helped to empower civil-society activism in countries without much of that experience. With Liz in Maputo and the ICBL deciding to hold our conference there, the Mozambique campaign grew increasingly active and influential in the country.

They hired a full-time coordinator and started a newsletter. The campaigners lobbied parliamentary committees and met with the speaker of the national assembly. They also were able to meet with their foreign minister. The national campaign grew to encompass more than seventy organizations and ultimately gathered more than a hundred thousand signatures on its landmine ban petition. Although the campaign repeatedly asked for a meeting with Mozambican president Joaquim Chissano to present the signatures to him, it wasn't until the week before the ICBL conference that they finally got the meeting.

During the months of Liz's nonstop preparations for the conference, she was also holding capacity-building and campaign-skills workshops throughout the region to help strengthen and build new African ban campaigns. Three were launched in SADC countries during the course of planning for the conference: Zambia in September, Zimbabwe in October, and Angola in November 1996. In February 1997, the Somali campaign was launched in the Horn of Africa.

Campaigning workshops and training sessions became one of Liz's important contributions to the ICBL overall. They've remained a hallmark of ICBL work since she became the campaign coordinator after I stepped down in February 1998. The skills training that the campaign offered these new activists could be used not only for their work on landmines but also on any other issues they wanted to tackle.

Maputo was an exciting NGO conference and a crucial step in the Ottawa Process. It proved to be an important setting for building support among African governments. More than 450 campaigners from sixty countries listened as Mozambique's President Chissano opened the conference, "Toward a Mine-Free Southern Africa."

There were four days of strategy sessions, workshops, and panel discussions. As we'd done in Cambodia, we planned visits to minefields to watch how mine clearance teams worked in Mozambique. We concluded Maputo with a final declaration endorsing the Ottawa Process and calling on all governments to publicly commit to signing the ban treaty in December.

The attention generated throughout the SADC region by the activities and work leading up to the Maputo conference, coupled with extensive work by national campaigns, was a catalyst for government action. The week before the conference, South Africa unilaterally banned antipersonnel landmines. During the conference itself, Mozambique did the same. Malawi and Swaziland used the occasion to announce their support for the Ottawa Process and for signing a ban treaty in December.

The ICRC followed up quickly with a seminar in Harare, Zimbabwe, in late April. There, foreign affairs officials and military from all twelve SADC states called for governments in the region to establish a mine-free zone, immediately end all new deployments of antipersonnel mines, and commit to signing the ban treaty in December. All this, and we were still only four months into the year.

For Goose and me, May was as crazy as all the other months since the Ottawa Process began. And even with all those activities that month, we were also involved in preparations for the June conference that would be hosted by the Belgian government. Brussels would be the last of the treaty meetings before the final negotiations in Oslo in September. It was considered a make-or-break meeting in the Ottawa Process.

But first, in May, we'd return to Africa for a continent-wide conference on landmines, held in Kempton Park, South Africa, which was sponsored by the Organization of African Unity and the South African government. Then we'd fly directly to Stockholm for a regional meeting of governments and NGOs. From there, it would be on to pro-ban Oslo, followed by antiban Helsinki for meetings with government officials and campaigners.

I recently dug up a calendar for 1997, and the amount of travel details scrawled throughout it looks insane. Even though I made all those trips, it's hard to believe I did. Sometimes just thinking about the jet lag seems to summon it up. At least Goose and I were always together and part of all official ICBL delegations at the meetings throughout the year.

An unbelievable element of that entire period is that only a small handful of people knew that Goose and I had a personal relationship at all. Even for years after we married in Geneva, in May 2001, there were multitudes in the campaign who still didn't know we were a couple, let alone that we were married. From time to time, I occasionally run into people from the ban movement who are shocked to learn that we've been married for years.

•   •   •

Forty-one nations of the Organization of African Unity attended the Kempton Park conference. ICBL involvement, particularly by the African campaigns, was significant. Along with South

Africa's vice president and Archbishop Desmond Tutu, I was asked to give one of the keynote speeches there. By then, I'd become a powerful speaker on behalf of the ICBL and banning landmines, but speaking alongside the archbishop was challenging, especially since it was the first time I met him.

That meeting underscored the fact that that Africa was on the move. There, Zimbabwe became the third SADC state to unilaterally ban antipersonnel mines. Nine other countries—Botswana, Lesotho, Mauritius, Sierra Leone, Cape Verde, Burundi, Uganda, Tanzania, and Guinea-Bissau—pledged full support of the Ottawa Process for the first time. Only Egypt voiced strong opposition. At the same time, though, that government felt such intense pressure that it declared it no longer produced or exported mines. In closing, Egypt also noted that it was in favor of the "eventual elimination" of landmines. Like the United States, Egypt's "eventual" still hasn't materialized.

The meeting closed with South Africa destroying 25 percent of its antipersonnel landmine stockpile. Six NGO representatives were invited to fly on a military plane to witness the destruction, which was set off by the country's defense minister. The very strong final declaration and action plan that came out of Kempton Park was forwarded to the annual Organization of African Unity Summit in June in Harare, Zimbabwe. It helped forge the basis of an Africa-wide commitment to ban landmines that proved critical in maintaining the integrity of the Mine Ban Treaty in the face of a direct U.S. assault during the Oslo negotiations later that year.

.   .   .

Oslo, August 31, 1997. The day before the Oslo treaty negotiations would begin. It was 6:30 in the morning when Goose and I were jolted awake by the phone. Bob Lawson was calling to say Princess Diana was dead after a car accident in Paris. The global reaction to her death is well documented but in many ways still defies the imagination.

Diana's first involvement with the landmine issue was her trip to Angola with the British Red Cross at the beginning of 1997. She made a second trip, just weeks before her death, with Ken Rutherford and Jerry White of the Landmine Survivors Network in support of landmine survivors and the global effort to ban landmines. Her support for a ban greatly irritated the British government, with one official labeling her a "loose cannon" on the subject of landmines, but she didn't particularly care.

Pressure on Diana because of her ban position diminished dramatically when the Blair government came to power in May 1997. Landmine policy in the United Kingdom, formerly in lockstep with the United States, immediately began to diverge. In the lead-up to the 1997 elections, a landmine ban had been part of the Labor Party's platform, so a change in policy was expected. The degree to which Diana's feelings about landmines influenced U.K. policy is probably impossible to determine, especially since we were already near the end of negotiating the ban treaty. But the silence of the U.K. delegation throughout the Oslo conference probably was a reflection of the emotional response to her death.

The pictures of Diana with landmine survivors in Angola and Bosnia were iconic at the moment they were taken and still are today. People around the world had followed her since her fairy-tale wedding to Prince Charles. The photos of her in minefields and with mine victims brought the plight of victims to the general public in ways few other things could have. Ken and Jerry attended the mobbed funeral in London.

．　　．　　．

The United States always denied that the reason it finally decided in mid-August to send a delegation to Oslo was to do everything it could to derail negotiations. But the U.S. delegation wasn't there in unbridled support for a complete and immediate ban of antipersonnel landmines. It didn't matter what Clinton or Albright or anyone else in the administration said about U.S. motives. What mattered was what the diplomats did in Oslo, which was to try to gut the Mine Ban Treaty.

Clinton had been under intense pressure from Senator Leahy and others in Congress, and from Bobby Muller and the U.S. Campaign to Ban Landmines, to send a negotiating team to Oslo. However, the ICBL overall, along with many pro-ban governments, didn't want the United States there at any cost. But with the U.S. decision to participate, the number of media types registered for the conference doubled. With Diana's death, it skyrocketed.

People inside the Washington Beltway had a hard time understanding that many others in the world didn't think U.S. involvement could make or break the success of a treaty banning landmines. Of course it would have been excellent if the United States had fully embraced the ban. But everything it did in the lead-up to Oslo demonstrated no such policy on landmines. A U.S. delegation in Oslo hell-bent on bending treaty negotiations to its will was much more threatening to the future of a mine ban treaty than no U.S. participation at all.

The United States had continued to promote its high-tech solution to the landmine problem, and it didn't go to Oslo with a change of view. The government had sent delegations to the Ottawa Process meetings as observers, not participants, and always with the goal of pressuring countries to support the U.S.

position. Many of us couldn't believe the lengths the United States would go to in its attempts to protect its landmines.

Less than three months earlier, the last major treaty conference before the final negotiations in Oslo had been held in Brussels. Campaign activists, complete with paraphernalia designed to bring some reality to the proceedings, were there in force. Some particularly creative people had built a simulated minefield. Its hidden sensors, if stepped on, would trigger the sounds of landmine blasts. They were able to position it in front of the building where the meeting would be held, so it was almost impossible to get inside without walking through the minefield.

Those who supported a total ban of landmines enthusiastically ventured across—such as Belgium's Princess Astrid. There's a great photograph of her walking across it, trying not to trigger landmine blasts, as she enters the conference site to address the participants. Not all shared her grace, and the expressions on some of the diplomats' faces as they tried to tiptoe across the simulated minefield without detonating an explosion were sights to behold.

Others worked hard to skirt the minefield, and some went so far as to sneak into the hall through a back entrance. However once the diplomats got inside the building, no matter how they got there, they couldn't avoid the landmine survivors themselves. These were people who'd gone through real minefields and lived to talk about it. They were waiting at the doors of the conference room to greet the government representatives, whose decisions about banning landmines would affect the lives of millions.

Some who attended the Brussels conference hadn't had to deal with the simulated minefield or the landmine survivors at all. U.S. diplomats and military had come to Brussels but not to the ban conference itself. The U.S. delegation had held meetings of its own outside the conference site. When one of the diplomats described the experience of attending one of these meetings to a few of us, the degree and crudeness of U.S. bullying was difficult to fathom. (I'm sorry to have to say that it hasn't changed much over the years.)

He'd been summoned, as he put it, to meet with U.S. officials. After being picked up in a big black vehicle, he was taken to a room in a hotel basement. People from the United States were seated along a table up on a platform. The diplomat sat in a chair below them in what he described as an "inquisitional setting."

After being stridently harangued for some time to support U.S. landmine positions, which he refused over and over again to do, noting that U.S. positions ran directly counter to those of his own government, he had been told that his government had better be careful. If they didn't change their policies to support the United States, "the next time they were invaded by Russia" the United States wouldn't "rescue" them.

Now the U.S. delegation would be bringing the arrogance evident in that type of "negotiating" to Oslo. We were anything but pleased. The minute the head of the U.S. delegation opened his mouth at the conference, he confirmed all of our worst fears. And that was only the beginning.

. . .

The historic negotiations opened in Oslo, and the ICBL was ready. Goose and I had gone to Norway a week earlier to help put the finishing touches on our plans for the three weeks of negotiations. Norwegian campaigners from the mine-clearance organization Norwegian People's Aid had been preparing for the arrival of campaigners for months. They'd been able to get an office and meeting space for the ICBL inside the negotiating site in Oslo. Even better, we were directly opposite the negotiation room itself, which gave all campaigners easy access to government delegates throughout the conference.

Some of us would be taking part in the negotiations themselves. Goose and I were part of the official ICBL delegation that was present at all sessions and in the smaller working group meetings. Although we couldn't formally propose treaty language, the ICBL informally circulated language that we wanted to see in the treaty and had a legion of campaigners available to push governments to consider it.

Another important part of our work in Oslo was a four-day NGO forum to plan campaign action after the treaty had been negotiated. Whenever campaigners were together anywhere for any reason, we took the opportunity to strategize and plan. The action plan we created in the ICBL forum in Oslo was fundamentally important to our ability not only to sustain but also to increase our momentum after Oslo.

Eighty-nine governments were full participants in the treaty negotiations. Many more came as observers. All were greeted with huge banners the ICBL had hung across the central square facing the conference center exhorting them to negotiate a treaty with "no loopholes, no exceptions, and no reservations." Goose had suggested that refrain minutes before I'd spoken months earlier at the Brussels conference. I'd used it then and it took hold, becoming the mantra of treaty negotiations.

South Africa's ambassador to the U.N. in Geneva, Jacobo Selebi, presided brilliantly over the Oslo conference. When it opened, rather than wasting significant time with the usual government statements and pontificating about great intentions, Selebi went right to the meat of the negotiations and opened discussion on core articles of the treaty. The strategy forced sticking points into the open within the first two days, which meant there'd be plenty of time to deal with them.

At the very outset the United States presented its so-called negotiating position, which was a set of interlocking demands. Eric Newsom, the head of the U.S. delegation, and who had worked for Senator Leahy when the ICBL started, informed diplomats that no single demand could be changed. They all had to be accepted as a package deal. They included an exception for the United States that would allow it to continue using landmines in Korea, and a change in the fundamental definition of antipersonnel landmines so that certain U.S. smart mines wouldn't be captured by the ban. Also, unbelievably, the United States demanded a nine-year delay before the treaty could take effect. How do you negotiate on all-or-nothing language designed to gut the treaty and render it largely meaningless?

Creative campaigners skillfully distilled seemingly complicated issues into simple slogans that left no doubt about ICBL positions. Every day, volunteers handed government delegates slips of paper with new slogans as they entered the conference room. For example, when the United States tried to redefine, more than once, its antipersonnel mines in order to prevent their inclusion in the treaty, the slogan read, "When is an AP mine not an AP mine? When it's American."

The United States cajoled and arm-twisted with great vigor, which was matched by our own. For almost two full weeks, despite U.S. efforts, things kept moving along remarkably smoothly, and the conference was on the verge of completing a treaty strongly supported by the ICBL. And days early! We could barely contain our excitement.

Then, in the most dramatic and threatening moment in Oslo, the U.S. delegation asked for the floor. We were livid when they asked for a twenty-four-hour delay in negotiations, and even more so when the Canadian government fully backed the request. Without Canada there'd have been no Oslo. Yet suddenly they were willing to support a U.S. maneuver to suspend negotiations, giving Clinton and other U.S. administration officials time to call leaders around the world in a last-ditch effort to save their package of demands.

With the crucial Canadian support, the suspension was granted. Effectively it was much longer than twenty-four hours. Twenty-four hours reached to the end of the day on Friday. Negotiations didn't take place on the weekend anyway. Then it turned out that the following Monday was election day in Norway, so there'd be no work that day either. The twenty-four-hour delay became four days of drama and tension. The tenor and tone in Oslo changed completely.

Now, we had to fight not only the United States but also Canada. Their capitulation was moving way beyond suspending negotiations. Jean Chrétien, the Canadian prime minister, was softening under U.S. pressure. Some pro-ban governments began to whisper that if Canada gave in, they'd "have no choice" but to do the same. It looked like everything was on the verge of collapse, and a decimated treaty would be the calamitous result of what had been stupendous work throughout the eleven months of the Ottawa Process until that point.

The jockeying was nonstop. Everything felt fluid up until the moment it finally wasn't. We strategized with the equally furious Norwegian delegation and diplomats from other unshakable pro-ban countries. We parlayed with Selebi as he tried to work something out so everything wouldn't be lost. But none of us could understand Canada, and we went after them as intensely as we did the U.S. delegation.

We made posters declaring Canada the new fifty-first state. Campaigners dressed up as Clinton and Chrétien laughing and shaking hands in collusion. It was physically painful when Bob Lawson, Jill Sinclair, and other Canadian diplomats we'd been working with so closely had to walk through our anti-Canada demonstrations. They were as ardently pro-ban as we were.

What was perhaps the most dramatic confrontation with the Canadians took place over the phone. A bunch of us were in the ICBL office when the phone rang. Somebody answered, then waved the phone at Goose and me and signaled that it was Ralph Lysyshyn, the head of the Canadian delegation. I had nothing to say to him. Until Goose started talking to him in diplo-speak. Everything was on the verge of falling apart around us and Goose was talking nice? As if what Canada was now doing was something to discuss and smooth over?

I was fulminating in the background, and a frustrated Goose handed me the phone. I was shaking with outrage, and my message was brief and unmistakably clear before I slammed down the receiver: "What the fuck is your government doing? You started all this! If Canada caves, we will publicly fry your foreign minister."

Ralph knew it wasn't an idle threat; the ICBL was already making Canada miserable. He once said in an interview about the landmine ban movement: "You don't want to take on Jody Williams publicly. When she speaks, she carries the room with her." I knew he'd be thinking about that and sweating, and would faithfully convey the message to Axworthy and Chrétien back in Ottawa.

The suspended negotiations finally resumed. Rumors were

swirling, and we'd started hearing some positive things earlier that morning, but we wouldn't believe anything until we heard the U.S. delegation speak. They were given the floor first. Attention was riveted on Newsom, the head of the delegation. The room was absolutely silent for a moment before he began to speak.

He somberly intoned that the United States had tried its very best to negotiate in Oslo but had been blocked at every turn. Therefore, he announced, the only option left was to immediately withdraw from the negotiations. With that, Newsom and the rest of the U.S. delegation got up and walked out. The silence held until they were gone. Then, after another brief, nerve-racking moment when Japan wanted to reopen discussions, Selebi proceeded to wrap everything up in short order and conclude the Oslo negotiations.

In the face of tremendous U.S. pressure, governments hadn't rolled over, as they too often did. They'd repeatedly said "no" to U.S. demands. In particular it was the African countries that had held firm as a solid bloc in staunch opposition to the United States. And each "no" empowered others to say the same, to hold firm in their intention to give the world a mine ban treaty with no loopholes, no exceptions, and no reservations.

A final action the ICBL took in Oslo was to make sure every government delegation had a copy of our post–Mine Ban Treaty action plan, which had been formulated during our NGO forum in Oslo. We wanted governments to have no doubt that the ICBL was committed to making sure the beautiful words of the treaty translated into reality on the ground. That meant signatures in Ottawa in December, ratifications after, and then making sure that the Mine Ban Treaty was implemented and obeyed. The ICBL was committed to the process for the long haul.

Later I sent this email to campaigners around the world who'd not been able to be in Oslo, to share with them in a small way what it had been like that afternoon:

Subject: A little after noon on 17 September in Oslo

It seems a while since I have written any personal musings on this incredible landmine campaign. But the moments shortly after noon on the 17th of September in Oslo will forever be some of the best in my life—and in many others'—so, for whatever they are worth, I wish to share them.

The buzz as we went into the room on Wednesday at noon was that the U.S. was withdrawing its proposals. And while we believed it, we still wanted to hear the words. And hear conference chairman Selebi say that the treaty had been approved.

Well, as you all know, the U.S. did withdraw its demands. And the next words were Selebi asking if the conference approved the text. We were holding our breath. And then Japan held up their nameplate to take the floor. The chairman was clearly not pleased.

Japan voiced its objection to the treaty and wanted to offer new proposals! Carl von Essen moaned!

After a bit of "quiet diplomacy" between the conference secretariat and the Japanese delegation, Selebi again asked the question "Does this conference approve this text?" Not once, but twice he asked. And then, when no one raised objections, he gaveled the approval of the treaty.

The entire ICBL delegation was on its feet, clapping and cheering. Then various delegations stood until the whole room was cheering.

Moments later when the meeting was adjourned (until the "formal adoption" and closing remarks of the next day), we began filing out. And outside our campaign office, right at the foot of the stairs facing the conference room doors, were our people!

Yes, our campaign people, who have busted butt to get this job done, cheering the delegates. Those of us who had been inside the conference made a beeline through the government delegations to stand with the ICBL-ers and cheer the delegations as they came down the stairs.

We got to chant for those who had made it really work—"Af-ri-ca" (those who held so firm in the face of the U.S. arm-twisting). "Norway. Norway." (Which never seemed to waver.) "Aus-tri-a" and "Thomas Hajnoczi," the author and "father" of the ban treaty text. "Can-a-da" for starting the whole thing. And on and on. We did not stop cheering until the last delegation left the room.

Champagne was popping. We got to hug those delegates who really made a difference.

I think it is fair to say that few negotiating conferences have ever ended with such applause by those who have lobbied so hard to make it happen. It was truly and absolutely a most wonderful moment. And despite the ups and downs at Oslo, the cheering of the delegates was something they deserved.

The treaty text was the culmination of so much work; and at the historic close of the conference, the French ambassador captured the amazingness of the moment with her comment that it was one of those rare moments in history when the actions of states come together to reflect the will of the people.

I wish you all could have been there for the cheering. Without all of us working together, it never would have happened. For me, nothing in our work to ban landmines—not even the treaty signing in Ottawa—will ever equal that Wednesday in Oslo.

CHAPTER ELEVEN

Whirlwind

October 10 to December 10, 1997

Is there such a thing as too much euphoria? In five short years we'd gone from launching the International Campaign to Ban Landmines to the creation of the Mine Ban Treaty. That already was so much more than, and phenomenally faster than, any of us had expected when we launched the ICBL. We were riding waves of joy and disbelief over that accomplishment. Now, only three weeks later, on October 10, 1997, we were awarded the Nobel Peace Prize. It was unreal. Surreal.

Even with all the speculation and hype about the ICBL as front-runner, almost nobody really believed a grassroots campaign like ours would receive such recognition. The increasing number of media calls in the lead-up to the Peace Prize announcement hadn't quite prepared Goose and me for what we'd feel when we actually heard it. And we never anticipated the media onslaught in Putney that day.

Most of the press had a hard time finding us. Journalists were driving the Putney town clerk crazy, stopping to ask for directions to the house. She was reluctant to tell them in any case, trying to protect my privacy. People who lived along our dirt road put up cardboard signs pointing to the house because they became sick of being bothered, too.

It was a media circus in an incongruous setting. The first few journalists had arrived even before Goose and I got the phone call from Norway to alert us that we'd soon hear the live announcement from the Nobel Institute in Oslo. We listened to the official announcement, and then I greeted the journalists with coffee shortly after throwing on the clothes I'd been wearing before I'd gone to bed not that many hours earlier. Black jeans, a tank top, and no shoes. I never wear shoes at home.

Despite what some thought, my "outfit" wasn't selected by design. It was no attempt to harken back to the hippie activism of the '60s. I wasn't trying to make a political statement, or for that matter a fashion statement. I wish I'd had the presence of mind to think about clothes as a political statement. I most definitely would have been wearing a ban-landmines T-shirt. But I wasn't that clever at that moment. I was overwhelmed and unable to give what I was wearing a moment of thought. I couldn't orchestrate anything that day.

The temperature rose to around eighty degrees that afternoon, and the field and beaver pond, which formed a backdrop to the house, didn't especially lend themselves to a press conference. Trying to arrange anything remotely formal with the press wouldn't have been easy under the circumstances. The entire day was a succession of journalists coming and going from before dawn until after eight o'clock that night. We managed the day—and the flow of people outside the house, and the journalists on the phone—as best we could.

Maybe if Goose and I had talked through possible scenarios, I'd have been a bit more clear-minded. I might not have referred to President Clinton as a "weenie" for giving in to the military and deciding to keep antipersonnel landmines. But even then I'm not sure. My choice of words wasn't premeditated either.

I'd never had such an experience with the media before in my life. I was kind of hyped up while, at the same time, in a comfort zone at my own house. I was comfortable enough that my unthinking smart-ass side blurted out that remark even as I heard myself saying it. If I do make such comments, I prefer to make them by choice, not by default.

But we were just completely unprepared, despite knowing that the landmine ban movement had been nominated by various people and in various configurations. Goose and I both thought that *if* there were a Peace Prize for banning landmines, it would likely be shared by Prime Minister Lloyd Axworthy, representing Canada's leadership in launching the Ottawa Process, the ICBL for being the engine driving the movement, and the ICRC for its important decision to actively campaign to ban landmines.

We'd learned that the Nobel Prizes can be awarded to up to three individuals and/or organizations each year. We believed that if the Nobel Committee did award the Prize to Axworthy, the ICBL and the ICRC, it would have made that decision to underscore the partnership among governments, civil society, and international organizations that had been key in achieving the ban treaty. Instead, it decided solely to highlight civil society's fundamental role in the process, to make it very clear that ordinary people can and do have important parts to play in contributing to peace.

When it decides to recognize an organization, the Nobel Committee prefers to also name an individual recipient. The committee does this when it makes sense and is warranted after the months of researching nominees of serious interest that it undertakes every year. So to emphasize civil society's part in banning landmines, it made the award that year, in equal parts, to the International Campaign to Ban Landmines and to me, its founding coordinator.

.   .   .

Work didn't stop after October 10. Right after the Oslo negotiations, we began implementing our action plan to get as many countries as possible to Ottawa to sign the treaty on December 3 and 4. If campaigners had already been pushing forward after the achievement of the Mine Ban Treaty itself, the Peace Prize announcement only energized us more. It mattered how many countries showed up in Canada.

On one of the last nights in Oslo in September, after the treaty negotiations ended, Bob Lawson, Susan Walker, Goose, and I had bet on how many countries would actually show up in Canada to sign the treaty. Our guesses ranged between thirty-three and sixty-nine countries. Mine was the low number. Oh me of little faith?

We all guessed low, even though we'd already agreed that if the number were not close to matching that of the eighty-nine states that had negotiated the Mine Ban Treaty, the treaty might be off to a shaky start. We were anxious about that and concerned about how much the United States would pressure countries not to sign. Anything was possible, so there was no time to relax and let down our guard.

The Peace Prize proved an unexpected boost, adding prestige and significant weight to our work. Most of the media attention that came in its wake was useful too. But some of it wasn't terrific at all. There was some tension after the Nobel announcement, primarily directed at me personally, that found its way into the press. It was fueled by handful of people on the ICBL steering committee.

Most hurtfully, it originated with Bobby Muller. Bobby, who'd hired me specifically to create the landmine campaign, and who later seemed increasingly angry after I did, especially when I was recognized for that work. He'd been such a close friend and had been so excited for so long as the ICBL had grown by leaps and bounds. I didn't publicly display my deep dismay, but kept my own counsel. I talked about it in private only with Goose and a couple of others. But Muller's personal attacks hit me very, very hard, and I felt a huge void with the loss of his friendship.

There'd always been tussles off and on in the steering committee, which had changed and grown along with the ICBL over the years. There were plenty of strong personalities and strong egos in the mix. Just like anywhere and in any kind of work. But we'd always been able to keep the focus on the campaign's goals. The Nobel announcement shifted the equation a bit. A few seemed more preoccupied with the Peace Prize than with focusing on getting their governments to Ottawa in December. Some who we'd not seen at steering committee meetings in ages suddenly started showing up again.

Goose and I talked and talked and talked as I struggled not to respond to media questions about the "tensions" which seemed designed only to create and fuel flames. No Mother Teresa myself, there were times I did so want to lash out. Maybe I even wanted to scream and cry and rend my garments. But for the most part I kept my anger in the kitchen to be shared with Goose. I ignored the few, and directed media attention to the amazing achievements of *all* the campaigners in the ICBL. We also stayed focused on the growing excitement as more and more countries announced they were coming to Ottawa.

One of the most important changes that occurred not long after the Peace Prize announcement was a shift in the policies of the Japanese government. Japan had closely mirrored the U.S. position. Its diplomats had even tried to promote U.S. objections in Oslo after the U.S. delegation itself had withdrawn from the negotiations. But surprisingly, Japan's foreign minister, Keizo Obuchi, announced a review of Japanese landmine policy, noting that "it would not make sense for Japan to oppose the Treaty while cooperating in demining activities in Cambodia."

Six days before the treaty signing conference, Japan announced it would be going to Ottawa. Because the country is an important U.S. military ally, its change in policy was a strong signal to other governments still sitting on the fence. Obuchi himself flew to Canada to sign the treaty on December 3.

· · ·

In the midst of everything else, I ended up coordinating ICBL involvement in the activities that would take place around the Nobel award ceremony in Oslo. The Nobel Committee had tried to leave me out of that loop so I could just enjoy my own part in it, but that wasn't working out very well. I reminded Geir Lundestad, secretary of the Nobel Institute, that coordinating the campaign was my job anyway so it would be easier on everyone if I coordinated this too.

The ICBL and I were each given forty tickets to the ceremony, but I didn't need that many. I invited my immediate family and my Uncle Chuck and Aunt Katie, as well as a handful of friends, including Mario Velasquez from my Salvador days. I'd not seen him in quite a while, but how could I not include him? Listening to Mario speak so many years earlier about the war in El Salvador had firmly set me on my path of activism. Susan

Whittaker and Antoinette Bill, who'd been stalwarts of various delegations to Salvador, had to be in Oslo. And Susan's husband, Noam Pitlik. The rest I gave to the ICBL so that more campaigners could be there to share in all the excitement.

Of course, the members of the campaign steering committee would be in Oslo, but we had to sort out who the rest of the fifty-odd remaining ICBL tickets would go to. There were other decisions to be made as well. Obviously I'd be accepting my own Peace Prize and giving my Nobel Lecture. But we had to decide who'd do the same on behalf of the ICBL. Understandably, there was a large pool of possibilities for the honor. The task lay in deciding how to make our selections equitably. It wasn't the easiest thing under the circumstances, but we managed to work it all out.

Reth—Tun Channareth—would accept the Nobel medal and diploma for the campaign, and Rae McGrath would deliver the ICBL lecture. When we were trying to make the decision, people felt that, with Reth, Rae, and me taking part in the award ceremony, the three main areas of the ICBL's call and work—support for survivors, support for mine clearance, and the political work of banning landmines—would be represented in the ceremony itself. Other members of the steering committee would have the opportunity to participate in other activities on behalf of the ICBL while in Oslo. It was all going to work out.

One of the things the Nobel Committee asks recipients for is a photograph. They'd be hanging my picture on the wall with those of all the other recipients of the Peace Prize since the very first, in 1901. I needed a good photograph to send them, but wasn't sure where I was going to get one. I didn't have to worry about it for long after *Vanity Fair* got in touch to see if I'd be willing to be photographed by Annie Leibovitz for their magazine. That was an easy "yes."

Then *Glamour* informed me they were naming me one of their ten women of the year. It turned out that Annie would be taking pictures for that as well. In the process of all the picture taking, we were having so much fun that I brazenly asked if she'd do my Nobel picture. She generously agreed. When my sister Mary Beth and I showed up at her New York studio for the shoot, Annie decided to play around taking pictures of my sister and me as well. They are among my favorites of all time and adorn the bookshelves in my office. Fortunately, they were taken *before* I gave myself a black eye that afternoon.

We left Annie's studio and were getting into the car to be driven back to the hotel to get ready for the *Glamour* event. Somehow I managed to smash my face on the pointed edge of the car door above the window and almost knock myself out. The driver was aghast, as if it were in some way his fault. Once I was sure I hadn't knocked my eye out, Mary Beth and I couldn't stop laughing. How much clumsier could I possible be? By the time we arrived for the *Glamour* ceremony, I did have a big black eye.

Another favorite photograph from that time was taken by Richard Avedon. A couple of hours before the appointed hour, his people arrived at our little rented house in Virginia to pre-pare a room for the shoot. They hustled about, covering win-dows to make sure the room was pitch black. Then Avedon himself swooped in, positioned me the way he wanted, quickly snapped his camera, and then departed. In less than twenty min-utes. The result was a wondrous black-and-white that also hangs in my office. It was all quite surreal.

· · ·

Clinton wasn't going to Ottawa, but the ICBL didn't give up trying to make him change his mind. Six amazing campaigners piled aboard what was called the "Ban Bus" to drive across the

United States and reach out to people and inspire them to pressure the administration to sign the treaty. Mette Eliseussen from Norway, Dalma Foldes from Hungary, John Rodsted from Australia, Michael Hands from the United Kingdom, Petter Quande from Norway and Mary Wareham from New Zealand made up the Ban Bus team.

They started on October 23 at Sproul Plaza at the University of California, Berkeley, the birthplace of the free speech movement and other grassroots efforts. For five weeks, they lived in that bus as they crossed the country carrying photo exhibits, posters, videos, and a slide show. They spoke at events ranging from talks at local high schools, colleges, and universities to public rallies, as well as protests outside American companies that produced landmines.

Their stamina was an inspiration. How six people endured such close quarters for five weeks is beyond me. I never could have tolerated it. Thankfully, the ICBL has always been made up of people with a wide range of skills and enthusiasms. From that we derive much of our strength.

The "Ban Bus Tour" ended on December 1, when the bus rolled into Ottawa to cheers, hoopla, and fanfare—including twenty-five television crews, along with radio and print journalists. We held a jam-packed press conference to talk about the tour as well as the Mine Ban Treaty Signing Conference that would begin in two days.

The next few days were a tumultuous celebration as more than twenty-six hundred people gathered in Ottawa. One hundred twenty-two governments signed the treaty while we were in Canada. That was far more than our feeble speculations and also more than the eighty-nine countries that had negotiated the Mine Ban Treaty in Oslo.

Three of them—Canada, Norway, and Austria—had also

completed all the necessary work to be able to present their ratifications of the treaty along with their signatures. Now we'd need only thirty-seven more countries to ratify it to make the treaty become binding international law. With those three countries already on board, the campaign almost immediately launched part of the next phase of our work, which was a competition for countries to ratify the treaty in time to be among those essential forty countries.

Big celebrations are often a blur of activities, as was the case in Ottawa. It was particularly so because there'd been no time to take a real break throughout the entire year. The Ottawa Process and the World Tour had been both heady and grueling. Then preparations for, and the accompanying angst over, the return to Oslo for the Nobel ceremony were complicated and time-consuming in and of themselves.

By the time Goose and I got to Ottawa, we were exhausted, exhilarated, and essentially fueled by adrenaline. We hoped it would hold us through the events there, and that we'd still have enough left over for Oslo, which would follow almost on the heels of Ottawa.

· · ·

Along with culmination of the Ban Bus Tour, two other moments emerge from the Canadian blur. Only governments could sign the Mine Ban Treaty, so the ICBL decided to create a "People's Treaty." While governments signed the Mine Ban Treaty inside the conference hall, ordinary citizens could sign the People's Treaty outside the hall. With their signatures, people would be committing to making sure that their governments would obey the obligations outlined in the Mine Ban Treaty.

The first person to sign was Song Kosal, veteran campaigner

and Cambodian landmine survivor. She was a strong spokesperson for landmine survivors around the world who also were committed members of the ICBL. It was fitting that she be the first to sign the People's Treaty.

For governments, signing began when Canada's foreign minister, Lloyd Axworthy, became the first government representative to put his name to the treaty document. Hundreds of people crammed into the room to witness the historic event. Axworthy was seated at a table, surrounded by Canada's prime minister, Jean Chrétien; Kofi Annan, secretary general of the United Nations; Cornelio Sommaruga, the head of the ICRC; and me. After Axworthy spoke, each of us had an opportunity to say a few words.

When I stood to speak I could see the biggest, most gorgeous smile shining through the crowd. It belonged to Kosal. She looked as if pure joy were radiating through her very being. I kept looking at all the campaigners in the audience but was always drawn back to her smile. I concluded by saying that when civil society comes together as we had in the International Campaign to Ban Landmines, we were truly a "new superpower." We'd shown that when we work together, ordinary people most definitely can achieve the extraordinary.

I put my hands together high up in front of my face and bowed as deeply as I could to Kosal. It felt exactly like the perfect way to end. That bow was meant as a gesture of love, admiration, and thanks to her and to all the landmine survivors who'd worked so hard to ensure that someday people everywhere would walk in a world free of landmines.

Whenever I think of that time in Ottawa, I can see Kosal's smile and feel a wonderful warmth spreading through my body.

·　　·　　·

Goose and I flew almost immediately after Ottawa into yet another celebratory maelstrom. Of course we had a schedule of the events that would be taking place, but a schedule can't possibly prepare you for the reality of the Nobel Peace Prize events. We didn't know what exactly to expect, which didn't diminish our excitement in the least.

Geir Lundestad, secretary of the Nobel Institute, and Francis Sejersted, chair of the Nobel Committee at that time, met us at the airport and whisked us off to the city in a limousine. We went directly to the Nobel Institute just in time for Goose and me to participate in a press conference there, which also included one other member of the ICBL steering committee.

We'd arrived exhausted, some would say "fried," and didn't have even a minute to try to pull ourselves together. Overnight flights can be especially grueling, and I felt particularly bedraggled as I took my seat in front of the media. The bags under my eyes were, as they say, hanging almost to my knees. I could almost feel sorry for myself when I look at the pictures from the press conference. Except I was there to receive the Nobel Peace Prize. With my ICBL friends and colleagues also receiving the Peace Prize.

The room was packed with journalists as well as members of the steering committee and other campaigners who'd already arrived for the Nobel events that would take place over the next few days. The press conference was pretty much like the many other media interviews and events I'd attended since the September treaty negotiations in Oslo, but with the added element of the Peace Prize.

One of the first questions was about the "tensions in the campaign." I'd expected it and said firmly that I'd entertain the question once. Period. We were all there to talk about the ICBL and its accomplishments, not to inflate rumor. After that preface, I said that whatever tension there might be stemmed from internal matters concerning one organization within the ICBL and had been blown out of proportion. What was an internal matter should have stayed inside that organization. It wouldn't affect the work of the ICBL.

I explained that the thousands and thousands of landmine campaigners around the world were anything but tense. We felt honored and were exhilarated. In fact, many campaigns were holding their own activities around the world at the same time as the Nobel ceremony in Oslo. End of story.

There was also another question we were already sick of hearing: "What impact does it have on the treaty that the United States will not sign it?" And in the same vein: "How do you feel as an American knowing that President Clinton won't sign the treaty?" There were also questions about both the terms of the treaty itself and the Ottawa Process that had brought it about. Questions about how to take mines out of the ground and about survivor assistance. And then there was the unavoidable "What's it like to win the Nobel Peace Prize?"

It's a question everyone wants to ask. Most will if they have a chance. But actually it's three questions. Sometimes it means: what's it like when you learn you've won the Nobel Peace Prize? Sometimes it means: what's it like to go to Norway and receive the prize? Other times it's really about how the Peace Prize changes your life. Some elements of the question are pretty easy to answer, but others aren't. Sometimes parts of an answer still feel like a work in progress.

When the press conference ended, we didn't have to go far. Members of the steering committee and Reth, who'd be receiving the Nobel Medal for the ICBL, simply moved to another room in the Nobel Institute. It was the room where the photographs of Peace Prize recipients hang. And there was my picture on the wall with all the others. Who would have ever thought?

Champagne bottles popped as we mingled and chatted with Geir and Francis and the other four members of the Nobel Committee. Two were women: Sissel Ronbeck and Hanna Kvanmo. There were two more men: Gunnar Berg and the Lutheran bishop Gunnar Stålsett. The bishop was quite an activist himself, whom I enjoyed meeting, and I also enjoyed talking with the two women a lot. Apart from the bishop, the other committee members were former politicians or businesspeople. As director of the Nobel Institute, Geir is a constant, but the members of the Nobel Committee are always changing as their terms expire.

One immediate question I had for them all was why photographs representing the organizations that had received the Peace Prize weren't also hanging on the wall. It should be pretty easy to frame an organization's name and logo and hang it along with the photographs of the individuals. Geir and the others looked a bit puzzled, and the answer essentially was that they weren't on the wall just because. It bothered me.

After the mini reception, we finally were taken to the historic Grand Hotel. Goose and I were given the Ibsen Suite. It's where most laureates stay each year. It was a grand moment indeed to go to our rooms and unpack. Rest. Take a shower and prepare for the evening, which was to be an intimate dinner for me and another member of the steering committee with Geir and the Nobel Committee.

I liked them. They weren't at all stiff and formal as I'd imagined. In fact, some were anything but. The night of the Nobel Concert, for example, I was sitting next to Hanna. Mariah Carey came on stage in a slip of a garment clearly showing the dreaded panty line. Hanna leaned conspiratorially toward me and said, "Nice underwear." We could hardly contain our laughter. The next time Mariah appeared, she was wearing a new sheath. This time Hanna leaned over and whispered, "*No* underwear." I could have died.

But that would be a couple of days later. There wasn't quite the same type of humor at the small dinner. But it was fun talking with them about aspects of the Peace Prize over the years. Nominees who shouldn't have been passed over. And others who should have been. The former most obviously was Gandhi; the latter you can speculate about on your own. It was a wonderful couple of hours' worth of bits of Nobel history.

After the dinner, I hurried back to the suite and met up with Goose and my family and friends, who were already there enjoying champagne without me! But nobody was ready for the night to end, so we continued to hang out and enjoy jokes and memories and friendship together. The champagne added a warm glow to the conversation. Everyone stayed until very late. It wasn't something we'd ever be doing together again.

·   ·   ·

About the feeling and happenings in Oslo then, a journalist for the *Washington Post* wrote:

> Norway's King Harald V will attend, as will his prime minister, most of parliament, the diplomatic corps and almost every other Oslo notable with the connections to get tickets. Thousands of children will leave school to cheer in the streets. There will be live music—Emmylou Harris and Mariah Carey, among others—a torchlight parade through dark winter streets, banquets and speeches.
>
> The 1997 Nobel Peace Prize will pass formally to the Interna-

tional Campaign to Ban Landmines and its American coordinator, Jody Williams, on Wednesday in a ceremony that will set off what amounts to an annual two-day national celebration. In the minds of many Norwegians, the peace prize is as much a part of their national identity as the fjords and the plays of Henrik Ibsen. Being Norwegian means being part of a once-a-year moral instruction to a world that is generally willing to listen.

I like the way he put it. Except for the bit where he said it "will pass formally . . ." It doesn't pass anywhere. Each is unique to the Nobel laureate of that year. But other than that, he was able to capture in summary the key elements of what Oslo is like then. I have mostly snapshot memories—as most of us do about the big events in our lives. And then we seem to clearly remember other things that are, for all appearances, insignificant, that seem like they shouldn't be remembered at all. Odd the workings of the mind sometimes.

. . .

Oslo's city hall is majestic. A fantastic, colorful mural stretches above the front of the huge room. That day, December 10, 1997, gigantic arrays of flowers that picked up the colors in the mural decorated the hall. More than one thousand people were there to witness the ceremony. In the center of the middle aisle sat the king and queen of Norway. Nine people were on the stage facing them all. And I was one of them.

When we'd arrived in procession, trumpets had ushered us into the hall. Rae and Reth and I and the members of the Nobel Committee had walked through the audience from the back of the hall and up to the stage. The king and queen had taken their seats in the center of the otherwise empty center aisle, with two aides sitting behind them. The trumpets fell silent, and then a tall, thin man stepped behind the bright blue podium bearing the profile of Alfred Nobel. Francis Sejersted, the chairman of the Norwegian Nobel Committee, stood for a moment taking in everyone in the room; then he began to read:

> There are those among us who are unswerving in their faith that things can be done to make our world a better, safer, and more humane place, and who also, even when the tasks appear overwhelming, have the courage to tackle them. Such people deserve our admiration, and our gratitude. We are delighted and honored to welcome some of them to the Oslo City Hall today. Our warm welcome to you, the representatives of the ICBL, the International Campaign to Ban Landmines, and to you, Jody Williams, the campaign's strongest single driving force. You have not only dared to tackle your task, but also proved that the impossible is possible. You have helped to rouse public opinion all over the world against the use of an arms technology that strikes quite randomly at the most innocent and most defenseless. And you have opened up the possibility that this wave of opinion can be channelled into political action
>
> It is in admiration, and in gratitude for their efforts to achieve that aim, that we honor the ICBL and Jody Williams today with the Nobel Peace Prize for 1997.

It's kind of overwhelming and in some ways disconcerting to hear such a description of yourself. I could see my family smiling broadly and was happy that they were so proud. But I also took great comfort in the fact that they really know all sides of me. And that they've loved and supported me in all my life adventures, and that the Nobel Peace Prize had nothing to do with that. To them, I'd always be just me.

I sometimes joke about me and Mother Teresa and the Peace Prize. My family will never get us mixed up. Even if some seem to imagine that after receiving the Peace Prize a person is somehow transformed into something resembling a saintly creature. It's rather frightening actually. But I wouldn't know about that until sometime later. And most certainly not during the Nobel ceremony and festivities.

Once Francis finished his words, he called Reth and me to the podium. There he gave the Nobel Medal and diploma to each of us, accompanied by the vigorous clapping of the audience. We returned to our seats and listened as Rae read the ICBL's remarks. After Rae, it was my turn to speak. I took my place at the podium and looked across the audience. I found Goose and Mom and Dad and the rest of my family and friends. It gave me immeasurable pleasure to wave to Mom and Dad before I started to speak.

"Your Majesties, Honorable Members of the Norwegian Nobel Committee, Excellencies and Honored Guests,

It is a privilege to be here today, together with other representatives of the International Campaign to Ban Landmines, to receive jointly the 1997 Nobel Peace Prize. Our appreciation goes to those who nominated us and to the Nobel Committee for choosing this year to recognize, from among so many other nominees who have worked diligently for peace, the work of the International Campaign.

I am deeply honored—but whatever personal recognition derives from this award, I believe that this high tribute is the result of the truly historic achievement of this humanitarian effort to rid the world of one indiscriminate weapon. In the words of the Nobel Committee, the International Campaign "started a process which in the space of a few years changed a ban on antipersonnel mines from a vision to a feasible reality."

Further, the Committee noted that the Campaign has been able to "express and mediate a broad range of popular commitment in an unprecedented way. With the governments of several small and medium-sized countries taking the issue up . . . this work has grown into a convincing example of an effective policy for peace." . . .

It is fair to say that the International Campaign to Ban Landmines made a difference. And the real prize is the treaty. What we are most proud of is the treaty. It would be foolish to say that we are not deeply honored by being awarded the Nobel Peace Prize. Of course, we are. But the receipt of the Nobel Peace Prize is recognition of the accomplishment of this Campaign. It is recognition of the fact that NGOs have worked in close cooperation with governments for the first time on an arms control issue, with the United Nations, with the International Committee of the Red Cross.

Together, we have set a precedent. Together, we have changed history. The closing remarks of the French ambassador in Oslo to me were the best. She said, "This is historic not just because of the treaty. This is historic because, for the first time, the leaders of states have come together to answer the will of civil society."

For that, the International Campaign thanks them—for together we have given the world the possibility of one day living on a truly mine-free planet. Thank you.

I didn't read anything to the audience, although I'd turned in written remarks for the record. I can't read a speech. I've almost never done it. I get bound up in the reading and forget what I'm meant to be communicating. But I didn't need to; how could I possibly mess up my remarks? I was talking about the ICBL. Its creation and the history of its work. The Ottawa Process. The Mine Ban Treaty. These were things I knew in my bones.

We had the power to bring about serious change because we worked together to do it. Ordinary people in about ninety countries around the world had come together and accomplished the truly extraordinary. We had most definitely demonstrated that the impossible is possible. The only real limitations we face are those we put on ourselves.

Epilogue

Peace. It's a tough word. For some it calls up images of weak-kneed utopians or tree-hugging liberals or any number of demeaning words meant to delegitimize the hard work involved in convincing people that aggression, violence, and war are choices and not the inevitable fate of humans. They are also words that can cut off real discussion about what peace is and isn't, and what it would take to build sustainable peace.

Real peace is not simply the absence of armed conflict, but it took me a long time to fully understand that. When I protested against the war in Vietnam in 1970, I was protesting to end *the war* not *war.* I wasn't thinking at all about sustainable peace or a concept of human security, which is much bigger than the security of the state alone.

Some describe human security as ensuring that people everywhere are free from want and free from fear. It also entails protecting this planet, because it is the only one we've got. Human security requires directing our resources toward providing for the basic needs of human beings so they are secure in their daily lives.

For too long, security has been defined in terms of the security of the state, not of individuals. We call it national defense. The United States spends more on its military and weapons systems than all of the other nations of the world combined. The billions and billions of our tax dollars that go to weapons systems and other aspects of "defense" is money that will never be spent on our public schools, or on an affordable health care system that gives everyone access to health care, or on creating jobs with dignity. Money for war will never be used to fight poverty and other social ills that tear apart the socioeconomic fabric of a country and often are fundamental causes of armed conflict. We have to change that kind of thinking.

To achieve such change we have to start educating people to see that war is nothing to glorify. Individuals may be fantastically heroic in war, but there is nothing heroic about war itself. It is a grisly, brutal endeavor generally revolving around power—whether to gain it, maximize it, or maintain it—and resources. If war and all its consequences were to be honestly faced, how many people would go? To make war palatable it is usually wrapped in banners of democracy, freedom, and liberty or other such terms to dress it up in glory. But if we need to understand that war isn't glorious, we also need to better understand what peace is.

Peace isn't "Kumbaya" or a dove and rainbow. When I think about a dove and a rainbow, I think about serenity. But serenity, personal peace, is not sustainable world peace. Confusing serenity with creating peace can make it even harder to really understand what it takes to change how we think about war and peace. Working to create a world with sustainable peace is hard work every single day. It means thinking in terms of human security, not just national security. It means demilitarization—another "dirty" word—and using our resources for productive ends for us all.

When I hear people scoff at peace, I think of Dr. Martin Luther King Jr. and all the work he did to end racism and inequality, and of his opposition to war. I think of Rosa Parks and the thousands of others who took nonviolent action along with Dr. King. There's nothing weak-kneed about that.

When people say *peacenik* with scorn, I think of Gandhi, who helped end an empire through the nonviolent actions of the tens of thousands he inspired to participate in making change happen. I think of Nobel Peace laureates Betty Williams and Mairead Maguire of Northern Ireland, who helped bring out tens of thousands of people, largely women, to protest the violence of "the troubles" there. Their nonviolent action contributed to the restoration of peace in Northern Ireland.

When people want us to believe that peace is something for the faint of heart, I think of other giants of peace, like His Holiness the Dalai Lama, Nelson Mandela, Archbishop Desmond Tutu, Sir Joseph Rotblatt, Aung San Suu Kyi, and the late professor Wangari Maathai. With moral fortitude and through nonviolent action, they have helped shift thinking and policies in our world.

·   ·   ·

The 1997 Mine Ban Treaty came about because a small group of us believed we could make it happen. October 6, 2012, marked the twentieth anniversary of the meeting at Human Rights Watch in New York where six organizations committed to working together to ban antipersonnel landmines and launched the International Campaign to Ban Landmines. October 12, 2012, was the fifteenth anniversary of the day that the International

Campaign to Ban Landmines and I learned that we'd both been awarded the Nobel Peace Prize.

I think most governments had probably expected, and many hoped, the campaign would declare victory when the treaty was successfully negotiated and would then close down operations after the December 1997 signing ceremony in Ottawa.

We immediately extinguished those thoughts when we gave the governments copies of our posttreaty action plan even as the gavel was swinging to close the Mine Ban Treaty negotiations in Oslo in September 1997. I've no doubt that, because of the ongoing work of the ICBL, the Mine Ban Treaty is one of the strongest examples of the successful implementation of and compliance with an international arms control treaty.

I stepped down as campaign coordinator in February 1998. We were fortunate that Liz Bernstein took my place, until December 2004, and that afterward Sylvie Brigot assumed the role. Both women have provided the ICBL with formidable leadership over the years. My role became that of "campaign ambassador." Landmine survivors Reth and Kosal also serve as ambassadors for the ICBL.

In that role, I continue to speak out on behalf of the ICBL and to promote the Mine Ban Treaty in countries around the world. My travels have taken me to most continents. I've been in Mozambique, Nicaragua, Thailand, Kenya, Croatia, Jordan, and Colombia with the campaign. These have been sites of some of the annual meetings of states that are party to the Mine Ban Treaty, at which we've assessed progress and the remaining challenges. And of course the ICBL and ICRC and U.N. agencies participate as well. I've been asked to be a keynote speaker on behalf of the ICBL in the opening ceremonies of many of these important meetings.

By early 2012, 160 states had become party to the treaty. That represents about 80 percent of the governments of the world. Some 44 million stockpiled landmines have been destroyed and will never go in the ground to claim a life or a limb. More than $4 billion has been spent on landmine clearance around the world and on assistance to landmine survivors.

The only country in the world that has consistently used landmines since the Mine Ban Treaty took effect is Burma. There has been no known trade in antipersonnel landmines since the mid-1990s. Only twelve countries have retained the right to produce landmines, but it is believed that only three of them do so.

Because we have been able to stigmatize the weapon, even countries that haven't joined the treaty are in essence obeying it. For example, Russia and China have stopped exporting landmines. This is significant, as both countries were huge producers and exporters of the weapon.

What is surprising, in some ways, is that the United States still hasn't joined the treaty. It's surprising because it has followed all of the treaty's obligations. The United States hasn't used antipersonnel landmines since the first Gulf War in 1991. There has been no export of U.S. mines since 1992 and no production since the mid-1990s. It has also destroyed millions of stockpiled landmines.

It would be logical for the country to join the treaty, but the military remains obstinate in its refusal. Presidents Clinton, Bush, and Obama have submitted to the military's insistence on keeping antipersonnel landmines. The primary issue is that the U.S. military doesn't want to bow to civilian influence in terms of which weapons it can and cannot use. It is concerned that if the government were to join the Mine Ban Treaty, it would mark the beginning of a "slippery slope" and other weapons could be at risk.

Weapons that don't comply with the laws of war *should* be banned. In fact, two other weapons have been—one in 1996 and the other in 2008. Almost unnoticed amid the whirlwind activity of the ICBL in 1996 was the work of the Human Rights Watch Arms Division (Goose is executive director of the Arms Division) and the International Committee of the Red Cross. Together they were able to push governments to ban blinding laser weapons in May 1996, before they were ever put into production and use.

Goose and his Arms Division were also primary founders, with other NGOs, of the Cluster Munition Coalition. Using the model of NGO-government partnership that came out of the landmine ban movement, a coalition of nongovernmental organizations again was the engine of a new treaty. The goal was reached with the successful negotiation of the 2008 Cluster Munition Convention. This time the government of Norway led the charge, and the treaty was signed in Oslo in December 2008. In January 2011, the ICBL and the Cluster Munition Coalition merged. Goose is the chairman of the board of the merged ICBL-CMC.

It is hard to imagine that two decades have passed, and that the ICBL is as creative and vibrant as ever. Campaigners around the globe continue working to ensure that the 1997 Mine Ban Treaty is obeyed by the countries who have signed and ratified it. And they keep pressing nonsignatory governments to join the treaty. Because of their commitment, there have been changes on the ground that have had a positive impact on the lives of people affected by antipersonnel landmines.

The success of the ICBL has been an inspiration to activists everywhere. We have demonstrated that civil society can work together to change the world. The response of activists to the Peace Prize was telling. So many that I worked with in my Central America days contacted me to say how proud they were, and that they felt all activists were in some way honored by the Nobel Committee's recognition of the work of the ICBL. I wholeheartedly agree.

. . .

On a visit to the Nobel Institute one time when I was in Oslo, I went with Geir Lundestad into the room where all the pictures of the Nobel Peace laureates hang. As he opened the door he was grinning like the Cheshire cat. He said, "Jody, I think you are going to be very happy." I was and I am. My lobbying campaign with the Nobel Committee bore fruit.

Today, if you go to the institute, you will find not only the pictures of the individual recipients of the Nobel Peace Prize hanging on their wall. Now the organizations that received the prize are represented there too. Organizations like UNICEF, Doctors Without Borders, the International Committee of the Red Cross, and of course, the International Campaign to Ban Landmines. Their names and logos are framed and on the wall as they long should have been.

. . .

Although I'm still with the ICBL in spirit, and sometimes in person, these days I'm the chair of the Nobel Women's Initiative. Six women recipients of the Peace Prize—Betty Williams and Mairead Maguire (Ireland, 1976), Rigoberta Menchú Tum (Guatemala, 1990), Dr. Shirin Ebadi (Iran, 2003), the late professor Wangari Maathai (Kenya, 2004) and I—launched the initiative in January 2006. We are exceptionally fortunate that my friend, colleague, and activist-coconspirator extraordinaire, Liz Bernstein, has been the executive director since its founding.

The initiative was actually Dr. Ebadi's suggestion, which she made when she and I were together in Nairobi at the end of 2004. She started talking about how many women Peace laureates were alive today, and said that together we could help other women working for peace. She suggested we start some kind of project to make that happen.

The next day we met with that year's recipient of the Peace Prize, Professor Wangari Maathai, at a Nobel Ladies' Tea, which also functioned as a photo op. The throng of journalists didn't know that, while they were snapping photographs, the three of us were conspiring to form what in 2006 would become the Nobel Women's Initiative.

It is curious that despite the fact that wars are and always have been overwhelmingly waged by men, and despite the fact that it is women who struggle to hold families and communities together in the midst of the fighting and to find ways to build lasting peace, only fifteen women in its more than 111-year history have been recognized with the Nobel Peace Prize.

In the Nobel Women's Initiative, we see it as our purpose to use the influence and access afforded by the prize "to promote, spotlight, and amplify the work of women's rights activists, researchers, and organizations worldwide addressing the root causes of violence, in a way that strengthens and expands the global movement to advance nonviolence, peace, justice and equality," as our website says. So often the efforts of women are carried out in the shadows, with little support and even less recognition. It makes me very happy to be a grassroots activist who is able to share my Peace Prize with other activists around the world.

We support human rights and democracy in Iran. We support the work of Aung San Suu Kyi and the Women's League of Burma and others in their efforts to bring democracy to Burma. In mid-2011, the Nobel Women's Initiative spearheaded a new effort, the International Campaign to Stop Rape & Gender Violence in Conflict, to bring together organizations around the world in a united global campaign to tackle this horror through coordinated and sustained action. While individual organizations have done some fantastic work on this issue, we believe we can amplify voices and broaden impact if we work together. I know it's true, because I've helped do it before.

As I write this epilogue, the Nobel Women's Initiative and, in particular, the International Campaign to Stop Rape & Gender Violence in Conflict, are works in progress. To follow what we do—and even better *to join in*—check us out at www.nobel womensinitiative.org. Consider this a personal invitation.

. . .

In October 2002, I was invited to speak at the Graduate College of Social Work at the University of Houston. As I always do when I have the opportunity to speak with students, I hung around after speaking and chatted, and gave out my email address and business cards. The dean, Dr. Ira Colby, said he was surprised at how accessible I wanted to be to the students. I thought it was normal.

He watched for a while and then, just about the time I was leaving, asked if I ever considered teaching. I answered, "Not really," to which he said, "Would you?" When I said, jokingly, "Send me an email," he did. Since 2003, I've taught at the Graduate College of Social Work, most of that time as the Sam and Cele Keeper Endowed Professor in Peace and Social Justice. I don't live in Houston, but go down for two five-hour seminars at the beginning of the semester and two at the end. In between I interact with the students via Skype.

For me, teaching is an extension of activism, perhaps particularly in the field of social work. I've come to see myself as an international social worker. One of the primary goals of social work, listed in the Social Worker's Code of Ethics, is "to enhance human well-being and help meet the basic human needs of all people." To me, that means looking at the world through the lens of human security.

In class we focus on the international aspects of social work that is, on considering issues that affect more than one country and which cross international boundaries. These range from meeting the basic needs of a particular population to complicated issues such as human trafficking and population displacement resulting from wars and famine. Social workers work in collaboration with international organizations—such as the United Nations, Doctors Without Borders, and the Red Cross—and governments to establish and implement programs to address these issues. When these programs are done well, individuals, communities, populations, and countries are empowered to promote change through international collaboration—the antithesis of war.

. . .

My brother Steve was finally properly diagnosed when he was in his forties. It was a rocky path to his diagnosis, and even for a few years after that. With the proper medication, which he now finally receives, he is no longer violent and hasn't been for many years. Like everyone in the family, I am sad that his life has been so difficult. It is almost a life not lived. But I can't think about it too much or too deeply. I get a crushing sensation in my chest, and my mind closes down in self-defense.

Steve lives with my mom, and they are quite the "odd couple." Strangely, maybe, they almost seem to make each other complete. My mom, in my view, is practically a saint when it comes to Steve. Despite all the trials and tribulations, she has maintained a vibrant sense of humor and positive view of life. She truly and completely rocks, and I absolutely adore her. Goose thinks she's pretty awesome too, as he does the rest of the family.

My other siblings—Mary Beth, Mark, and Janet—are all happily married, and we remain extremely close. Whenever I can, I escape to Vermont to be with them. My family and Vermont are in my blood and my bones. I'm very lucky that way.

. . .

Goose and I were married in Geneva, Switzerland, on May 13, 2001. The Rev. Dr. Rebecca Larson, a Lutheran minister and landmine activist, officiated at the ceremony. We celebrated with family and friends for about four days. It was fabulous.

We really and truly are living happily ever after—in our life together, and in what we do together and individually as activists working to contribute to making the world a better place for us all.

There's little in my life I would change. It has been a long and winding road, with family tragedy, job burnout, idealism, heartbreak, and grassroots activism. Most of my work has been like that of the other activists I know: grinding, sometimes frustrating, and with highs and lows. However, I've been privileged to be part of a movement that achieved political success and has affected the lives of millions of people around the world. Few of us in the International Campaign to Ban Landmines really thought it would bear such lush fruit.

For me, receiving the Nobel Peace Prize hasn't been all joy and wonder. At first I was perplexed about how to understand it in relation to my work, but over time it has resulted in my feeling a huge sense of responsibility to work harder for sustainable peace. In the last fifteen years I've had times of doubt and conflicting emotion—that is real. But I've remained crystal clear that I am a grassroots activist to the core. My life still revolves around the daily nature of struggle, of pushing limits, and of defending human rights on the ground. It's been a fascinating, wild ride so far, and I can't wait to see what happens next.

ACKNOWLEDGMENTS

Thanks to my agents, Lynn Franklin and Doug Abrams, who believed in the message of this memoir and without whom this book would not have been finished. And my editor Naomi Schneider, whose suggestions only made the book stronger, and everyone else at University of California Press in any way involved in this effort.

Different people read parts of the book in its various incarnations. And thanks to them all. But my special appreciation goes to Lisa Sparrow, Marta Tannenhaus, and Eileen Rosin, whose readings at the final stage of the manuscript helped make it stronger. And a special thanks to my friend, screenwriter Audrey Wells. Audrey, Goose, and I spent many hours talking through aspects of my life, and Goose's and my life, with her as she worked on a script that reflects much in this memoir. Those conversations affected my thinking for the better and in ways I'm not even aware of.

And Goose, Stephen Douglas Goose, my husband and work

colleague. He has read every variation of my writings over the years that I kept hoping, but wasn't sure, would become a book. I know I've read them all more than he has, but he is a close, close second. I know he's as happy as I am that it passed to the hands of others.

CALIFORNIA SERIES IN PUBLIC
ANTHROPOLOGY

The California Series in Public Anthropology emphasizes the anthropologist's role as an engaged intellectual. It continues anthropology's commitment to being an ethnographic witness, to describing, in human terms, how life is lived beyond the borders of many readers' experiences. But it also adds a commitment, through ethnography, to reframing the terms of public debate— transforming received, accepted understandings of social issues with new insights, new framings.

Series Editor: Robert Borofsky (Hawaii Pacific University)

Contributing Editors: Philippe Bourgois (University of Pennsylvania), Paul Farmer (Partners in Health), Alex Hinton (Rutgers University), Carolyn Nordstrom (University of Notre Dame), and Nancy Scheper-Hughes (UC Berkeley)

University of California Press Editor: Naomi Schneider

1. *Twice Dead: Organ Transplants and the Reinvention of Death,* by Margaret Lock

2. *Birthing the Nation: Strategies of Palestinian Women in Israel,* by Rhoda Ann Kanaaneh (with a foreword by Hanan Ashrawi)

3. *Annihilating Difference: The Anthropology of Genocide*, edited by Alexander Laban Hinton (with a foreword by Kenneth Roth)

4. *Pathologies of Power: Health, Human Rights, and the New War on the Poor,* by Paul Farmer (with a foreword by Amartya Sen)

5. *Buddha Is Hiding: Refugees, Citizenship, the New America,* by Aihwa Ong

6. *Chechnya: Life in a War-Torn Society,* by Valery Tishkov (with a foreword by Mikhail S. Gorbachev)

7. *Total Confinement: Madness and Reason in the Maximum Security Prison,* by Lorna A. Rhodes

8. *Paradise in Ashes: A Guatemalan Journey of Courage, Terror, and Hope,* by Beatriz Manz (with a foreword by Aryeh Neier)

9. *Laughter Out of Place: Race, Class, Violence, and Sexuality in a Rio Shantytown,* by Donna M. Goldstein

10. *Shadows of War: Violence, Power, and International Profiteering in the Twenty-First Century,* by Carolyn Nordstrom

11. *Why Did They Kill? Cambodia in the Shadow of Genocide,* by Alexander Laban Hinton (with a foreword by Robert Jay Lifton)

12. *Yanomami: The Fierce Controversy and What We Can Learn from It,* by Robert Borofsky

13. *Why America's Top Pundits Are Wrong: Anthropologists Talk Back,* edited by Catherine Besteman and Hugh Gusterson

14. *Prisoners of Freedom: Human Rights and the African Poor,* by Harri Englund

15. *When Bodies Remember: Experiences and Politics of AIDS in South Africa,* by Didier Fassin

16. *Global Outlaws: Crime, Money, and Power in the Contemporary World,* by Carolyn Nordstrom

17. *Archaeology as Political Action,* by Randall H. McGuire

18. *Counting the Dead: The Culture and Politics of Human Rights Activism in Colombia,* by Winifred Tate

19. *Transforming Cape Town,* by Catherine Besteman

20. *Unimagined Community: Sex, Networks, and AIDS in Uganda and South Africa,* by Robert J. Thornton

21. *Righteous Dopefiend,* by Philippe Bourgois and Jeff Schonberg

22. *Democratic Insecurities: Violence, Trauma, and Intervention in Haiti,* by Erica Caple James

23. *Partner to the Poor: A Paul Farmer Reader,* by Paul Farmer, edited by Haun Saussy (with a foreword by Tracy Kidder)

24. *I Did It to Save My Life: Love and Survival in Sierra Leone,* by Catherine E. Bolten

25. *My Name Is Jody Williams: A Vermont Girl's Winding Path to the Nobel Peace Prize,* by Jody Williams (with a foreword by Eve Ensler)

26. *Re-Imagining Global Health: An Introduction,* edited by Paul Farmer, Arthur Kleinman, Jim Kim, and Matthew Basilico

Text:	10.75/15 Janson
Display:	Janson
Compositor:	BookMatters, Berkeley
Printer and binder:	Thomson-Shore, Inc.